Seasons of Misery

Christmas, 2013

To Geri and David
With all my love –
Kathleen

EARLY AMERICAN STUDIES

Series editors:
Daniel K. Richter, Kathleen M. Brown,
Max Cavitch, and David Waldstreicher

Exploring neglected aspects of our colonial,
revolutionary, and early national history and culture,
Early American Studies reinterprets familiar themes
and events in fresh ways. Interdisciplinary in character,
and with a special emphasis on the period from about
1600 to 1850, the series is published in partnership with
the McNeil Center for Early American Studies.

A complete list of books in the series
is available from the publisher.

SEASONS OF MISERY

Catastrophe and Colonial Settlement
in Early America

KATHLEEN DONEGAN

PENN

UNIVERSITY OF PENNSYLVANIA PRESS

PHILADELPHIA

Published by
University of Pennsylvania Press
Philadelphia, Pennsylvania 19104-4112
www.upenn.edu/pennpress

Printed in the United States of America
on acid-free paper

2 4 6 8 10 9 7 5 3 1

Library of Congress Cataloging-in-Publication Data
Donegan, Kathleen.
    Seasons of misery : catastrophe and colonial settlement in early America /
Kathleen Donegan. — 1st ed.
        p. cm. — (Early American studies)
    ISBN 978-0-8122-4540-0 (hardcover : alk. paper)
    1. Frontier and pioneer life—United States—History—Sources. 2. Frontier
and pioneer life—United States—Historiography. 3. United States—History—
Colonial period, ca. 1600–1775—History—Sources. 4. United States—
History—Colonial period, ca. 1600–1775—Historiography. 5. United States—
Social conditions—To 1865—History—Sources. 6. United States—Social
conditions—To 1865—Historiography. 7. United States—Colonization—
History—Sources. 8. United States—Colonization—Historiography. 9.
Barbados—Colonization—History—Sources. 10. Barbados—Colonization—
Historiography 11. Great Britain—Colonies—North America—History—
Sources. 12. Great Britain—Colonies—North America—Historiography. I.
Title. II. Series: Early American studies.
E162.D66 2014
973—dc23

                                                            2013015743

For David—sine qua non

CONTENTS

Unsettlement

In August 1611 the Reverend Alexander Whitaker, newly arrived in Virginia, wrote to the Reverend William Crashsaw, one of the colony's major promoters in London. Whitaker had a strange story to tell: "One night our men being att praiers in the course of guard a strange noise was heard coming out of the corne towards the trenches of our men like an Indian '*Hup hup*' with an '*Oho Oho.*' Some say that they sawe one like an Indian leape over the fier and runne into the corner with the same noise. At which all our men were confusedly amazed. They could speak nothing but *Oho Oho.*"[1] Confusedly amazed, each man suddenly believed that he was surrounded by Indians. They all grabbed their firearms and began to attack their fellows with the butts of their guns. Whitaker said that the melee lasted about seven minutes. These were not sleeping soldiers startled by a strange sound in the cornfields. These were men awake and on guard, Whitaker reported, who suddenly began to shout Indian words and reach for their guns. One of the men remembered other details of the incident: "a fantasy possessed them that they imagined the Salvages were sett upon them, eache man Takeinge one another for an Indiyan And so did fall pell mell one upon an other beatinge one another downe and breakeinge one anothers heades, that Mutche mischiefe mighte have bene done butt that it pleased God the fantasy was taken away whereby they had bene deluded and every man understood his errour."[2] Whitaker used similar terms to describe how the men snapped back to reality: "Suddenly as men awaked out of a dream they began to search for their supposed enemies, but findeing none remained ever after very quiet." Though they eventually recognized their error, they struggled to understand it. Perhaps, one later wrote, the delusion was "ocassyoned by the Salvages Sorceries and Charmes," a supernatural retaliation against the colonists after a year of atrocious violence. Whatever happened, those who were there agreed that the incident was "one thinge amongste the rest . . . very remarkable."[3]

What should we make of the affliction that beset those men that night, when they suddenly saw themselves and their fellows as Indians? A fantasy possessed them; they were no longer English, and yet as English soldiers, they were compelled to attack their non-English selves. The figure running outside was only "like an Indian," but the settlers' chant of "*Oho Oho*" and their "breakeinge one anothers heades" were real. They were both the aggressors and the victims of their own violence. What happened that night was an extraordinary materialization of the settlers' pervasive confusion about their own identity. This pell-mell self-attack stands as a remarkable example of what one colonist called the "mixed suffrances of both body and mynd" that were experienced in early settlements "daylie."[4] As the story demonstrates, incidents such as this could be recalled and narrated in part, but they were also defined by mystery and silence. And while the tale reflects the escalating hostilities between natives and settlers that characterized early English settlements in America, it is also marked as "colonial" by the aggression and delusion it portrays, by the material and psychic expression of the men's disorder, and by the self-strangeness of their unresolved bewilderment. Englishmen at evening prayers suddenly breaking into Algonquian chants and attacking each other becomes a most uncanny scene of colonial estrangement. Always *tassantasses* (strangers) to the natives, the colonists were also often strangers to themselves.

This book is a study about the unsettling act of colonial settlement, and how English settlers became colonial through the acute bodily experiences and mental ruptures they experienced in their first years on Native American ground. It is also a study about writing, and how the first distinctively colonial literature emerged out of the crisis of colonial settlement. Settlements were brutal places characterized by disease, death, factions, violence, starvation, ignorance, and serial abandonment. When settlers wrote of these things, they told the truth. But their accounts reveal more than factual descriptions of their circumstances, and the texts they produced provide more than evidence about a material world. Settlers were not simply reporting on present conditions; they were also struggling to construct an identity out of the incommensurable experiences of being English and living in the New World. Catastrophe was more than a description of calamitous events. It became a discourse through which settlers witnessed themselves and registered their shock at unprecedented circumstances that they could neither absorb nor understand. Both as an event and as a discourse, catastrophe marked a threshold between an old European identity and a new colonial identity, a state of experiential and narrative instability wherein only fragments of Englishness were retained amid the upheavals of New World experience. Most profoundly, writing settlement as a catastrophe linked the settlers' own suffering to their acts of violence, and this conjunction between suffering and violence came to express for them the inescapable condition of becoming colonial. Understanding early colonial identity, then, requires telling a new story about its beginnings, a story in which crisis and catastrophe are placed at the center of the first years of English settlement in America.

A World of Misery

"There were never Englishmen left in a forreigne Countrey in such miserie as wee were in this new discovered Virginia," one settler wrote, decrying a state both physical and psychic.[5] In this lamentation the settler tries to make a connection between Englishmen who were never "left in a forreigne Countrey" and those who were. However, the wished-for connection is doomed from the start because of the vastly different worlds that define the two subjects. The audience to this plea necessarily exists outside the nature of the settler condition; indeed the claim that this condition is unprecedented, even unimaginable, is exactly the point. The speaking subject, "left" at the outpost of a fledgling empire, becomes colonial through the deep estrangement that "such miserie," suffered at such a distance, effects upon his former ties. As the psychoanalysts Françoise Davoine and Jean-Max Guadillière write, in situations of social or historical catastrophe, "the destruction of all reference points" leaves "the subject who is confronted . . . in a state of total estrangement, of absolute aloneness with regard to all the ties that, up to that point, were familiar."[6] The breakdown of those alliances and customary identifications is a disaster that subjects "reveal at the price of their own identity."[7] And yet in the literature of settlement, such expressions of colonial misery were everywhere. In Roanoke "the country was to them miserable & their reports therof according."[8] In Virginia settlers lived in "a world of miserie."[9] In Plymouth the "First Comers" were in such "sad conditions and trials" that subsequently arriving immigrants "fell a-weeping, fancying their own misery in what they saw now in others."[10] In Barbados the settlers lived "wearisome and miserable lives" and suffered "miserable long sicknesse."[11] What does this excess of misery tell us about the colonial condition apart from the unforgiving New World environment? It is an indication that misery was not only a material condition but also a language through which new settlers revealed how the social links that tied them to England, and to their own sense of Englishness, were breaking down. Never, they attested, were there Englishmen like them.

Given the acts they undertook in England's name, why does it matter if settlers suffered as they colonized? One reason to pay attention to settlers' misery and the discourse surrounding it is to complicate an account of conquest that sees English colonists as imperial agents who imported and enacted the prerogatives of possession based on convictions of cultural superiority, legal entitlement, and religious imperative. Imperial agents they were, and enact these prerogatives they did, but such an account is incomplete. The colonizers' power, agency, and subjectivity were often tenuous, at times crumbling in the face of catastrophic hardships and at times desperately asserted in panic. Here there is a distinction to be made between colonization as an imperial project and becoming colonial as a lived condition. Settlers were charged with possessing and holding the land, and they came armed and ready to do so. Their personal intentions to acquire land and wealth accorded with the overall mission of colonization. However, the cultural and ideological foundations that undergirded the initial act of colonization depended on a conviction that the colonists were bringing civilization to the uncivilized. As the fantasy of taming a wilderness and ruling its "natural" people gave way to the radical uncertainties of life in the New World, the miseries of settlement proved deeply destructive to the ideals of individual and group civil life. In the spaces of settlement, both *habitus*—the sense of being surrounded by customary behaviors that reflected cultural identity—and *civitas*—the knowledge of belonging to a body of people ruled by the same laws—easily broke down. If the English defined themselves as an advanced people existing in well-ordered, civilized groups, that image was shaken by the extreme suffering endured and violence perpetrated in the settlements. Because of their radical displacement, mental confusion, and struggles for survival, early settlers experienced an alienation—epistemological, social, corporeal—that was inseparable from their colonial status. Alien to themselves, they could not control, and many could not even survive, the world they were supposed to possess.

In the language of the English charters, the discovery and possession of the New World were supposed to follow in quick succession. The strings of verbs that described colonization predicted no interval. For example, Queen Elizabeth I granted Walter Raleigh the right to "have hold occupy and enjoy" what "heathen and barbarous" lands he might "discover search fynde out and viewe."[12] Written in London, the charter gave away distant lands with the stroke of a pen, but occupying that land had to be done in person by the settlers who were left to "inhabite or remayne there." Once on the ground, they immediately found that they had no such powers as the charter granted. Habitation and possession turned out to be two entirely different things, and the directives that assumed otherwise were written in a language increasingly irrelevant to the exigencies and atrocities of colonial life. The charter's broad, confident outline of the colonial mission tells us little about the events that marked the colonial condition: mass starvation, sieges, mutinies, desecrated corpses, slaughtered children, shipwrecks, fire, delusional fantasies, and abandonment. These destructive events defined the colonial experience as much as did the inscriptive right to "have hold occupy and enjoy."

Though the colonial context of these disasters was new, when colonists wrote of them, they had a long English tradition of writing about crisis from which to draw, and this tradition informed their New World discourse. English literature had long employed a variety of rhetorical forms to express the shock of sudden calamity, the pain of personal hardship, and the sense of social decay. These ranged from biblical traditions such as psalms of exile and the book of Lamentations; to medieval traditions such as the formal complaint, the litany, or the invective; to contemporary variations on the almost universal theme of providence. Providential thinking especially was a mainstay of popular belief in the pulpits, in the presses, and on the streets at this time, despite (or perhaps because of) the fact that God's messages could be interpreted in multiple and competing ways.[13] Recurrent social disasters such as famine, plague, and other diseases likewise produced what we may call an early modern literature of crisis. The publications that came from plague years included a range of medical, literary, and theological texts, as well as widespread news of the spread of the plague, bills of mortality, and weekly tolls of burial.[14] All of these discursive systems were flexible, and writers could use even the most ancient of them in response to situations they themselves might have seen as unprecedented. As the literary historian Lawrence Manley writes, "[T]raditional vocabulary was transformed by the circumstances of its application."[15] These traditions provided tools for making meaning out of crisis; however, they did not fully discipline the jarring details of lived experience. For example, in a 1623 broadside publication entitled *The Dolefull Even-song*, published on the heels of the collapse of Black-Friar's Catholic Church in London, the writer is convinced that the sudden tragedy is the work of God's justice. But even given this providential conclusion, he does not omit the image that must have been burned in his memory: "that Tragicall spectacle of so many bruised and battered carkases, so many smothered corpses, which yesterday breathed the same English aire with us."[16]

Colonial writers too drew on prior modes of expression to capture their experiences of catastrophe. Their texts are literary creations as much as they are historical artifacts, and in them we can find traditional vocabularies persisting, even if they are transformed. However, the crises that settlers suffered and tried to represent took place far from the material and social world of printing presses and street criers, bookshops and broadsides, preachers and readers that contextualized other crisis literature. Settlers most emphatically did *not* breathe the same English air as the battered corpses in *The Dolefull Even-song* did just yesterday. The distance and the difference were immense, and defined their experience. Even everyday life in the early settlements exerted what the historian Robert Blair St. George calls "a kind of emergency pressure."[17] How much more did disaster confirm a state of unparalleled crisis? While it is difficult to construe this colonial experience apart from its modes of representation, it is precisely by reading the literature of settlement *as* literature that we can see gaps, omissions, turns, confusions, falls, excesses, urgencies—all of which point to junctures where the adaptive capacity of older, collective forms no longer worked to translate colonial situations. Their new "world of miserie" thus not only represents their lived experiences but also represents the fractures between those experiences and a literary heritage that often could not contain them. Although English discourses could sometimes give colonists a language for their pervasive crises, at other times that language did not suffice; and this too colonists revealed "at the price of their own identity."

Seasoning

Settlements are liminal places that exist between the wonder of New World exploration and the stability of established colonies. In a trajectory that moves from New World contact to European hegemony, settlement marks a central but fraught moment: central because it represents the decisive moment when European people decided to stay permanently and import their culture with them; and fraught because these efforts so often resulted in chaos and failure. Therefore creating a developmental narrative that links early settlement to viable colonies always requires the turning phrase "but then": but then the settlers adapted their English lifeways to the American climate; but then family-based migration stabilized the population; but then they developed a staple crop and a consumer market was created; but then Indian resistance became weakened by the rampant spread of European diseases; but then they created a vast labor force through the enslavement of Africans; but then a society began to form. These constructions indicate a shift between the messy uncertainties of early settlements and the moment when their settled colonial histories began.

Following this trajectory, the disasters of early settlement can be likened to a process of seasoning writ large. "Seasoning" was a term that originally referred to hardening wood by exposing it to environmental conditions. Seasoned wood was strong and dry and would function in a wide variety of conditions. By the turn of the seventeenth century, "seasoning" was also used in reference to people who were fortified through exposure to difficult circumstances. "Seasoned" people were either metaphorically or literally acclimatized. By the century's end, however, "seasoning" was being used specifically in reference to what happened when people moved to the colonies.[18] As the historian Joyce Chaplin writes, "A seasoned colonist was an altered person, a contrast to untested newcomers."[19] Seasoning was something to pass through, an inevitable by-product of settlement, just as historiographically settlement is an inevitable stage to pass through in the establishment of colonies.

I have titled this book *Seasons of Misery* because I want to dwell in this seasoning time rather than pass through it. I am interested in the present tense of this moment because I believe that colonial settlement can be more fully understood if we try to see it as a cluster of unassimilated events rather than as an established body of forward-leaning facts. Hayden White elucidates this distinction: "An event cannot enter into a history until it has been established as a fact. From which it can be concluded: events happen, facts are established."[20] According to philosopher Alian Badiou, the event must contain a supplement to "what there already is—the situation of knowledge as such—generated by nothing other than repetition. . . . This supplement is committed to chance. It is unpredictable, incalculable. It is beyond what is."[21] Thus, while the "situation" is defined by an ordinary state of affairs in which all things can be accounted for, the "event" forces a rupture, a break with previously known forms. It is "something that happens in situations . . . that they and the usual way of behaving in them cannot account for . . . something that cannot be reduced to its ordinary inscription in 'what there is.'"[22] In this way, the event forces change because it suddenly reveals that the rules of a given situation, which once appeared total, are in fact inadequate to comprehend a new and insistent reality. Following Badiou, White writes, "*Event* occurs when knowledge of some hitherto unknown aspect of being has to be added to what had been previously known about being. It is, as it were, this 'shock' to the knowledge-system by the insistent nature of a newly discovered truth about being that registers as an event to consciousness."[23] In my reading, the unpredictable, incalculable initiation of colonial experience happened in this kind of evental space and registered as a series of shocks to what had earlier been considered a stable cultural sense of being.

My contention is that before the establishment of socially authorized narratives that told how settlements became colonies—that is, before the translation of events into facts—the insistent nature of these newly discovered truths about being were expressed largely in a discourse of catastrophe. My goal is to recognize this new, unsettling, and insistent state of being as the state of becoming colonial by restoring the sense of the event to the history of settlement. Of course, to write that history is already to give it order, structure, and plot. However, writing about colonial settlement through the lens of the event also means to suggest that settlement itself was a time when the event was ascendant over the fact. The power to provide meaning to what was happening, to narrate what was happening as a series of facts, and to connect what was happening to a previously known situation defined by repetition was constitutionally compromised. Events happen; facts are established. English soldiers spoke nothing but "*Oho, Oho*" and battered themselves with their own guns. In one sense this is a historical fact. We can locate the episode in time and space and find evidence of its occurrence in corroborating sources. And yet it was also an event; the blows here were not only physical but also assaults on cognition and recognition, on identity and being. The incident was a shock to the settlers' sense of reality and reference, a deep disturbance that was left unresolved. It was "one thinge amongste the rest . . . very remarkable." To stay inside this colonial seasoning, then, means deliberately representing these events in a different narrative form and historiographical frame, one concerned more with the ongoing present of crisis than with the forward movement of chronology. Progressive narratives that are concerned with how rough settlements developed into successful colonies can easily turn proleptic or teleological, structured as they are by retrospectively imposed historical chronologies. To adopt a different temporality, one concerned with what it meant to inhabit the ongoingness of the present, is in turn to recognize the central importance of unsettlement during these acute seasons.[24]

Many historical accounts treat settlement as a prelude, a period that presented a set of problems that needed to be solved in order to create colonies. In this view, settlement was a rough start on the road to more viable social formations. In contrast, this study concentrates precisely on that perilous time after the English formulated the intention to establish permanent colonies but before those colonies could maintain themselves as social and economic entities, viewing the period not as anomalous but as foundational to colonial identity and its modes of representation. Reperiodizing settlement in this way allows for an analytic account of colonial incursion that incorporates its extreme contingencies instead of summarizing and then resolving them. Distinguishing this period and identifying a discourse of catastrophe operating within it offer a way of reading in the documents produced by the first settlers evidence of the traumatic origins of colonial identity. Such an approach finds in our "founding" American texts a story of unfounding. It turns the critical emphasis from settlement to unsettlement, from knowledge production to epistemic rupture, and from adaptation to social and personal breakdown. The creation of colonial identity is often described as an incremental, adaptive process of accommodation that took place gradually over a period of time. However, I would argue that in its first instances, becoming colonial happened more abruptly, through a convulsive series of "nows." It was an unmaking, it was nonadaptive, and it emerged precipitously as a profound reaction to life in extremis. When natives withdrew food, when sickness spread, when settlers died in droves, and when "home" was an ocean away, Englishmen became something they were not before: colonial.

They Settled There

In many ways this field of inquiry is an old one. Colonial historians have long recognized the struggles of early settlement. Writing over fifty years ago, the historian Oscar Handlin proposed that early seventeenth-century colonial life was marked by inescapable hazard and chaos: "Every aspect of their existence combined to produce disorder. . . . The precariousness of existence was at the root of the disorder that overwhelmed them."[25] Handlin argued that as settlers struggled to account for this pervasive chaos, they increasingly relied on a providential worldview to create meaning for their lives in this strange land. If suffering was everywhere, they told themselves, significance must be everywhere too. Indeed these trials, they reasoned, must be the signs of a great mission. Even as they struggled, they saw suffering and survival as emblems of having been selected to pursue a special destiny. The seventeenth century, Handlin argued, was significant because it was in this period that this sense of mission became an essential aspect of English lives in America. Handlin's movement from struggle to meaning is characteristic of his generation of early American scholars. As exemplified in Perry Miller's classic *Errand into the Wilderness*, struggle was located within the context of American exceptionalism, part and parcel of the Puritans' search for their special fate and mission in America. Thus, Miller could recite a long list of colonial disasters and failures without challenging this exceptional status of the Puritans: the land "had been laid in the covenant before even a foot was set ashore," and there "New England should rest." They settled there, the story goes, and oscillating between failure and fulfillment, they "launched themselves upon the process of Americanization."[26]

The next generation of scholars saw things differently, and focused on a darker aspect of settlement: Europeans invading Native American lands and wreaking havoc on native people, culture, and history. In 1976 Francis Jennings's *The Invasion of America* performed what one scholar called "the academic equivalent of a scorched-earth campaign" that "changed the landscape of American Indian history forever."[27] Jennings turned settlement history on its head by putting forth an account of violent invasion and brutal expansionism. "The implications of the use of this word *settlement* are worth noticing," Jennings wrote, noting how the term simultaneously erases the existence of already "settled" Indian populations and masks the Europeans' primary intention to conquer and exploit. From the beginning, he argued, "what made trouble was the European purpose of settling on top."[28] Richard Slotkin too, in *Regeneration through Violence,* foregrounded the history of violence in both colonization and nation building, arguing that colonial and later American anxieties about "the wilderness" created archetypal dramas unfolding at the edges of settlement. In these dramas an intimacy with Indians threatened a white descent into "savagery," which whites combated through violent acts that renewed or regenerated the progressive march of "civilization" across the American West. Beginning with the first European settlements, Slotkin wrote, "the myth of regeneration through violence became the structuring metaphor of the American experience."[29] They settled there, these scholars asserted, and violence was at the heart of that settlement.

Although conquest continued to structure subsequent histories of the settlement era, looking at cultural interactions during this period led another group of scholars to focus on the theme of adaptation.[30] There is a long tradition of studying the transfer of English culture to the New World, but the inclusion of Native American and African American cultures caused the story to be told in a different way. "The tale of the peopling of the New World is one of human creativity," claims the historian T. H. Breen. Although "the challenges were staggering," he writes, each of these groups responded to those challenges through a process of "creative adaptation."[31] The model of creative adaptation has structured local, comparative, and synthetic histories of the colonial Americas, particularly those concerned with the emergence of creole identities and societies. In the study of early settlement, the capacious concept of adaptation has enabled scholars to emphasize the complexity of the process whereby ideas and practices from those contact cultures—cultures which were themselves dynamic and diverse—were modified by daily negotiations under the changing circumstances of the New World. When natives and newcomers "faced off," to use the historian Karen Kupperman's apt phrase, both groups tried to stabilize interpretations of their mutually defining relationships by adapting traditional structures to a changed world. In Kupperman's account, they settled there and eventually made sense of themselves by incorporating their colonial experiences into preexisting social, cultural, and ideological categories.[32]

Suffering, violence, adaptation: each of these successive historiographical approaches to the struggles of settlement gets important things right, but each also closes down some aspect of crisis in the colonial condition. Handlin and Miller understand disorder, but push it toward a meaningful resolution. Jennings and Slotkin understand violence, but overlook the misery and incoherence of the settler experience. Breen and Kupperman understand the complexity of English adaptation to the colonial world, but sublimate rupture into adjustment. The field of historical work around colonial settlement is broad and varied, but a few more examples might suffice to find similar closures. For example, Mary Louise Pratt and Richard White supply the enormously useful models of the "contact zone" and the "middle ground" to interpret cross-cultural interactions; however, reading the discourse of catastrophe, we find that contact zones were also chaos zones, and the middle ground often became visible as a kind of breach appearing discursively as the unmaking of English subjectivity.[33] A range of scholars write about imperialist forms of knowledge production in the New World, but a focus on mastery misses what the anthropologist Michael Taussig calls "the epistemic murk."[34] The colonists' narrative literature shows that even as they were counting tribes and measuring rivers, their experiences in the New World often remained incomprehensible to them. Atlantic studies of migration and settlement patterns provide us a global view of mobile populations, but in that larger frame, interiority is lost in the establishment of broad-scale models.[35] Oceans connected, but they also separated, and early colonial texts record a sense of isolation, distance, and difference in the context of physical incursion and psychic entrenchment.

My purpose is neither to debunk these approaches to settlement history nor to totalize the wide variety of critical discourses that explicate significant aspects of the early encounters. Nor is it to claim that misery has gone unacknowledged. Indeed such seminal works as Andrew Delbanco's *The Puritan Ordeal* and Mitchell Breitwieser's *American Puritanism and the Defense of Mourning* have brilliantly concentrated our attention on the central experience of loss in the colonial world.[36] My purpose is rather to use the framework of catastrophe to stay close to what is often sealed off in accounts of colonial development: irresolution, misery, incoherence, unmaking, breaches, interiority, murk. I intend to stay close, that is, to acute experiences and their textual representation and, by staying inside the seasons of misery, to find coloniality in crisis rather than in accretion.

This emphasis on crisis has caused me to think through the relationship between my reading of the settlement period and the critical field of trauma theory. I do think that many of the texts I read are acts of witness to nearly unspeakable things and that, in Cathy Caruth's words, "they become themselves the symptoms of a history that they cannot entirely possess."[37] Further, I believe that settlement crises did represent the breakdown of subjects in response to traumatic events, what Judith Herman defines as "threats to life or bodily integrity, or a close personal encounter with violence and death." According to Herman, traumatic events "confront human beings with the extremities of helplessness and terror, and evoke the responses of catastrophe."[38] Certainly this was the case for settlers. In addition I am fully convinced by Dominick LaCapra's insistence on negotiating the affective element of historical understanding and by his model of "empathic unsettlement," in which one recognizes the affective impact of writing about historical trauma but maintains a structure of historical specificity and "a respect for the otherness of the other."[39]

However, my readings of catastrophe in colonial settlement also differ from theorizations of trauma in important ways. First, I am interested in both settler misery and settler violence, and in using the framework of catastrophe to keep both suffering and violence in view. This complicates the premise of the subject primarily as the victim of trauma, because settlement was a historical crisis in which colonists inflicted tremendous harm on others. Indeed exploring that connection is one of my goals. Second, I am interested in the production of historical subjects as well as in the fracturing of subjectivity. I want to trace how the intensities particular to colonial settlement effected a separation from Englishness as it had previously been understood and, in doing so, produced colonial subjects. In the failed attempts to transport and maintain stable forms of Englishness—and amid frequent situations of violence, chaos, bewilderment, and fear for physical survival—settlers became something other. This disordered "becoming" is as much my topic as is the collapse of a former sense of belonging.[40]

Text and Story

As a reader of the texts of early settlement, I am interested in both literary exegesis and historical recovery, and throughout this study I use the tools of both literary criticism and narrative history. Textual analysis serves to find pattern, form, and structure in these accounts; to attend closely to their language; and to treat them as literary constructions. Narrative serves to give a deep account of events and experiences as recounted by eyewitnesses, preserving their time-bound, fragmentary perspectives while also creating a wider historical view. These textual and narrative techniques combine to produce what might be called "narrative readings" of the primary source material. Through these readings I recognize the relationship between language and event to be complex, but take up that complexity in order to understand how historical actors grappled with their ability to represent colonial experience. Entering this critical space generates material for constructing new historical narratives about these people, places, and events by acknowledging not only that these writers of "true relations" struggled with their own testimonial imperatives but also that the struggle itself was part of their story.

Doing narrative history from a literary perspective can be said to have two antecedents: the New Historicist anecdote and the new Narrative History. The anecdote, as it was used by the New Historicists, was designed to both import and impart "the touch of the real," to reconnect literature to the unique and eccentric realities of lived experience in the everyday world.[41] Because the intense particularity of the anecdote interrupted broad and supposedly comprehensive historical narratives, it destabilized "history" as a context for any literary work, allowing us to see both the past and the literary work anew. "Old Historicists" selected what they saw as typical and representative, standard and reproducible: small stories that told the one big story. New Historicists did the opposite, choosing the anecdote that would reveal enigmatic fragments, express unarticulated possibilities, or conjure up the "'effect of the real'-via-the-strange."[42] Employing the thickly described, side-shadowing anecdote thus became a move that signaled a new set of questions about literature's relationship to culture—a relationship these critics saw as neither autonomous nor reflective but rather as performative, dialectical, and multiple.

New Narrative History did something similar in replacing overarching historical narratives based on quantitative, structuralist, or scientific methods with thick descriptive accounts of individual events or lives that resisted absorption into those other broad-scale analytic techniques. Questions about local histories, mental structures, or lived experience necessitated a turn back to narrative method. In the wake of scientific historiography, this return to narrative seemed retrograde to some. However, the new narrative studies were distinctly different from the epic narratives of old. They combined narration and analysis; they concentrated on previously obscure populations; they moved from economic and demographic concerns to cultural and emotional ones; and they used accounts of intimate human behavior to shed light on cultures of the past. Narrative History tried to get inside a person's head while attempting to comprehend that person's world through a combination of description and analysis. The new narrative move was "from circumstances surrounding man, to man in circumstances," as the historian Lawrence Stone puts it.[43]

New Historicist and new Narrative methods had key features and influences in common, but there were also important disciplinary differences. New Historicists told the story on the way to analyzing the text, while new Narrative Historians used texts on the way to telling the story. I place myself at the crossroads of these different practices by drawing on both exegetical tools and a sustained narrative schema. I read the documents using well-established tools of literary analysis: an awareness of the differences between signifier and referent; an interest in the operation of discourse; an attention to structure, form, and genre; an ear for tensions, ruptures, and silences. But I also extract a narrative from the texts, constructing a history with an aim to restore the sense of the "event" and include questions of perception and multiple viewpoints in its telling. In this method of critical writing, the narrative arc runs in tandem with the analytic arc, so that "narrative reading" itself becomes a form of argument. A narrative practice yoked to literary analysis tells us about what was happening in a time and place, but it simultaneously makes "happening" itself a point of inquiry. The narrative produced by this method becomes a form of literary exegesis because it is produced by a sustained and close encounter with textuality. The method also arrives at historicity because it shapes the primary source into a sustained narrative that can be mobilized as an argument about the history of settlement. Thus close literary readings of the texts provide the groundwork for new narratives of events, which in turn make critical interventions into received ideas about colonial history.

This method is particularly appropriate to the study of colonial settlement for several reasons. First, it slows things down. Slow movement allows one to linger in the uncertainty of "present" moments that mark these texts as colonial. It allows one to grasp the strange, the inchoate, and the "underdetermined," as Myra Jehlen puts it, to better express the violent, the disavowed, the taciturn, and the disorderly in these texts.[44] In a world of radical epistemic shifts, slowing down can ultimately challenge the broader chronology of both standard periodization and synthesized historical narratives by avoiding the teleological thrust of each. Second, narrative readings reframe the question of what counts as evidence. While traditional methods demand that evidence be stable and iterable, we can construct different historical accounts by understanding that textual evidence can also test the limits of iterability. Seeing this instability itself as a form of evidence can change the way we understand disruptions along the horizon of meaning, especially in the situation of settlement, where lack of recognition often precisely signals the colonial event. Extracting narrative from a crisis rather than a stabilization of meaning can capture that unforeseeable break with the known. Third, using literary criticism to open up the historical texts allows us to read these accounts of settlement in terms of their own discursive structures and to narrate settlement from inside the conditions in which colonial representation took form. By foregrounding the document and the reading of the document, the narrative radiates from the space wherein what is internal to the text meets or grapples with the material world. Such a strategy reveals both the junctures and disjunctures between the inner and material world so that we can see how earlier systems of thought and states of being faltered and gave rise to new forms of coloniality.

Sites of Unsettlement

In each chapter in this book I analyze this transformation and its representations in a distinct context: epistemological crisis at Roanoke; abjection and atrocity at Jamestown; mortality and material remains at Plymouth; and excess and ungovernability in Barbados. In each case I am interested in the period of settlement before the organization and stabilization of self-replicating colonial societies. Over the course of the seventeenth century, colonies in New England, the Chesapeake, and the Caribbean were consolidated around different social, religious, economic, and racial systems, which profoundly shaped not only their cultural practices but also their regional identities. However, I have chosen to compose a lateral study of an intensive period across these four sites rather than a longitudinal study of any one region or a comparative account of regional development. This is because I am interested in the phenomena of early settlement itself, and in locating commonalities that become muted when the disorders of settlement function as a prelude to the development of regional colonial formations. When we hold an end goal in sight, we tend to read this early breakdown in terms of its eventual recovery. In doing so, we lose the close grain and critical distinctiveness of the first colonial period, because our interest remains in what comes after. In contrast, when we forgo that resolution, we can read the breakdown on its own terms. This asks us at once to reconsider the temporality of this period and to pay closer attention to its forms. It also asks us to do analytic work within a time of chaos, instead of narrating a linear progression from chaos to order. While this approach presents a more limited archive, it also brings into sharper critical focus the role catastrophe played in colonial settlement—a role that has been both over-read ideologically as an originating act of heroic perseverance and under-read historically as a rough, but brief, transition to colonial societies.

Chapter 1 presents a history of three separate failed attempts to construct a colony at Roanoke. From accounts of these attempts, two interrelated themes provide a discursive lens through which to view early colonial experience: disordered cognition and the threat of abandonment, or put another way, not being able to read and not being able to leave. The chapter's central text is a report by Ralph Lane, governor of the first colony in 1585. Historically, Lane's report has not been a focal point for scholars, especially in comparison to the attention paid to the work of the scientist Thomas Harriot and the artist John White, whose collaboration effectively shaped knowledge of the colonial world for much of Europe.[45] Yet Lane's unstable narrative, with its chaotic structure and many departures from reality, is important precisely because it maps out a disordered epistemology. What looks like flawed rhetoric is actually a volatile consciousness textually preserved. The chapter explores Lane's surreal river journeys, his growing conviction of an Indian conspiracy, and his ongoing relations with the Roanoke werowance Pemisapan, who is ultimately murdered and beheaded. After narrating Lane's ouster from Roanoke and the quick eradication of a skeleton colony left there in its wake, the chapter turns to John White's account of his subsequent colony, the one that was ultimately lost. It concludes by considering everything else that was lost in the attempt to settle Roanoke, including the assumptions that the New World could easily become a known world and that settlement would lead directly to possession.

Chapter 2 turns to Jamestown and contends with the predominance of John Smith as a figure in the history of early Virginia. I argue that Smith's sagas of power and possibility do not touch on the darker discourse that came into being at the same time, one in which extreme suffering and extreme violence defined the colonial position. The central texts are two long narratives by George Percy, whom I read against Smith to argue that while Smith creates the panoramic map of Virginia, the neglected Percy is the key writer of Jamestown itself. In this chapter, I seek to revise our understanding of the settlement through both textual recovery and historical discovery by bringing to light untold histories embedded in Percy's accounts and, even more important, by offering a model of the history of early Jamestown as a descent into abjection. The focus here shifts from identifying the material causes of the settlement's disasters to theorizing the critical function of disaster in settlement writing. Catastrophe almost ruined Jamestown, but it also had a hand in implanting it. Connecting the story of the "Starving Time" to the viciousness of the first Anglo-Powhatan war, I argue that as structures of meaning crumbled in Jamestown, the arena of settlement became a theater of atrocity wherein settlers did "things that seemed incredible." The chapter ends with a reconstruction of the textual traces of Paspahegh, the site where the English set their fort, and with a telling of that story of tragic confrontation through its harrowing human particulars.

Chapter 3 addresses the issue of mortality in the Plymouth colony by taking up William Bradford's famous report that the settlers were "scarce able to bury the dead" in the first years of settlement. During the desperate mortality crises that defined the period from 1616 to 1622, both Indians and English around the Plymouth settlement struggled to account for their scarce-buried dead. I argue that in this context the ability to read death properly was at once crucial and deeply compromised. Dead bodies became highly charged sites of cultural crisis, and I analyze the problematic presence of those bodies for both natives and newcomers, paying particular attention to how each group looked upon the other's dead. Reading William Bradford's *Of Plymouth Plantation* alongside other contemporary reports of the colony, letters, biblical narratives, and a critical piece of court testimony, I tell the story of a complex landscape of power relations among people in Plymouth, in the nearby Wessagusset settlement, and in the Massachusett tribe. Multiple strands of rumors and fear, alliances and competition tied these groups together; those connections also unraveled into starvation, massacre, and social collapse. Violence thus becomes the disavowed underside of the discourse of misery that Bradford stages in his text, as he tries to clear the past of its most visible remains and make a bid for possession based on Pilgrim faith and humility. Despite his efforts, however, the dead, and with them the catastrophe of settlement, come in and out of view, continually threatening the stability of both the settlement and its written history.

Chapter 4 turns to Barbados and reflects a shift in early American studies that recognizes the central place of the Caribbean in the colonial Atlantic world. Because this chapter works up to the mid-seventeenth-century sugar revolution rather than taking the sugar economy as an established condition of colonial relations, it traces a much closer connection between tropical and mainland settlements while still registering the unique situation of the West Indies.[46] For English settlers in the first half of the seventeenth century, the

West Indies existed as a place of intractable extremes, of tropical excess that was seen to infect those who settled there. Catastrophe lived in that excess, not only in the staggering mortality rates but also in the natural, social, and economic worlds that were considered to be inescapably immoderate. After analyzing the earliest accounts of English lives in the West Indies, I turn to Richard Ligon's *A True and Exact History of the Island of Barbados*. Although Ligon's history strives for order, it is continually interrupted by a narrative ungovernability, exposing sites of decrepitude, avarice, violence, and inhumanity. Despite the author's intent to be methodical, this eruptive ungovernability destabilizes his efforts to rationalize colonial activity "beyond the line." Ligon's text represents the multiple orders of colonial knowledge that were being produced in the mid-seventeenth century, and seeks to offer "the sum" of all he knows—both of the prodigious nature of the island and of the exact calculation of what one could extract from it. But even as *A True and Exact History* demonstrates the production of that knowledge, it is persistently vexed by the violent extremes of Anglo-Caribbean coloniality as the plantation complex was coming into its full expression.

When I began this study, I wanted to write about the first years of colonial settlement because I could not get the stories out of my mind. It seemed to me that they were too easily passed over in formal arguments about how colonies developed or in discussions about the ideological implications of colonialism. The catastrophes of the first seasons could astound, but what could one do except explain the external conditions that led to such acute states and move on? How else could one write it? In his book *Metahistory*, Hayden White defines the historical work as "a verbal structure in the form of a narrative prose discourse."[47] He identifies three strategies historians use within that construct to achieve something that will be accepted as an explanation of what happened in the past. One of these strategies is formal argument; it applies the laws of cause and effect onto historical conditions, which results in conclusions that occur "by logical necessity."[48] Another explanatory strategy is ideological implication, whereby the knowledge of past events sheds light on the present day and gives us insight into how ideological structures shaped history then and still do now. A third strategy is emplotment, in which sequences of events are ordered and given meaning by being told as a particular kind of story. Each mode of historical writing formalizes a different kind of "poetic insight" into the materials out of which history is made, and each results in a different style of narrative prose.[49] Historians use and combine all of these techniques in different measure, and the strategies themselves go in and out of style. As White says, there is a choice among interpretive strategies, and the grounds for making that choice are "ultimately aesthetic and moral rather than epistemological."[50]

I have moved through this study primarily by means of emplotment in order to make an argument that remains committed and closely connected to the difficult testimony from this period. I have aimed to articulate both the crisis of colonial settlement and the relationship between its acute conditions and the construction of coloniality by bringing these historical actors and their writing up close. My contention is that we must grapple with this difficult period because it was through early catastrophe that colonial identities were first formed. The shock of early settlement—its suffering and its violence—happened in unknown places that were, by the settlers' very presence, supposed to become English. They did not. What happened instead is hard to read and write about: confusing and often horrid, unthinkable and yet undeniably true. The testimonies and histories from this moment grew out of the rhetoric of exploration and encounter, but it was the charge of settlement—to stay and to possess—that crucially led to the discourse of catastrophe. Catastrophe and colonial settlement became my theme because in my reading of these documents, nothing was more unsettling than that.

CHAPTER 1

Roanoke: Left in Virginia

An account of the particularities of the imployments of the English Men
Left in Virginia . . .

—From the title of Ralph Lane's account of the first
Roanoke settlement, 1586

Of the countless writings about the beginnings of English America, perhaps none condenses the story of a settlement as radically as the three letters "CRO." When John White came to Roanoke in 1590 to relieve the colony he had left there three years earlier, all 110 settlers were gone and this cryptic message, carved into a tree that stood in front of the abandoned English fort, was left behind. The whole existence of the colony—its population, its habitation, its past, and its potential future—was concentrated into this "secret token," and yet John White believed that it was a history he could read. In his narrative of these events, published by Richard Hakluyt in his *Principall Navigations* of 1598, White describes why: "upon a tree, in the very browe thereof were curiously carved these faire Romane letters CRO: . . . a secret token agreed upon betweene them & me at my last departure from them . . . to write or carve on the trees or posts of the dores the name of the place where they should be seated . . . if they should happen to be distressed in any of those places, that then they should carve over the letters or name, a Crosse ☧ in this forme, but we found no such signe of distresse."[1] Seeing no cross, White believed that his people voluntarily moved to the Indian village of Croatoan, forty miles south of Roanoke. However, John White never made it to Croatoan to recover his colony or even to detect any further "signes or certain knowledge" of them. The small English fleet that carried White to Roanoke in 1590 was interested in finding an established colony only if it could be used as a base for privateering, a place to spend the winter months while waiting to seize Spanish ships traveling through the West Indies in the spring. On White's urging, the fleet briefly considered going on to Croatoan to look for the settlers, but the vagaries of ship faring on that piece of coastline intervened. Weather grew foul, cables broke, anchors were lost, ships almost grounded, fresh water dwindled, and victuals grew scarce. Given these conditions, White's case for further exploration came nowhere close to prevailing. He was left to commit "my discomfortable company the planters in Virginia, to the merciful help of the Almighty" (716).

The first English families who came to live in America were abandoned, became lost in the woods, and were never heard from again. This story, about innocents enticed into the forest and then absorbed by wild nature, has long occupied the American cultural imagination. As Richard Slotkin and Toni Morrison have shown, American uses of the archetype convert a long history of racialized violence against Native American and African American people into a story about a white hero's journey into "untamed," "dark" territories.[2] In this chapter I position the story of Roanoke's lost people differently: not as a prelude to the mythos of the American wilderness but rather as a coda to the forced expulsion that ended England's dream of inhabiting a New World Eden almost as soon as it began. Before the English colony at Roanoke was lost, other attempts at settlement had repeatedly failed. Before some unknowable thing happened to whoever carved the letters "CRO" on the brow of a tree, the question of what happened—and an incapacity to answer that question—already pervaded English reports from Virginia. We might even consider the legend of the "Lost Colony" as a culturally negotiated settlement, a kind of screen memory for this early history of colonization. That legend transforms a history of deep indeterminacy into a story about indeterminacy; it replaces the violence that arose from not knowing with a melancholy arising from loss; it disavows a history of failed colonization through a mystery about wandering off into the woods. The image of John White halted at the root of the cryptic tree thus becomes an emblem obscuring a far more problematic record of colonial history: reports of earlier attempts at settlement in which the failure to understand or account for events in Virginia was a central feature.

Between 1584 and 1590 the English took up residence in America under the specter of profound dislocation. The Roanoke ventures established an English colonial presence in the New World, but it was a presence whose features were defined by chaos and disappearance. This chapter analyzes events and their contemporary representations from the 1584 charter for settlement, to the 1585 exploration of the territory, through three different attempts to establish a colony, and finally to White's failed rescue mission in 1590. In this time, to be "left in Virginia" signified a radical departure not only from a known world but also from a world of knowing. Two connected themes run through these sources and structure the discursive frames through which this early colonial experience was represented: disordered cognition and the threat of abandonment; or, to put it in a slightly different way, not being able to read and not being able to leave.

Although the 1584 charter for the future Roanoke colony ceremoniously bequeathed an unknown land, and the glowing exploratory report of the next year remained willfully ignorant of warnings about inhabiting it, the colonial incursion itself was a different matter. There on the ground, not knowing what was happening was a deadly matter. While the material from those who look forward to a colony is confident and predictive, the settler narratives that look back on it are characterized by disturbance and unpredictability, both in their subject matter and in their formal structures. At its center, therefore, this chapter pursues the state and stakes of not knowing in the first settlement at Roanoke and suggests that the disorganized narrative evidence from that mission, in its very confusion and incapacity to tell what happened, leaves a most telling record of colonial incursion. The Roanoke ventures failed to "settle" the New World for the English, but they did leave behind a record of unsettlement that began to associate colonial space with bewilderment as much as with discovery, and with what was lost there as much as with what was found.

Modern histories agree about the problems that consigned the attempted settlements at Roanoke to failure: the influence of privateering and its lures of quick money; the lack of economic and political will to support colonization; a shallow shoreline that jeopardized every boat that came in; and hostilities between a militarized colony and the native people they intended to dispossess.[3] For example, Alan Taylor writes of a colony in a "poor location" that "lacked supplies from and contact with England" and of English sea captains who, knowing that the area was "a graveyard for ships and sailors," much preferred to pursue "immediate wealth" in the West Indies.[3] Along with this consensus about the material circumstances that shaped the would-be Roanoke settlement, almost every account of the colony also employs the same rhetorical effect to end the story, trailing off into an evocative

silence in which the lost or abandoned settlers are neither absent nor present but finally unlocatable, even to history: . . . *and they were never heard
from again.* While popular sources pluck this string with varying degrees
of theatricality, academic treatments also contribute to the aura of mystery
around Roanoke by drawing on a similar dramatic effect. Thus Taylor writes
that "the mariners abandoned any surviving colonists to their still mysterious fate."[5] Karen Kupperman concludes that not even splinter parties of the
Roanoke group were ever "seen again": "There were persistent rumors that
some English people had escaped . . . and were with other tribes. John Smith
claimed that Powhatan showed him 'divers utensils of theirs,' and another
Virginian, George Percy, reported seeing an Indian boy whose hair was 'a
perfect yellow.' But that was all."[6]

I want to enter the field of mystery around Roanoke in order to replace
the persistent reiteration of this final echo into silence with close textual
readings of how the colonists represented their often unaccountable experience. Mine is an attempt to discover a different idiom for a colonial incursion that shuttled between messy, fractious fields of action on the one hand
and long stretches of bewildered idleness on the other by acknowledging
that both states—active and inactive—exhibited the same confusion about
where one was and what was happening.

Focusing on the centrality of the unaccountable in the early records requires a shift in the evidentiary basis of analysis. The most extensive records
of colonial knowledge produced in this era come from the first colony in
Roanoke: Thomas Harriot's *A Briefe and True Report of the New Found Land
of Virginia* and John White's watercolors of the people and material culture
in the area. Both provide detailed and exhaustive eyewitness evidence and
were the foundational primary texts through which the New World was represented to European eyes.[7] It may seem slightly perverse to accord these
important documents so small a role here, but the choice is deliberate. For
all the knowledge gathered and preserved in the Harriot and White collaboration, neither work is primarily concerned with direct events or their representation. White does depict the practices of daily life, and Harriot famously
attempts to summarize Algonquian responses to the English, especially in
terms of disease, technology, and religion. However, both studiously avoid
the uncertainties of contingent temporality in favor of a perpetual present
tense that is able to stabilize, authenticate, and transmit information.[8] They
represent colonial presence in America in terms of what is becoming known.

Harriot and White were expert at their tasks, but they also worked in genres—the catalog and the portrait—most likely to depict the New World in a controlled fashion. As long as the scientist and the artist could be mobile and get close to their subjects, they could list or limn, describe or depict them with an authorizing verisimilitude. Consequently their texts tend to displace the forms of chaos that shaped colonial experience with forms of certainty that shaped the production of European knowledge. Promoting and endorsing a future of success for the colonizing venture, their records do not leave traces of a history of failure. That history, by contrast, is embedded in narrative texts written about Roanoke, especially in a long report by the governor of the first colony, Ralph Lane. Though this chapter analyzes several texts that represent both events and nonevents in Roanoke, Lane's report is the central document used to explore narrative disorder as a mark of catastrophic discourse in the earliest literature of English colonists. A critical engagement with that disorder reveals that a crisis of meaning was among the many forms of unsettlement in the first, failed attempts to settle an English colony in America.

Trouble in England's Eden

One of the earliest texts to enact English prerogatives in the New World was Elizabeth I's 1584 charter to Sir Walter Raleigh.[9] The language of the charter is grandiose in every sense, an elaborate textual performance that mimics the spectacular processions and rituals that were the cultural index of the queen's power. The charter is more than an enumeration of Raleigh's rights and holdings; it is also a performative utterance that, by its mere motion, asserts England's dominion over remote and unknown lands by giving Raleigh permission to go forth and possess them. One way in which the charter enacts its manifold powers is through an elaborately enfolded syntax. The royal subject appears in temporally successive form as "us our heires and successors." Likewise rights are granted to Raleigh, "his heires and assignes and to every or any of them." Raleigh can "discover search fyde out and viewe . . . have holde occupy and enjoy." Conditions apply "from tyme to tyme and at all tymes for ever hereafter."[10] As there is nothing known of the actual territory that Raleigh is going out to possess, there is no end to what the charter can give away: "all the sole of all such landes Countryes and territories so to be discovered and possessed as aforesaid and of all Cities Castles townes villages and places in the same, with the rightes royalties, franchises and jurisdictions as well marine and other within the sayd landes or Countryes or the seas thereunto adjoining."[11] Language ceremoniously swags and drapes over the window to the unknown. The work of the charter is to dictate comprehensively the contours of a land it cannot see and the terms of a future it cannot predict. The enfolded forms of speech extend the reach of the decree by seeming to contain all potentialities: from time to time in all times, for any and all such things, in each and every or any way whatsoever.

This capaciousness is one of the functions of legal language (and not necessarily limited to New World decrees), but in this context the rhetorical redundancy has a particular effect. The charter granting Raleigh license to create an English colony in the New World says everything because there is nothing particular to say. Its central site and action are unknown. If there is a castle, it is his to keep. If there are enemies, they are his to fight. On the one side stands the benefactor and her limitless power to give, and on the other stands the beneficiary and his limitless capacity to receive. Between the two is a colonial space whose principal characteristic is that it is unknown, which is precisely why the English are intent on going there. The unknown is the center around which the entire performance turns. Verbs referring to colonial activity come in strings, but the actions they describe are indistinct, and the relationships between those actions are less distinct still. Lands are "to be discovered or possessed"; territories are "to be possessed and inhabited." But it is unclear whether "the fynding out discovering or Inhabiting" of these places are meant to be alternative activities or equivalent ones. In early modern parlance, the infinitive form of the verb "to possess" included an easy slippage between finding, viewing, claiming, taking, and inhabiting that apparently was to be clarified on the ground, whether by Raleigh or his assignees or whomever.

Although it is unclear how a settlement might figure among the proliferation of possessive possibilities, the charter does grant to Raleigh (and/or others) "full and mere power and aucthorty" to run one. Much clearer is the Crown's strictly limited obligation to such a potential settlement. The charter ends with what may be justly called an abandonment clause. If Raleigh "or any of them or any other" should decide to rob, steal, or in any way fleece the Crown or anyone in league with the Crown, a public proclamation would be made in all Atlantic ports that the English in Virginia were no longer under anyone's protection and thus fair game for all comers: "And that from and after such tyme of puttying out of proteccion of the said Walter Raleigh . . . and the said places within theire habitacion possessyon and rule shalbe out of our proteccion and allegiaunce and free

for all Princes and others to pursue with hostility as being not our Sub-
jectes nor by us any waye to be avouched mainteyned or defended nor to
be holden as any of ours nor to our proteccion of Domynyon or alliaunce
any way belonging."[12] Of all the clauses in the charter, the abandonment
clause is the most crucial. It establishes that for all that is unknown about
the potential risks and rewards of colonial activity, the Crown would take
only the rewards. The threat of withdrawing protection is actually spe-
cious because the charter offers no protections in the first place. The public
"putting out" would allow the Crown officially to fend off any demands
for reprisal should the English in remote lands turn to privateering, even
though setting up a wintering port for English privateers was the primary
motivation for establishing a North American foothold. More germane
to the history of settlement, however, is that from the very point of initiation, England's overseas colonies could instantly be cut loose from protection, alliance, or any means of belonging to the home country. Settlers at
Roanoke were later shocked when supply ships failed to come to their aid,
but abandonment was literally written into their constitution. That failure is generally described as circumstantial, but the "especiall grace" and
"certeyne science" that chartered English colonization indicated otherwise. The protecting cover of dominion could be extended by mere motion, but it could also by mere motion be withdrawn.

In April 1584, a scant month after receiving his charter, Raleigh sent out
two ships to explore the newly expanded reaches of England's realm. The
ships returned to England in September with assurances of vast potential
and future returns. By December the propaganda campaign for investment
in an American settlement was in full swing. Confirmations of the journey's
success circulated among potential backers in the written form of a glowing
report from Capt. Arthur Barlowe, in the material form of pearls and skins,
and in the startling and spectacular human form of two Algonquian Indians, Manteo and Wanchese. The Indians and the English each had strong
motives for having Manteo and Wanchese accompany the expedition back
to London. Colonial promoters wanted to display the men as living, breathing proof that the reconnaissance mission had established ties with coop-
erative natives, and they also hoped that sheer curiosity would capture the
attention of potential investors. For their part, the Indian leaders of Ossomocomuck, the region where the two cultures made contact, hoped that the
two high-ranking men would act as scouts to gather firsthand information
on this new group of potential allies and trading partners, to assess their

homeland, and to investigate their intentions.[13] As Michael Leroy Oberg notes about their mutual observation, "The English people gawked at Manteo and Wanchese, but the two Algonquians returned the English gaze."[14]

In one important respect, Indians and English had a common goal: to learn each other's language. For both groups, the ability to communicate effectively was crucial to facilitating trade and preventing misunderstandings that could lead to violence. Having capable go-betweens who held positions of status and trust in the respective groups was essential to constituting an alliance, however each group's plans for that alliance differed. Although Thomas Harriot is credited for conducting these language lessons while back in England, the tutelage surely went both ways. The English were in Ossomocomuck for six weeks, not nearly enough time for the language barrier to fall, but Manteo and Wanchese remained with Harriot and others at Raleigh's estate for eight months. During that time the English and the Indians communicated their impressions of Ossomocomuck and London and sought to clear up any misunderstanding, but each group kept its ultimate goals for a continued association to itself.[15]

Arthur Barlowe's report, published in Hakluyt's 1589 edition of *The Principall Navigations* under the title "The First Voyage made to the coastes of America, with two barkes, where in were Captaines M. Philip Amadas, and M. Arthur Barlowe, who discovered part of the Countrey now called Virginia, Anno 1584," both claimed the primacy of discovery and promised the imminent fulfillment of England's goals.[16] "The First Voyage" is still read as possessing a thoroughly optimistic outlook, and it is true that its salient features are wonder at the splendor of the New World and enthusiasm about establishing a peaceful, profitable relationship with its native people.[17] What is largely ignored, however, is the role Manteo and Wanchese played in the text's composition. Recognizing this composition history prompts a significantly different critical analysis of the text, one that ties it more closely to the failed attempts at settlement that followed in its wake. Barlowe's report actually has two time frames. One describes the things he saw and did during his six weeks at Ossomocomuck; another fills in the backstory to some of those events, a history that could have been provided only by Manteo and Wanchese. Thus, while Barlowe's descriptions of his direct experiences are organized according to the perceptions and desires of an Englishman on the threshold of colonization, the interpolated narratives are translations of Indian intelligence well outside that frame. The former contain misreadings, but embedded in the latter are warnings from an Algonquian history that neither Barlowe nor future colonists had the skill or inclination to heed.

The guiding fantasy of Barlowe's discourse is that the New World is a kind of rediscovered Garden of Eden.[18] He declares, "We found the people most gentle, loving, and faithful, void of all guile, and treason, and such as lived after a manner of the golden age" (108). In examples such as these, Barlowe's descriptions inaugurate English colonization of America with an idyllic flourish, an alluring portrait of the land to be possessed.[19] This Edenic discourse was shaped by promotional, ideological intentions and was fully coherent with the aims of England's New World colonization. However, a striking textual dissonance exists between Barlowe's rhapsodic refrains and the underlying Algonquian leitmotif of resistance. The complex, interpolated narratives from Manteo and Wanchese are far more predictive of future English experiences in Roanoke. These tales are about shipwrecks, lost people, an astoundingly resilient native leader, and a long-standing history of intertribal conflict in the area. Manteo and Wanchese's accounts linger outside the report's primary discursive mode, remaining internally alien to the narrative's projected message even as they become part of its record. Inside the English report, they remain Indian stories.

Manteo and Wanchese tell two shipwreck narratives, both part of local Indian oral and material culture. These stories, which depict white people becoming lost in Ossomocomuck, belie Barlowe's representation of his English arrival as a scene of first encounter and provide prescient knowledge that the shoals of the Outer Banks would often be fatal to European ships. Furthermore they demonstrate how Indian knowledge is transmitted and preserved as history, the significance of which never registers with English colonists.[20] Earlier in the text, Barlowe depicts the "first" Indian coming aboard the English ship and marveling at the vessel's power and beauty, but one of the Algonquian shipwreck stories begins with a contrasting tableau: Indians on their own shores gathered around the wreck of a European ship from which no white person survived. They pull the nails and spikes out of the wreckage and use them to make what Barlowe calls "their best instruments" (104). Here is another reversal. Instead of being passive beneficiaries of European manufactures, the Indians, without the instructive or monitory presence of colonists, engage in a material syncretism in which the nails of the ship become raw material for their own manufacture.

The second shipwreck happens near the village of Secotan, where John White later made many of his watercolors. Two sailors survive and stay in the area for three weeks. The interpolated Secotan narrative of the castaways figuratively turns White's gaze in the other direction, as the Europeans, descriptions of whom circulated widely, become the objects of Indian curiosity. When Barlowe reports that the people at Roanoke "wondered marvelously when we were amongst them at the whiteness of our skin, ever coveting to touch our breasts, and to view the same," he again implies first contact, ignoring the long-standing dissemination of the story he has just been told and recorded. The second shipwreck narrative concludes when, at the urging of the castaways, the Secotan lash two canoes together and watch the castaways set off to sea, their tattered shirts fashioned into makeshift sails. The results are predictable: "shortly after it seems they were cast away, for the boates were found upon the sea coast cast aland in another island adjoining" (111). Thus these mariners end their story by being lost twice, once from their European fleet and once again from their native rescuers.

Manteo and Wanchese also tell the colonial promoters gathered at Raleigh's estate about an ongoing war between the Secotan and the nearby Pomeiooc. Barlowe calls it a "deadlie and terrible warre" and relates only certain episodes from what is clearly a larger history of massacres and malice, pitched battles, and treaties made and broken. "[A]s these men which we have brought with us into England, have made us to understand," Barlowe writes, "there remaineth a mortall malice in the Sequotanes, for the many injuries and slaughters done upon them" (113). While the English were in Ossomocomuck, the Roanoke, allies of the Secotan, tried to exploit the presence of English guns and iron weapons to overwhelm their enemy, the Pomeiooc, appealing to the newcomers' interests by promising loot of rich commodities in Pomeiooc territory. The small English company demurred, Barlowe noting that as to the natives' real intentions in this matter, "we leave to that to the triall hereafter" (114). The ideological and promotional framework of Barlowe's report allows it to rhapsodize about a future English America even as it records its current malice and slaughters. The text Barlowe wants to write has to remain ignorant of the Indian stories circulating within it. However, there is a practical force behind this willful blindness as well as a rhetorical one. A report from a six-week sojourn could withstand inconsistencies—the portrayal of native inhabitants as gentle and tractable souls alongside the history of a people in a bloody war—because most of the men from the reconnaissance mission did not have to sort out these contradictions in lived experience. Manteo, Wanchese, Ralph Lane, and the colonists involved in "the triall hereafter" did.

In terms of that "triall," it is important to pay attention to depictions of the Roanoke werowance Wingina, who would come to be a defining figure in the first English attempt at settlement. Throughout Barlowe's report, Wingina is both absent and present. Barlowe mentions him but never meets him; though the English hear of him often, they "saw him not at all." It is abundantly clear to the English visitors that he "is greatly obeyed." Barlowe infers Wingina's authority from seeing the respect paid to Granganimeo, his brother, but Manteo and Wanchese make the point explicitly: "[we] have understood since by these men, which we brought home, that no people in the worlde carry more respect to their King" (103). All throughout the six weeks of Barlowe's stay, Wingina kept his distance, remaining at his seat in Dasemunkepeuc while recuperating from wounds suffered in the war. Barlowe reports that though the king was "shot in two places through the body, and once clean through the thigh," he was "recovered" (100).[21] However, his wound was not the only reason Wingina did not meet with the European newcomers. The English could not comprehend that Wingina's status so exceedingly surpassed any they could ever hope to have that he would never be the one to make the initial contact, much less leave his principal seat to do so. While Barlowe understood that the "King" was respected, he failed to grasp that Wingina, watching from afar, was in fact superior.

When Barlowe's "First Voyage" appeared in Hakluyt's 1589 edition of the *Principall Navigations*, one evocative line read: "The earth bringeth forth all things in aboundance, as in the first creation, without toil or labour."[22] In the second edition of 1600, that sentence was excised completely. Between the writing of that sentence and its disappearance lies the history of the Roanoke settlements. By 1600 the English were still not at all sure what their "Virginia" would become, but certainly it was not to be an Eden. Despite the hopes outlined in Raleigh's charter and Barlowe's report, it had become abundantly clear that to find a land did not mean to possess it.

Writing the Incursion

In April 1585, only months after Barlowe's luminous report was circulated among backers of England's new colonial venture, seven ships carried over six hundred men to Virginia. Just over one hundred were to stay there to establish a permanent base. Fourteen months after arriving, they frantically pulled up stakes and returned to England, leaving a trail of violence in their wake. Shoreside their onetime hosts, the Roanoke, were incensed and deeply set on reprisal. What happened?

To learn what happened in Roanoke in 1585 and 1586, there is at once no better and no worse place to look than Ralph Lane's narrative, the full title of which neatly encapsulates its intentions: *An Account of the Particularities of the Imployments of the English Men Left in Virginia by Richard Greenevill under the Charge of Master Ralph Lane Generall of the Same, from the 17. of August 1585. until the 18. of June 1586. at Which Time They Departed the Countrey; Sent and Directed to Sir Walter Raleigh.*[23] There is no better place to look because Lane was in command of the settlement, and his is a detailed record of this first English incursion. As governor, Lane had the charge of creating and fortifying a base from which English privateers could raid Spanish galleons laden with New World gold. While this plunder was the immediate objective, Lane was also supposed to assess and describe the location's potential for a full-fledged colony: its geography, its resources, and its people. In addition he was tasked with giving an account of all that transpired there. If a successful mission required careful accounting, then a failed one demanded a more thorough explanation still. Lane's English company had been forced to abandon Roanoke, leaving the fledgling enterprise hanging on the edge of ignominy. Perhaps just as damaging to the company's reputation were the scores of unsettled men returning from the debacle and telling tales in London. Lane's report was expected not only to deliver the facts but also to halt the rumors and justify the colony's dismal outcome. He had no choice but to give an account of, and account for, what exactly happened when Englishmen were, in his jarring phrase, "Left in Virginia."

There is also no worse place to learn about what happened that year in Roanoke because, to put it bluntly, Lane's report is a mess. It lacks fluidity, has maddening omissions, and is poorly organized. It tells too little, leaving gaping holes in the story, except for when it tells too much, laying out everything Lane intended to do instead of describing what he actually did. The text declares allegiance to certain structuring principles—order, division, particularity—and then immediately subverts them. It requires the reader to engage in uncomfortable reading practices: to discount what is on the pages because each is filled with nonevents; to search for what is not on the pages because information is suppressed everywhere; to riffle back and forth between pages because the text refuses chronology. Having failed at his commission, Lane also fails to account for it.

One reason Lane's report is difficult to read is that he was unable to secure a position from which to write. Ostensibly, Lane's first job was to express "what I (Lane) can do for you (Raleigh)." This is the grammar of the colonist as subject, one existing in a remote relation to the imperial powers with whom and by whom his actions are identified. In this configuration Lane's intentions count. Instead, throughout the report he continually finds himself speculating about "what they (the Natives) can do to me (Lane)." This is the grammar of the colonist as object, one existing in a local relation to the Native American power that both thwarts his actions and potentially renders them meaningless. In this configuration Lane's intentions are often entirely irrelevant. There is also a third grammar at play here, a particularly colonial one that expresses fear and reproach: "what you (in England) promised to do for us (left here in Virginia)." When the expedition's lead ship returned to England in August 1585, the commander, Sir Richard Grenville, promised Lane that a supply ship would arrive in Roanoke by the next Easter at the latest, bringing sufficient men, munitions, and provisions to grow the colony. The ship did not come. Obligation, vulnerability, abandonment: among the shifting positions of these colonial relations Lane could not put his report in order even in retrospect.

While the report's author inhabits multiple subjectivities, its content offers up multiple versions of reality. Lane's strangely indeterminate relationship to facts actively refuses knowledge production, frustrating both his primary audience and modern scholars who take up his text. Some scholars have read the report as an elaborate justification for a bungled mission: the governor of the colony denies responsibility for the mission's failure by tacitly casting blame on his careless sponsors. This view sees Lane as the resentful apologist.[24] Others have read the report as a text that one must filter and radically condense. Indeed the purely informational content of Lane's report can be summarized in just a few sentences, and able minds have done just that.[25] The vast majority of readers in search of historical specificity usually jettison Lane's account and concentrate instead on the work of Thomas Harriot and John White, members of Lane's colony. Why read Lane's torturous and unreliable prose when we have at hand the very model of evidentiary reportage about the initiation of English colonial history? Harriot and White simply radiate historicity. Although Lane's report was published in Hakluyt's *Principall Navigations* of 1589, Harriot and White's are clearly the ones to follow from an archival point of view. Compared to the scholarly attention lavished on the work of Harriot and White, Lane's work remains understudied.[26] And among those who do study Lane, I believe something essential about Lane remains unread.

Part of my aim in focusing on Lane is to explore why he could not have written his *Account of the Particularities* as Harriot wrote his *Briefe and True Report* and to ask what that incapacity says about larger issues of narrative representation in the writing of settlement. Harriot and White were charged with gathering as much information as possible about the newly discovered land and with rendering that information as hard evidence that could circulate and promote colonization. The team was chosen because each man had exceptional skills suited to the task: Harriot was a leading scientist of his day, and White was a painter of precise miniatures. Detailed, accurate, comprehensive, methodical—the work they produced accomplished every goal set for it. Taken independently, each man's contribution captured the New World with greater precision than any other text had up until that point; published together, the effect was groundbreaking. In 1590 Theodore de Bry presented the collaborative work as the first part of his *Great Voyages* series. The volume was simply titled *America*.[27] It was, according to its modern editor Paul Hulton, "the first of its kind which can justifiably be described as scientific in both text and illustration."[28] By the time the English settlements failed in 1590, the work's original promotional intention was decidedly outweighed by the extraordinary value of the knowledge that volume contained.[29] Harriot and White offered an emphatically realistic record of what *was* there. Ralph Lane's job was to give a narrative of what *happened* there. He had to write the incursion itself, which proved the more challenging, and less valuable, task by far.

I use the term "incursion" to specify and explore the important interval between early contact and permanent settlement that the failed experiment of Roanoke represents. This historical space is regularly considered a contact zone, using Mary Louise Pratt's term for those "social spaces where cultures meet, clash, and grapple with each other, often in contexts of highly asymmetrical relations of power."[30] Pratt's model is a broad one that can be used for situations of contact, settlement, expansion, frontiers, and for the continued interactions in the presence of colonial or unequal powers. Within those parameters, Pratt writes not only of the arts of the contact zone, but also of its perils: "miscomprehension, incomprehension . . . absolute heterogeneity of meaning."[31] Given the prevalence and consequences of these perils during the time between contact and permanent settlement, I would like to think more specifically about the contact zone of colonial incursion as a "chaos zone." I use this term to refer to both social and mental spaces within the colonial contest where the ability to understand what is happening is recurrently and threateningly disturbed. Whether such failures of recognition result in uncanniness, paranoia, misprision, panic, physical violence, or (most frequently) a dangerous combination of all of these, they must be understood as something other than a temporary sense of disorientation. In the chaos zone, explanatory structures do not steadily accrue by adapting and realigning new data with a new ability to decipher. Instead, disorder is eruptive, endemic, and usually unresolved. While the model of the contact zone traces transcultural behavior over time, the model of the chaos zone concentrates more intensely on those states of confusion that resist linear integration, and that just as often inhibit cross-cultural interaction as occasion it. Therefore, if the contact zone describes that arena where two cultures actively meet, clash, and grapple, the chaos zone adds to this theater of interaction the often dangerous situation of isolation, where the perils of incomprehension are played out in a tense stand-off. Reading the writing of incursion through the lens of the chaos zone thus not only allows us to treat the chaotic atmosphere that surrounds not-knowing as a form of, rather than a failure of, evidence; it also preserves the strange combination of suspension and crisis that these accounts often depict.

This critical approach is related to Myra Jehlen's concept of "history before the fact," in which historical actors are deeply uncertain of, and unable to settle on a meaning for, what they observe around them, and yet document their experiences even as those experiences themselves remain contingent and not yet processed into ideological coherence. Jehlen describes this state as "underdetermined" and claims it is pervasive in colonial interactions, where there is often not "enough evidence to make certain an explanation of observed phenomenon." She further contends that a more totalizing treatment of colonial writing as a literature of European domination often forecloses textual traces of this instability.[32] By considering that moment of "never enough evidence" as itself a species of evidence, we can bring Ralph Lane's writing about the first attempt at a colony more fully into the textual and critical history of Roanoke. My purpose here is to create a critical framework in which the elaborate failures of Lane's report coalesce into a map of its meaning. In this reading, Lane's unsettled narrative is important for exactly the same reason it is difficult to read: because it maps a disordered epistemology.

It is tempting to put the narrative back on track, to forgo its wayward path, ignore the detours, and merely pin down what happened. Instead, I want to make "happening" itself an object of inquiry, for I believe the question of "what happened" in this settlement attempt and throughout the field of colonial incursion is multiform. It includes things that seemed to happen but did not happen, things that never happened but were imagined as if they happened, and things that were never acknowledged or perhaps never even experienced as happening but did indeed happen. One value in opening a line of reading in which the question "what happened?" does not strive for closure is that it introduces a different kind of evidence. Texts can have literary and historical merit precisely because they are confused about the status of happening—a recurrent state in colonial settlement. Lane's is just such a confused text, and because it marks a shift from English exploration literature to colonial settlement literature, I argue that its "flaws" need to be reconsidered as evidence of that shift. Possibly the text's confusion is exactly the point: what looks like flawed rhetoric is instead volatile consciousness textually preserved.[33]

Lane initiates the story of his year in Roanoke not as an action to be followed but as a problem to be solved. His first sentence is already constructed as a stammering reply: "That I may proceed with order in this discourse, I thinke it requisite to divide it into two partes" (255). These two parts are supposed to be, first, a description of how he and his men explored the country and, second, an account of the problems that forced their return to England. Lane's resolve to split his discourse into these two discrete modes—exploratory and military—demonstrates his intent to respond to English objectives for colonization, but his failure to uphold that division shows how the logic of those objectives disarticulated when preliminary plans were put into practice in Ossomocomuck/Virginia. Even as Lane tries to chart the path his discourse will follow, that path disappears beneath him. First, he promises to describe the explorations but instead makes a preemptive defense of their inadequacy by pointing to the weakness of his small company, its dire lack of supplies, and its consequent incapacity to accomplish much. Next, he promises to parse his rationale for his men's sudden departure but instead discharges a jumble of allusions, lurching back and forth in time to narrate their rescue and resupply as well as tales of hurricanes, conspiracies, and retroactive declarations of war. Indeed the opening gambit itself stops in medias res: "in the beginning wherof shall bee declared the conspiracie of Pemisapan, with the Savages of the maine to have cutt us off, &c." (255–56). The sentence, itself a quite accurate figure for the stalled Roanoke ventures, does not end at all but trails off in an overwhelmed, indeterminate et cetera.

It is not that Lane is an especially bad writer. In his letters, for example, he often demonstrated rhetorical command and a keen awareness for his

audience. In August 1585 he wrote to Sir Francis Walsingham, a high ad-
viser in Elizabeth's Privy Court, that he was confident about staying in Virginia "with a good compagnye, moore as well of gentlemen as others." At
the same time, he confided to Sir Phillip Sydney, a military commander like
himself, that in addition to living among "savages," he had to contend with
"the herdedge of wild menn of myne own nation" (202, 204). In September
he sent Richard Hakluyt a glowing letter "from the new fort in Virginia,"
which in its language and selection of details mirrored Arthur Barlowe's
1584 report almost perfectly. From his post in Virginia, Lane claimed that
he was on "the goodliest soil under the cope of heaven . . . the goodliest and
most pleasing territorie in the world" (207–8). Hakluyt expressed his ap-
proval by including the letter as in introduction to Lane's own report, publishing them together in *The Principall Navigations*.

However, in moving from the letter describing the goodly soil to the narrative of what happened on it, one detects a sudden change for the worse.
The space of incursion in which Lane found himself could not be adequately
narrated because, unlike the catalog form, the logic of narrative structure
could not be relied on to effect its organizational work: to shape, articulate,
and order events. This structural failure explains why Lane's report is more
than an apologia outlining how things would have gone better under different circumstances. Apologia is a systematic defense written in response to
charges, but Lane's account of his tactical failure goes beyond that. It departs
from systemic expression and wades into a struggle to signify other failures
of cognition and representation, a struggle that, even in retrospect, is still
caught up in the colonial chaos zone. In both the actual and alternative scenarios Lane describes, a surreal quality overwhelms a discourse of sequence,
causation, and consequence. This narrative that cannot establish temporal
boundaries, that imbricates real and imagined events, and that actively refuses chronology represents an early discursive turn in which the disrupted
epistemologies that arose from colonial experience also gave shape to its
narrative forms.

As for the task of settling Roanoke, conditions were bad from the start.
As the Algonquian shipwreck narratives indicate, the English ships approached a shore that was shallow and rife with crags and shoals. The English flagship *Tyger* repeatedly knocked against the hidden outcroppings
and nearly wrecked. Left with few provisions and never resupplied, completely unprepared to meet the challenges posed by the new environment,
and flummoxed by the area's power relations, the prospective colonists were

in no way equipped to survive, let alone to possess and hold "barbarous lands." Still, Lane was commissioned to explore.

By the time Lane began exploring the rivers of Ossomocumuck/Virginia, the English had been there for seven months. According to David Quinn, most of that period remains in something of a historical fog:

> We have no adequate account of the progress of the first colony under Lane after the departure of the last of Grenville's vessels in September 1585, until Lane provides us from March 1586 onwards with the materials for a story which carries us down to Drake's visit in June 1586. We should like to have some clear account of conditions at the fort and the houses near it, of the day-to-day relations between Lane's men and Wingina's village nearby, and of how White and Harriot proceeded with their task of surveying the ground and investigating the fauna and flora of the surrounding territory. (244)

In other words, we should like to have something better than Lane's account, but we do not. The narrative Quinn constructs for this period uses introductory phrases such as "So far as we can judge," "It is just possible," and "Very conjecturally, we may suggest." These are not the kind of phrases historians like, and Quinn's frustration is obvious. "It is most exasperating," he interrupts himself, "that we have no detailed knowledge of the progress of this party."[34] Other historians, Karen Kupperman and Michael Leroy Oberg most effectively, have been able to construct a workable narrative for Lane's settlement within the larger framework of Roanoke's history, but they too are wary of what Lane's text does and does not offer. "It is a difficult document to read," Oberg writes, "owing to the author's imprecise language and the palpable confusion his work manifests."[35] Kupperman characterizes Lane as having a "limited sense of reality."[36] Another critical consensus: although Lane's report is an essential document, it should be held at arm's length.

However, it is possible both to integrate the text more fully into the historical record and to realize its significance if our questions are as much about disorder as they are about order. For this reevaluation to occur, the total closure between the accuracy and and the value of evidence must be eased. The task is complicated because any reading of a text requires constructing a narrative around that text, and in this case both Lane's text and my own express much interest in what happened in Roanoke. Therefore, while part of my intention is to create a narrative about the first settlement in Roanoke, I also intend for that narrative to be a form of exegesis, not of summary. Instead of putting aside the report's methods of representation to mine it for facts, I stay closely involved with a discursive reading—not only what Lane says but also to a great extent how he says it—in order to resist a historical closure that the primary materials do not allow. My aim is to treat those elements of Lane's report that represent his "palpable confusion" and "limited sense of reality" as critical tools and not liabilities, so that a wish for the report "we should like to have" does not replace a reading of the report we do have.

Three River Journeys

Ralph Lane writes about three different river journeys: two that actually happened and one that he only imagines.[37] The first journey Lane describes in detail is a 130-mile trek up the Chowan River to the northeast. Lane and his troops were an aggressive bunch. By that point the Roanoke werowance, Wingina, had taken on the new name Pemisapan. The linguist James A. Geary proposes a possible translation of the name that portends increased vigilance: "he looks out as he goes."[38] It was a season of growing wariness, discipline, and change in the political landscape as Indian leaders tested their relations with these forceful, disease-spreading strangers. When Pemisapan learned of Lane's intended journey up the Chowan, he warned Lane that at the main town of Choanoac, the exploring party would find nearly three thousand warriors preparing to mount an assault on the English outpost back at Roanoke. Choanoac was the principal seat of the most powerful and populous tribe in the region. Its werowance, Menatonon, held loose control over the people of eighteen surrounding towns and had over seven hundred fighting men at his immediate command. The English company arrived fully armed and expecting a fight. When Lane did indeed find thousands of warriors in congress, he felt no need to inquire as to their purpose. Breaking into the center of the group, he seized Menatonon without warning. To Lane and his sixty men, this was a brilliant preemptive strike. To Menatonon and his thousands of tribesmen, the seizure was an outrageous act committed by uninvited guests. To Pemisapan, the fact that Lane had commenced the journey deeply suspicious of the Indians he would encounter was victory enough.[39] In the first pages of his report, Lane offers the following account of the scene: "Choanoke it selfe is the greatest Province and Seigniorie lying upon that River, and the very Towne it selfe is able to put 700 fighting men into the fielde, besides the forces of the Province it selfe" (259). That is all Lane reveals. There is no mention of the enormous Indian assembly, or his conviction about their intent, or his seizure of Menatonon. Again, Quinn notes his dissatisfaction: "Lane's failure to provide a narrative sketch for this expedition leaves us in some doubt at this point as to the circumstances" (259). But since Lane's stated mission at this point is to report only diagrammatic information (land elevation, river depth, town names), he feels the need to occlude the more alarming conditions—real, imagined, or arising from deliberate misinformation—that defined his journey. The stabilizing knowledge that would encourage future colonization has to replace the destabilizing knowledge about what actually happened: that dark forebodings of extermination led to the seizure of the valley's most powerful king. After all, while geographic features remain comfortingly stable, shadowy reports of a massive, plotting confederacy might later be revealed as erroneous. Lane does not report the episode because, despite his confusion, the overriding goal of his territorial survey is to offer "particularies" and to avoid being mistaken about the often baffling conditions on the ground.

However, Lane's account cannot continue in this nonnarrative mode because his explorations cannot proceed without the intervention of Menatonon as a source of information. The site of his disavowed confrontation is also the site of his most valuable intelligence. Lane first records Menatonon's presence as a simple matter of identification ("The King of the sayd Province is called Menatonon"). He then paints Menatonon as harmless but valuable, a powerful ally but not someone to fear. He describes the man as elderly and infirm ("a man impotent in his lims") but also grave, wise, and expert in the politics of the entire region: "When I had him prisoner with me, for two dayes that we were together, he gave mee more understanding and light of the Countrey than I had received by all the searches and Savages that before I or any of my companie had had conference with" (259). Except for the one jarring word, "prisoner," Lane entirely elides the episode's violence and swirling rumors.

Menatonon tells Lane that there is a king even farther to the northeast of Choanoac—three days' journey by river, then four more days by land—who controls such a vast resource of pearls that all the people's houses, beds, and garments are bejeweled and "a wonder to see" (260).[40] In addition to wanting the pearls, Lane also wants to discover the deep water in which they are found. Menatonon offers to provide guides to take Lane's men there but warns that the land and its possessions are fiercely protected by a king who is "loth to suffer any strangers to enter into his Countrey, and especially to meddle with the fishing for any Pearle there" (261). Lane's report on his company's discoveries begins on target: listing the directions of the compass, the course of the river, and the names of towns. Each section is mapped out and offered as stable intelligence possessed through direct experience. Yet to write within those parameters, he suppresses other events: Pemisapan's warning; the massive Indian assembly; the hostage taking; and the huge risk incurred in following such an aggressive course of action. Several paragraphs into his report, however, Lane loses that highly selective surveying position. Now the most important but still virtual "facts" come through an interpolated source, the host/hostage Menatonon. The werowance is in Lane's "possession" for two days, but the information Menatonon provides possesses Lane for the rest of his journeys. Lane thus goes from following the course of the river to following the discourse of Menatonon, his own geographic survey displaced by Menatonon's report of an unseen king in an unseen land.

At this juncture in the narrative—where the potential for riches, the promise of aid, and the threat of violence are all present—Lane begins to braid descriptions of a second imagined journey into his account of the real one. Addressing Raleigh directly, Lane writes, "Hereupon I resolved with my selfe, that if your supplie had come before the end of April, and that you had sent any store of boats or men . . . I would have sent a small Barke with two Pinnesses . . . to have found out the Bay he spake of" (261).[41] Lane does not simply register this resolution as an unfulfilled intention. Rather he proceeds to outline the journey-not-taken at length and in detail, and as he does, the imagined story begins to overwhelm the eyewitness report. This virtual journey is conceived of as a two-pronged attack. One deployment would take the river and overland route Menatonon described, while another would loop around seaward from Roanoke Island to meet the first group in the bay described by Menatonon. Lane's narrative departure, which begins with the premise "if your supplie had come," then forks out to describe and confront various contingencies along the virtual path. As Lane is a military man, playing out alternative scenarios is part of his job. However, Lane does not know the rules of engagement that would properly structure such a thought experiment. Even in his retrospective writing position, Roanoke remains mostly unknown to him.[42] Lane is not sure where he is/was to begin with, nor is/was he sure exactly what or who surrounds him. Nor, for that matter, is there any reliable, experienced source for such knowledge except, in this case, Menatonon, and then only if the werowance does not have a hidden purpose. We should remember that just days before providing his wise counsel, Menatonon was thought to be gathering a fatal force against the English. At this point, both the map of Lane's journey and the plot of his story are imaginary acts in a completely foreign territory.

Instead of assessing these gaps in information, the discursive preference for the imagined journey simply overrides them. As a writer, Lane is already deep immersed in that other territory. Charting the two routes to the deepwater pearls, Lane creates a material world of forts, bases, headquarters, and meeting points along the way. All the verbs are conditional (*I would have sent; I would have found; I should have ridden; he would have given me*), but the profusion of practical details of the journey overwhelms the narrative's conjectural forms. After marching in with as much food as they could carry, his men would end in "some convenient plot" and raise a fort "upon some corne fielde, that my companie might have lived upon it" (262). The troops would continue on, building small garrisons and leaving holding parties behind, colonizing the route by ensconcing every other day, until they came to the deep bay. Lane "would there have raised a mayne fort, both for the defence of the harboroughs, and our shipping also," before moving the "whole habitation" from the rocky Outer Banks near Roanoke into this better place (263).

What is happening in this narrative detour? Doubtless part of Lane's intention in describing this journey must have been to offer an example of what he could have done, and hence what others might do, given the proper supports. But the journey is described at such length and in such particularity that the fact that it never happened soon gets lost in a welter of details. Narratively, it happens. Moreover, even if Lane intended the plan to act as a guide for future explorers, the scenario is impossible. For example, the inland journey as Lane wrote it would leave him with only thirty, and not two hundred, men. Lane's imagined journey also flies in the face of the few things he did know: that the territory surrounding him was well populated and its people well armed. He also knew he had enemies. As he reveals later in the report, Lane was convinced that Pemisapan was creating a deadly environment by sending "continall worde" to the Choanist "that [the English] purpose was fully bent to destroy them: on the other side he tolde me that they had the like meaning towards us" (265–66).[43] Given all this, why should the prospect of relocating the colony appear so seamless a task? One answer is that precisely because it did not happen, the expedition can be narrated in great detail and without undue complications, Truly, the events and environment of Lane's actual journeys seem more surreal than the completely virtual world of the elaborately imagined "second" trek. This is part of the function of the imaginary in the incursionary account. Virtual courses are more explicable because they proceed from thought alone, whereas events remain inexplicable because they proceed from a world that is unfathomable. The overland voyage to a deeper port, the strong fort they would have built there, the fields they would have planted—these are all clearly defined because they are freely imagined. They accord with what Lane thinks should have happened, while what is happening does not intervene to challenge or trouble his expectations. Another reason Lane needs to relocate the colony with skill and dispatch at this point in the report is because he is gearing up for another, more complicated maneuver ahead. The establishment of this new fort is only part of the strategy of the imaginary journey, and Lane's first excursion into the discourse of "if" loosens up the text for the major departures that follow.

Lane's plan is as follows: he will leave several boats behind on the Chowan River before beginning the overland phase of the journey because, he declares, "My meaning was further at the head of the River" (262). According to this "further" plan, the two-pronged pincer movement headed to the northern, deep-water bay would be joined by a secret third prong: a journey to the west. Because in this scenario the surrounding land would be held and a new fort established, the concealed boats could then take Lane and a smaller company farther into the interior via the powerful Moratuc River, which shared the Albemarle Sound with the Chowan but then headed west.[44] At the source of *this* river, the westerly Moratuc, Lane would find a much more rewarding mission, and perhaps even discover a larger meaning for having been left in Virginia.

The river's head was a full thirty (perhaps even forty) days passage beyond the principal town of Morotico. "Not onely Menatonon, but also the Savages of Morotico themselves doe report strange things of the head of that River," Lane reports (264). The Indians claim that the Moratuc River springs violently from a huge rock behind which is a sea and that the churning water is sometimes brackish with salt. Was this the Northwest Passage? Lane does not separate the long Moratuc River journey from his Chowan narrative or frame it as a proposal for the future. Instead his report continues to braid together the imagined and real journeys without establishing distinctions between the two.

In fact, Lane does eventually travel up the Moratuc River. This "third" river journey begins by flowing seamlessly out of the "second," imaginary journey to the northeast, but soon Lane's account of this westward journey begins to shuttle among several time frames, each frame interrupting and disorienting the others. Lane resolves to take forty men upriver until he meets the Moratucs and Mangoaks who live there, and who, Lane thinks, have agreed to provision and support his further explorations—in essence, to welcome a deployment of armed, hostile newcomers wending through their territories.[45] However, Lane introduces his plan and its eventual failure at the same time: "the hope of recovering more victuall from the Savages made me and my company as narowly to escape starving in that discoverie before our returne, as ever men did that missed the same" (265). Directly after this quote, Lane returns to the massive gathering at Choanoac, revealing for the first time the three thousand warriors in "confederacie against us" and entering the swirl of rumors that circulated before, during, and after that meeting. It is unclear when Lane began to suspect that Pemisapan's warning was a ruse, or why he thought he could make important alliances at an assembly of tribes supposedly gathered against him. Instead of elucidating these matters, the narrative jumps forward to the river trip, only to break the spatial and temporal frame again to report that, in retrospect, he believes the Moratucs and Mangoaks were convinced that the English were coming to destroy them and so abandoned their towns. And so begins, and begins again, Lane's story of abandonment on the Moratuc River. The narrative keeps going back to go forward, forward to go back, breaking spatial and temporal continuity as Lane struggles to communicate his journey and its meaning. Each time the narrative goes off course, it exposes a chaos zone where events are unreadable but in which the stakes of confusion are life or death.

Despite Lane's attempts to shield the exploration part of his report from the battle zone in which that exploration occurred, they are parts of the same story. That story, told straight on, is as follows. In Lane's absence Granganimeo, the strongest native supporter of the English presence in Ossomocomuck, died. It was after Granganimeo's death that Wingina took on his new name, Pemisapan. As Wingina, the werowance debated the merits of an alliance with the English, but as Pemisapan, he recognized that the death and disorder they carried everywhere posed an acute threat. Pemisapan's first tactic was informational: to spread what some claimed were rumors and others saw as fair warning. The English, Pemisapan claimed, were brutal killers, and if they remained unchecked, their violent course would continue on to a bitter end. If Lane traveled upriver, it meant that he was coming to kill the tribes of the interior. Pemisapan's second tactic was positional: to withdraw physically from the English and encourage others to do the same. In the Algonquian world, separation was a common means of disciplining and controlling crisis. The people would create distance, separating themselves from the destructive contagion of the newcomers and making the country appear empty. In matters concerning Lane and his company, they would simply disappear.[46] Although an uninhabited landscape may have accorded with English fantasies of a New World ready to be possessed, in reality the prospect of such isolation was deadly. Because of the *Tyger*'s wreck, Lane's colony had lost most of its imported stock; the people lacked the skills to grow or catch food; their supply ship was nowhere in sight; and if they had not already exhausted local surplus food stores, they had certainly exhausted the local people's willingness to feed them. Whatever arguments existed among Indian groups up and down the Moratuc River, they all decided that they would not come for trading and would not even be visible to the English boats traveling by.

Though Lane's exploring party was not sure what to expect on its long journey up the river, the men did think they knew whom to expect: those Mangoaks and Moratucs with whom Lane thought he had "entered into a league" (266). Instead the riverbanks became an uncanny landscape of silence and empty villages. In his report Lane registers the creeping realization that they have been abandoned, and attempts to take stock: "having passed three dayes voyage up the River, wee could not meete a man, nor finde a graine of corne in any their Townes: whereupon considering with my selfe, that wee had but two dayes victuall left, and that wee were then 160 miles from home, . . . [I] advertised the whole companie of the case wee stoode in" (266–67).

Despite Lane's image of starving on the river with "all the Countrey fledde before us," the company nonetheless decides to move forward rather than to return. The men volunteer that "if the worst fell out," they would sooner boil their two great mastiff dogs into a porridge than turn their boats back to Roanoke.[47] In a typically circuitous sentence, Lane writes, "This resolution of theirs did not a little please mee, since it came of themselves, although for mistrust of that which afterwards did happen, I pretended to have bene rather of the contrary opinion" (268). We can translate this passage as follows: "I was happy they decided to go on, but I pretended not to be happy because I was afraid of what might end up happening, which is exactly what did end up happening." But what happened? We cannot be sure for at least two reasons. First, we are deeply unsure of what the word "happened" means by this point in the report. Nothing has happened so far on the Moratuc River, and that "nothing" is what is haunting the journey. Second, it is precisely at this moment that Lane again interrupts his story to describe a fabled golden city at the river's end, thus transporting us to another world entirely. He now confesses that he has learned of yet another mystery at the river's head: "[I]t is a thing most notorious to all the country, that there is a Province to which they sayd Mangoaks have recourse and traffike up that River of Morotico, which hath a marveilous and most strange Minerall" (268). Distracted by the fantasy of this metal, Lane takes a long time in his report before returning to the men in the boats.

Why at this moment does the story break into a descriptive account of the "marveilous and most strange" mineral at the river's head? Why now—when every Indian village they expect to feed them has been weirdly abandoned; when the men have decided to face starvation rather than "be drawen backe a foote"; when they have resolved to "fully and wholly" accept the wretched prospect of eating their dogs; when they have stopped caring whether they befriend or kill any native person they happen to meet—does a dream city appear? Just at the crux of this reckless journey into the unknown, Lane's narrative imaginatively spirits us away to the head of the Moratuc River, a place of fabulous resources and brisk trade, a famous center that draws Indians from everywhere, and which may even be a gateway to the sea.

The city is called Chaunis Temoatan; it is a Virginian El Dorado. Many details are lavished upon the unreal. Lane describes Indians employed in alluvial mining, houses decked in plates of shining metal, and the helpful guides his friend Menatonon would provide to take him there. His depiction of the place is rich with Indian knowledge, Indian bodies, Indian voices. In almost each and every line, we see and hear a lively world made up of "them." These are a people who take the world in hand. In Lane's words: they say, they call, they take, they wrap, they watch, they chop, they collect, they cast, they melt, they receive, they adorn, they trade, they beautify all things. Meanwhile, traveling up the river and hungrily eyeing the empty banks, Lane and his party never see a man. Lane admits as much, finally pulling the story back into itself: "These things I say. . . . But it fell out very contrarie to all expectation, and likelyhood" (270). According to Lane's private thoughts just pages earlier, "all expectation and likelyhood" were exceedingly dire, but the detailed invocation of Chaunis Temoatan has succeeded in completely reversing the terms—only to rebound back to the strangeness of the journey he is on.

Obviously, Lane never finds the golden city, but what does happen? When Lane refers to "what fell out," he is referring to eating the dogs. After his narrative diversion to the shining mines of Chaunis Temoatan, Lane is compelled to describe how his wretched company was "nowe come to their dogs porredge, that they had bespoken for themselves, if that befell them which did" (272).[48] Lane does not omit the ugly details, even the method used to prepare the dogs as food: in a pot, with sassafras. Although the contrast could not be starker, the narrative puts the fabled mine and the fated dogs in proximate terms. The taboo-breaking scene—the boiling of the mastiffs— is first predicted and then enacted, but between prediction and enactment is a shining city conjured up by hearsay and fantastic desire. Lane's deep narration and glorious vision of the glimmering mining wonderland are all about particularity. However, the awful meal of dogs is equally about particularity, the embodied and abject truth of the journey. Back in England, the rumor of finding gold may go in one direction and the rumor of eating dogs in another, but in Lane's report they are meaningfully yoked. Textually, a story of gold had to fill the uncanny, empty narrative space of the silent banks and hungry boats. The golden city seemed tantalizingly close, but it was imagined. The silence along the riverbanks seemed surreal, but it was inescapable. The material event forced by these two forms of ghostliness was the reality of eating the dogs—an alarming turn of events that was already assented to half way up the river. The space between the inscrutable silence, the imagined gold, and the tabooed act inscribes a chaos zone, both mental and material.

At the end of his section on discoveries, Lane again addresses Raleigh directly: "Thus sir, I have though simply, yet truley set downe unto you, what my labour with the rest of the gentlemen, and poore men of our company, (not without both payne and perill, which the lorde in his mercy many wayes delivered us from) could yeeld unto you, which might have bene performed in some more perfection, if . . ." (275). How much is left to balance on that slim conjunction "if": if they had not lost all their provisions upon arriving; if they had been supplied, as promised; if Lane's imagined journeys were as real as he wrote them. But even in a language of "payne and perill," these parting salvos depended on Lane embracing yet another conceit: that he had indeed written a brief and true report, the very report he was unable to write. He claims to have painstakingly "set downe" his voyages so that "it may appear unto you (as true as it is)" (272). He claims that the whole story is here "simply, yet truley set downe unto you." Despite its tortuous method, the narrative must be presented as simple and transparent so that Lane can claim that he has reported the truth of the country, "(as true as it is)," exactly as it seemed.

"We Be Dead Men"

In the empty landscapes of his river journeys, as Lane traveled into the extremes of desire and abjection, the stakes of life and death rose. Returning to Roanoke, his confusion is more profound still: not only the stakes but even the states of life and death become disorganized. A strong sense of self-otherness pervades the second half of the text, one that persists even in retrospect. As the report enters its more dangerous scenes, the interpretive cognitive breach becomes more ontological. There is a gathering uncertainty around distinguishing a living state from a dead state, a state of confusion contributing to Lane's already unsteady handle on events. Lane, Pemisapan, and others in the narrative appear at times to operate within an existential limbo, an unsettling but potentially strategic condition in this field of colonial incursion.

The most ready example of this dead-or-alive state was the Indians' suspicion that the English might be dead people returned to life who could shoot invisible bullets at their enemies, resulting in terrible sickness and quick death. Thomas Harriot's *Briefe and True Report* has been treated as the ur-text for interpretations of this belief since Stephen Greenblatt's seminal treatment of it in his 1981 article "Invisible Bullets: Renaissance Authority and Its Subversion."[49] Scholars have built upon, dissented from, or gone beyond Greenblatt's theory, but they all read the same text: Harriot's.[50] Lane also gives an account of the invisible-bullets hypothesis, but as is the pattern, Harriot's account garners critical attention while Lane's knottier account remains largely ignored.[51] Although both accounts describe Indian theories about why native people were dying of previously unknown diseases after the arrival of Englishmen, the differences between the two highlight the insistent, divisive, and yet confusing incursionary politics that shape Lane's text. Harriot discusses the matter as a general phenomenon, summarizing occasions and opinions spread across times and places. He concentrates on patterns rather than on discrete events, noting that death spread rapidly in "*everie* such towne" where "*any* subtle devise [was] practiced against us," which "moved *the whole country* . . . to have us in wonderfull admiration."[52] In his surveying mode, Harriot refers to native people in the plural and most often in the indefinite form ("*Some* therefore were of the opinion," "*Some* would likewise seeme to prophicie," "*Some* also thought," "And *other some* saide"), removing these articulations from their immediate, historical, and interpersonal contexts.[53] Therefore, even as Harriot reports on what he calls a "rare and strange accident," he still maintains the framework of index and synopsis that structured his earlier catalogs.[54] And, as in the catalogs, Harriot remains concerned with the future use of what he observes; in his account, he famously speculates that the consequences of English health amid Indian death would likely bring the stricken native people "to honour, feare and love us."[55] However, instead of reading the invisible-bullets theory through the lens of Harriot's proto-ethnographic survey, I wish to situate it within its immediate local and political contexts, and within the discursive context of Lane's war story. This shift allows us to recover how even the most potentially ideological readings of the wages of life and death become increasingly convoluted when read from the perspective of the chaos zone.

Unlike Harriot, Lane does not report on a general phenomenon but rather on a specific event: a speech made by the Roanoke elder Ensenore to his deeply divided village. While Lane does mention that many people hold these opinions, it is the individual Ensenore who vividly embodies the wisest among them, and Ensenore who mobilizes these Indian beliefs for political purposes. In Harriot's account, Indians in general have conceived a "wonderful admiration" for the English and their God, even conflating the two: "some people could not tel whether to thinke us gods or men" (379). But in Lane's account, Ensenore speaks to a group of Indians who have begun to openly chide the settlers, belittling the helpless newcomers who are on the verge of "starving out of hand" (276). Hosilities toward the English were mounting, as was the intention to unseat them. Lane's narration is about these local politics, sketched out in all their ontological complexity. He places the "invisible bullets" speech at a moment in the text when the English settlers are extremely vulnerable but one in which the conception of them as dead men might actually save their lives.

Although Ensenore speaks in an atmosphere of growing contempt for the Englishmen and the English God, he asserts that it is a mistake to think that the English are weak. Even in Lane's translation and summary, the speech is worth quoting at length because, although briefer than Harriot's account, it is a more complicated version. In short order Ensenore lays out six claims about death, life and the spirit that moves between them. First, the English are servants of a powerful God. Second, not only are they immortal, but they also can reverse the pathways of death, so that whoever seeks to kill an Englishman will himself die. Third, to kill a living Englishman is hazardous because Englishmen grow even more destructive after death. Fourth, Englishmen can shoot invisible bullets from a hundred miles away. Fifth, the English are in fact already dead, having returned to this world on an inexorable mission of destruction. And finally, a warning: no Englishman ever remains dead for long but instead circulates between dead and living states. Lane's translation of Ensenore's speech is as follows:

> For he [Ensenore] had often before tolde them, and then renewed those his former speeches, both to the king and the rest, that wee [the English] were the servants of God, and that wee were not subject to be destroyed by them: but contrariwise, that they amongst them that sought our destruction, should finde their owne, and not bee able to worke ours, and that we being dead men were able to doe them more hurt, then now we could do being alive: an opinion very confidently at this day holden by the wisest amongst them, and of their olde men, as also, that they have bene in the night, being 100 myles from any of us in the ayre shot at, and stroken by some men of ours, that by sicknesse had dyed among them: and many of them holde opinion, that wee be dead men returned into the world againe, and that wee doe not remayne dead but for a certaine time, and that then we returne againe. (278)

In Ensenore's speech, the claim that the English have powers beyond those of normal men implies that they are not so much gods as dead men walking. Are the English more dead or alive? The answer is not so clear. Throughout the text, they inhabit states of "being alive" and states of "being dead men." "Wee be dead men returned into the world againe," Lane writes and takes is as a statement of alliance from the "only frend" he had left among the Roanoke (275).

Chronologically, Ensenore delivers this speech after Lane and forty men return from their nearly fatal trip up the Moratuc River on April 4, 1586. While Lane's company faced starvation on the river, famine had encroached on the fort as well. Word spread that half the English company was slain and the other half was starved, plausible even if it did not strictly align with fact. Lane admits as much: "One part of this tale was too true, that I and mine were like to be starved, but the other false" (277). True or false, the exploring group was believed to be dead, and the specter of English ruin charged the atmosphere around the fort. According to Lane, it opened a season of unbridled contempt for all things English: the settlers; their absent governor; their helplessness; their forced dispersal and exposure in quest of food; and worst of all, their so-called God. "Nowe they began to blaspheme, and flatly to say, that our Lord God was not God, since hee suffered us to sustaine much hunger, and also to be killed" (277).

If the English God was not providing, neither were the Indians. While Lane and his crew ventured into silence up the Moratuc River, Pemisapan "was advised and of himselfe disposed" to leave Roanoke Island and return to his seat at the town of Dasemunkepeuc on the mainland. Lane realized full well that to exterminate the English, all Pemisapan needed to do was "runne way from us" and leave "his ground in the island unsowed" (276). It was a long-standing practice for the werowance to return to his principal seat, but to leave a contingent of dependent and dangerous foreigners behind was something entirely new. Lane interpreted Pemisapan's plan to relocate to the mainland as an outright act of war, "a ready meane to have assuredly brought us to ruine" (276). Warming to the scenario, Lane projected "no possibility" for English survival, "[f]or at that time wee had no weares for fish, neither could our men skill of the making of them, neither had wee one grayne of corne for seede to put into the ground" (276). Imagining how the scene would play out, Lane leaves it to "common reason" to finish the story he has begun (276).

However, between that hostile, hungry March and Ensenore's death in April, the landscape shifted slightly. That Lane and his company returned from the Moratuc River alive was itself a crucial event.[56] Believing that they had been slain or starved, many, including Pemisapan, were amazed to see them return as living men. Though Lane's crew returned half-starved to a half-starving colony, they did return. Ensenore's speech clearly took advantage of the aura of these men to make the extraordinarily persuasive case that the English could cross the boundaries of life and death. Pemisapan's loyalties were divided between the elder's advice and his own calculations, but he was finally coaxed to act in favor of the settlers. Although Pemisapan maintained his stance against the English, Ensenore convinced him that in this time of unprecedented disease and volatile, potent forces, it would be wise to make sure the "English" ground on Roanoke Island was sown with corn. That accomplished, Roanoke Island was planted, and Ensenore died two days later.

Without Ensenore as a calming force, Pemisapan decidedly turned his back on the English. The English supply ship was supposed to arrive before Easter, but Easter was long passed. The new crop, planted in April, would not ripen until June. Now, although the corn would survive Ensenore's death, it was unclear whether the English would survive the two months until harvest. To Lane, the sight of corn growing on Roanoke was on some level "a marvelious comfort." A legacy of Ensenore's influence, their "owne store" might last them a whole year after harvest, even without "a newe supplie out of England" (280). At the same time, it was still just as easy for Lane to consider his colony dead as it was to consider it alive: "All our feare was of the two moneths betwixt, in which meane space if the Savages should not helpe us . . . wee might very well starve, notwithstanding the growing corne, like the starving horse in the stable, with the growing grasse, as the proverbe is" (280). A harvest in June does little to relieve starvation in May. A held fort matters little if the supply ship never arrives. Amid such uncertainties, it followed that what was happening in the incursion might never matter, or even count as having happened. Even as the corn grew, Lane saw his colony descend into extreme famine in an increasingly hostile environment. He was forced to weaken his forces by dispersing the people into the country in groups of ten to twenty, both to gather what food they could and to look for the supply ship on the horizon.

Depicting his company as vulnerable both inside and outside the fort, Lane states his conviction that not only was "the conspiracy of Pemisapan" well under way but that its goals were already half accomplished (275). The English, dead men returned to life, were on their way to being dead again. At this pitched moment in Lane's account, the report splinters into a number of virtual narratives. It is difficult to distinguish what is happening from what is obsessively being imagined. When Pemisapan announces that men from many tribes are to gather at Dasemunkepeuc for a tribute to Ensenore, Lane sees it as a ruse to disguise the convocation of a great force of warriors planning to exterminate him. With starvation and/or attack seemingly imminent, Lane's report then wagers all possible courses of destruction, all possible defenses, all possible battles. But again, the past time of the report is textually preserved as a present time of eruptive unreadability. Verbs vacillate; referents blur; perspectives are skewed. The terminology of command even switches; now it is "Pemisapan with his troup [who] ... should have executed me and some of our Weroances" (281). Strands of truth and fiction are woven together as the narrative is pulled simultaneously in alternate directions toward alternate realities. The text becomes not about what happened, but about what Lane or others should have or would have done, what they meant to or imagined to find. Refusing to settle down and state its business, the war report swirls to dizzying effect, re-creating conditions that in all their surreal seemingness also possess a frightening immediacy. A surprise assault, a co-coordinated siege, a miraculous rescue—each of these extreme (and extremely detailed) scenarios becomes equally possible, equally true, equally false.

Entering a dead time, Lane describes his own murder in vivid detail: "In the dead time of the night they would have beset my house, and put fire in the reedes that the same was covered with: meaning (as it was likelye) that my selfe would have come running out of a sudden amazed in my shirt without armes, upon the instant whereof they would have knocked out my braynes" (282). Having been thus killed, Lane continues as an omniscient narrator to plot out the rest of the destruction. Thomas Harriot would be murdered in the same fashion ("The same order was given"), as would all of the "better sort, our houses at once instant being set on fire" (282). If such a vision seems phantasmal, Lane hastens to confirm its reality by recounting the parts of the "plot" that had already been "immediately put . . . in practise" (282). The Indians had withdrawn all food and would not trade; the fishing weirs had been broken, and the English could not repair them; and "the King stood assured" that Lane's company was forced to disband "into sundry places to live upon shell fishe" and watch hopelessly for ships (283). Even at the level of the text's grammar, the mixture of conditional forms (what the Indians "would" do), past forms (what Lane "had done"), and future and subjunctive forms (what clearly "must be" done) keeps the lines between real and imagined narratives barely discernible. Meanwhile, the Meapemeoc and Mangoak and perhaps the Chesepian were on their way to Dasemunkepeuc, generating a force that, at one point, Lane estimated to be nearly fifteen hundred bowmen. What "common reason" could deny the meaning of that?

Pemisapan's attack on the English fort, which was rumored to have been planned for June 10, 1586, but which had already happened imaginatively, spurred Lane to act. The event "instantly upon" him and the event "to be put in execution" were simultaneous, leaving no time for inaction: "These mischiefes being all instantly upon mee and my companie to be put in execution, it stood mee in hand to study how to prevent them, and also to save all others, which were at that time as aforesaid so farre from me" (285). Lane responds to this imperative by sending word to Pemisapan that the long-awaited English supply ship has finally arrived and is waiting to greet them at Croatoan. In order to reconnect with his countrymen, Lane explains, he would need Pemisapan to give him guides, four days' provision for the journey, and some men to fish and hunt for the rest of the English company in the meantime. For the starving and dispersed English, even a calculated lie that relief had come must have seemed a painfully cruel deception. Lane writes, "I in trueth had neither heard nor hoped for so good adventure" (285). Spreading the fiction of a gratified English fantasy is Lane's final resort: they were not abandoned, their ship had come in, and the Indians would help them every step of the way. Pemisapan's response to Lane's message is cagey at best. He would be pleased to help the English to Croatoan, but only, it seemed, after his many visitors arrived to celebrate the memory of Ensenore.

On June 1, 1586, Lane led an attack on Dasemunkepeuc. Hakluyt's marginal note in Lane's printed report adds the descriptor "the slaughter, and surprise of the Savages," but Lane's discourse focuses almost entirely on the individual fate of "the King" Pemisapan.[57] He narrates the confrontation as if he were an outsider observing a peculiar, almost preternatural episode—as if he had not been contending with Wingina/Pemisapan in thought, word, and deed for nearly an entire year. This part of Lane's report is critical for several reasons. It tells us how Pemisapan died, it tells us how Lane framed the action and meaning of the crisis around that death, and it memorably demonstrates how unstable the boundary between life and death had become in the chaos zone.

As to the manner of Pemisapan's death, these are Lane's words: "The king himselfe being shot thorow by the Colonell with a pistoll lying on the ground for dead, & I looking as watchfully for the saving of some of Manteos friends, as others were busie that none of the rest should escape, suddenly he started up, and ran away as though he had not bene touched, insomuch as he overran all the companie, being by the way shot thwart the buttocks by mine Irish boy with my Petronell" (287). Colonists repeatedly record their utter shock that Indians who suffered grave wounds could run off and survive. Implicit in their shock was the realization that what would kill an Englishmen may not necessarily kill an Indian. Here, the "king," counted as dead, preternaturally leaps up "as though he had not bene touched." Being shot through, Pemisapan runs. Another Irish servant is sent into the woods to search after the wounded werowance. The two disappear for so long that Lane thinks, "we had lost both the king, and my man by our owne negligence." Eventually, Lane sees the servant "returning out of the woods with Pemisapan's head in his hand" (288). The full stop at the end of Lane's agitated story thus arrives in the shape of the slain werowance's head.

Even as we register this grave token, what shall we make of Lane's description of Pemisapan's flight between death and life? No existing history of Roanoke, not even the few that record the incidents at Dasemunkepeuc, registers the circumstances or meaning of Pemisipan's death flight.[58] Perhaps the best way to proceed is to compare this narrative treatment to a visual one. John White made a watercolor labeled "A Chief Herowance"; Harriot's commentary on de Bry's engraving of this portrait identifies its subject as one of "the cheefe men of the yland and twone of Roanoac."[59] He stands with his arms folded across his chest, a posture that communicated gravity and wisdom among the Algonquian Indians. Around his neck is a large, square copper medallion, another sign of status. The pearl chain from which it hangs and the copper and blue beads ornamenting his ears and wrists are all tokens of authority. He does not look at the viewer. Although presented as a specimen, the man's personal presence is unmistakable. Lane's narrative is, and has to be, different. Pemisipan in motion has both form and agency. He is shot, falls, lies still, and then bounds up in full strength and runs to his escaping warriors, putting himself at their lead despite his wounds. Lane sees him in each of these states in rapid and alarming succession, first as dead and then as shockingly alive. He does not know whether Pemisapan is killed, rallying, or disappeared until he sees the severed head. Compared to this, the werowance in White's miniature and Harriot's gloss represents not only a still form but also a form of comprehension that does not have to follow, trace, or account for the man in his unreadable acts and astonishing changes.

Lane says nothing of what happened in the week following Pemisapan's death. In his report, that period is glossed over in the space of a single sentence. Immediately after describing his servant emerging from the woods carrying Pemisapan's head, Lane writes, "This fell out the first of June, 1586 and the 8 of the same came advertisement . . . [of] a great Fleete of 23 sailes" approaching Roanoke (288). The consequences of attack on Dasemunkepeuc are thus fully concealed in the text by this new miracle coming over the horizon: not the supply ship but Sir Francis Drake sailing into Roanoke as a conquering hero. Fresh from sacking Spanish forts at Santo Domingo, Cartagena, and St. Augustine, the famous Drake was loaded with plunder and offered to supply Lane with whatever was needed to sustain the English colony. They arranged for a transfer of commodities from Drake's spoils to Lane's settlement: food, clothes, munitions, healthy sailors, a large labor force, and most important, ships and boats adequate either to continue explorations, or to move the colony, or to return to England if need be. But while the men were finalizing these plans, another intervention blew into the bay, this time a miracle of disaster: an awe-inspiring, three-day-long, hurricane-strength storm that destroyed many of Drake's ships and all of Lane's plans.[60] The storm, Lane writes, felt like "the very hand of God as it seemed, stretched out to take us from thence" (292). Clearly for many of Lane's colony this was an act of deliverance. Lane gives a litany of reasons why he and the settlers boarded Drake's remaining ships and left Roanoke behind, but he never again mentions the beheading of Pemisapan or the native forces gathering at his doorstep. The problems he does enumerate were insurmountable enough, but it is also plain that the certainty of retaliation made it too dangerous for the English to continue at Roanoke. While Lane describes the decision to depart as judicious, his depiction of the leave-taking belies such solemnity. Drake "immediately" sends pinnaces to the island "for the fetching away of fewe that were left there with our baggage." More than a few do not make it to the ships. The weather is still "so boisterous," the ships "so often on the ground," that Drake is "in more perill of wracke" in Roanoke than in all his "actions against the Spaniards" (293). If even Drake's hardened sailors are "much agrieved with their long and dangerous abode in that miserable road," we can only imagine the desperation of Lane and his soldiers to be gone (293).

In another account of Lane's leave-taking, Hakluyt describes the storm as the hand of God punishing the settlers, not rescuing them: "[They] left things there so confusedly, as if they had bene chased from thence by a mightie armie, and no doubt so they were, for the hande of God came upon them for the crueltie, and outrages committed by some of them against the native inhabitants of that Countrie."[61] Hakluyt's image of an army chasing "our English Colonie out of the paradise of this world" neatly encapsulates the difference between Barlowe's paradisiacal exploratory report, which promises a golden age, and Lane's incursionary one, which cuts off at the point that "a mightie armie" was in fact gathering at Dasemunkepeuc.

Despite the deliberate silence regarding its final days, the first settlement's panicked escape from Virginia left much in its wake. What did Lane's colony leave behind? They left three men whom Lane had sent into the interior on an assignment and who were not heard from again.[62] They left the sodden shreds of the colony's amassed "Cards, Bookes, and writings," including a substantial collection of papers from Harriot and White. These documents "were by the Saylers cast over boord" in order to lighten the ballast and get the ships out of "that miserable road" as quickly as possible (293). They left behind avowedly hostile local tribes, who, instead of seeking trade, now sought revenge for the attack on their principal seat and for the murder of their leader. They left behind an abandoned English fort and abandoned English houses. They also left behind the prospect of finding a deep-water port, a possible northwest passage, and beguiling mines. In their place, members of Lane's colony brought back to England an uncontainable flood of stories. And Ralph Lane brought back the makings of what could not have been anything but a deeply flawed report—a report that did not satisfy, a report that we cannot read straight, a report that we also have largely left behind.

Skeleton Colonies

Only days after Lane's colony departed with Drake, the supply ship came. The relief crew spent several days "up in the Countrie" searching for signs or any news of the settlers left there the year before.[63] The ship's long-awaited arrival enacted a strange reversal. The colony no longer looked for a ghost ship; now the ship looked for a ghost colony. Failing to find any colonists to supply, it returned to English with its cargo intact. Perhaps two weeks later, Sir Richard Grenville arrived with a larger expedition carrying significant reinforcements of every kind, including nearly four hundred men. Like those on the supply ship, Grenville's crew approached an uncannily silent fort, but this time they found two bodies hanging there—one English, one Indian. There is no way of knowing how the bodies got there or what they meant, but it was proof enough that hostilities continued after Lane's departure. This was not at all the scene Grenville expected to find; indeed it must have seemed an utter mystery to him. He stayed for two more weeks, searching the coasts around Roanoke and trying to gather intelligence, but the people of those villages kept a willful distance from this third round of English arrivals. Grenville managed to capture three men. Two escaped before being interrogated, but the third man reported that Lane's colony had boarded a fleet of English ships and fled the country.

We know of this conversation between a Roanoke Indian and an English captain because of a Spanish prisoner in Havana: Grenville's former captive Pedro Diaz. The context, as it was from the beginning of the Roanoke ventures, was privateering. Diaz was a pilot on the *Santa Maria*, the Spanish treasure ship Grenville captured while returning from Roanoke for the first time in 1585. Diaz had been in Grenville's custody ever since: in England, while Grenville outfitted his fleet; off the coast of Galacia, where he took two French ships; in Puerto Santo, where he tried to burn the island but was repelled by its native inhabitants; and then to Roanoke, where, according to Diaz, the English "had left settlers."[64] After escaping from the English, Diaz was debriefed in 1589 by Spanish colonial authorities in Havana. He testified that Grenville's party found the colony abandoned but for the two hanging bodies, took an Indian captive onto the ship, and "got an account of how Fransisco Draque had brought away the people who had been on that island . . . finding them in poor condition and greatly in need of provisions."[65] Diaz also reported that Grenville did not leave the garrison on Roanoke Island as he found it, but deposited eighteen men there to hold the fort until further notice. Thus finding the Roanoke colony abandoned except for "the bodies of one Englishman and one Indian hanged," Grenville left a skeleton crew behind to secure England's claim to settlement in North America and then went on about his real business: privateering.[66]

There is a critical consensus that this was an outrageously bad judgment on Grenville's part. Quinn writes, "In view of the evidence of Indian hostility which Grenville had, this was very rash."[67] Kupperman states frankly, "He should either have left a large force with all the food and equipment or abandoned the site altogether."[68] Although some refer to this unfortunate group left behind as "the holding party," we may also think of them as a second, bare-bones English occupation of Roanoke. Quinn refers to them as settlers of the second colony, and Hakluyt counts them as an occupying force.[69] In his voluminous *Principall Navigations* filled with first-person accounts, Hakluyt himself writes of them and does his best to justify their meager presence: "after some time spent therein not hearing any newes of them [Lane's colony], and finding the place which they inhabited desolate, yet unwilling to lose the possession of the Countrie, which Englishmen had so longe helde: after good deliberation he [Grenville] determined to leave some men behind to retain possession of the country: whereupon he landed

15 men in the Ile of Ronoake furnished plentifully with all manner of provision for two years, and so departed for England" (480). Hakluyt's language of deliberation and determination, as well as his contention that the land was long held by Englishmen and could be possessed and retained by a tiny company, is a cover for the facts. The truth was that a succession of groups had either disappeared or been run out of Roanoke: Lane's entire colony; an unknown number of Drake's passengers; one hanged sailor from the supply ship; and now eighteen (or fifteen, depending on the source) more men "left in Virginia," as Hakluyt's marginal note has it. By the time Diaz gave his testimony, he was also able to report that the next English ships that came in "did not find the eighteen men who had been left there, nor any trace of them."

One needs to extract the story of the second settlement from records in which the facts, of which many were reported secondhand, are only glancingly mentioned. On the English side, both Harriot and Hakluyt touch on the fort's occupation between 1586 and 1587, but they do so ever so briefly because the story of the skeleton colony does not align with the promotional thrust of their writing. Harriot barely alludes to the Grenville party in his introduction to the *Briefe and True Report*, and then only to deny their significance: "the others after [Lane's colony] were onlie for supply and transportation, nothing more being discovered than had been before" (320–21). The real purpose of Harriot's introduction is damage control, specifically to refute the "slanderous and shamefull speeches bruited abroad" by men returned from Lane's colony. The introduction's confrontational and irritated tone indicates a writer eager to be done with the exculpatory part of his business. In short, before opening onto the detailed, measured, and exquisitely controlled performance of his own discoveries, Harriot makes quick work of the "many envious, malicious, and slauderous reports" already in circulation, not concerning himself with the silent men marooned in Virginia (324). Hakluyt, filling the gap between Lane's escaping colony and White's lost one, also quickly focuses elsewhere. Within a single sentence his account brings Grenville, laden with Spanish spoils, back from Roanoke to England: "Not long after he fell with the Isles of Acores, on some of which Ilandes he landed, and spouled the Townes of all such things as were worth carriage, where also he tooke divers Spanyardes: with these, and many other exploits done by him in this voyage, as well outward as home, he returned into England" (480). It proved easier to erase these stranded men and instead describe a captain returning home with spoils from his exploits.

I do not claim that the failed searches of the supply ship and Grenville's fleet, or the bodies they left behind, constitute major historical episodes. I do claim that they represent the acute nature of these first attempts at colonial settlement and therefore should be part of its critical analysis. These episodes are consistent with the experiences of most English people who spent any time in Roanoke because they represent a pattern of abandonment and expendability. Moreover they indicate serious breaches in the ability to interpret or account for events in the first English incursion into Native America, while also emphasizing the proximity of violence and indeterminacy. The stories are left unresolved; either the corpse silently absorbs the unreadable narrative into itself or the body goes missing, leaving no trail behind. These abandonments indicate that the cultural longevity and elaboration of the mystery of the Lost Colony is a legend that screens but also repeats a suppressed history of other people left behind in Virginia.

In 1587 John White led yet another group of English colonists to try again to plant a permanent and self-perpetuating English settlement in North America. The ships that brought these colonists were the sixth round to arrive at Roanoke in three years: Barlowe's, Lane's, Drake's, the supply ship, Grenville's, and now White's. White took passage on four of these voyages, as did Manteo, who accompanied him.[70] After Lane set the deadly terms of Anglo-Indian engagement with the murder of Pemisapan, Roanoke had grown increasingly dangerous for the English with each arrival. Although White and his company originally planned to settle in the Chesapeake, they first stopped in Roanoke to check on the men Grenville had left garrisoned there. As members of Lane's colony, both White and Manteo knew the situation created by the raid on Dasemunkepeuc and Pemisapan's murder, but somehow they thought Grenville's men were still alive, albeit in need of relief. Even before reaching the fort, however, it was clear to White that they were mistaken, seeing no "signe that they had bene there, saving only we found the bones of one of those fifteen, which the Savages had slaine long before" (524). This was the third time English people had found the same patch of land mysteriously forsaken in two years. In 1586 the supply ship found Roanoke deserted by Lane's colony. Two weeks later Grenville's fleet found only two bodies swinging from the posts and left a small company behind to hold the fort. White found the post again vacant, marked only with one skeleton of the skeleton colony. He returned to the larger company "without hope of ever seeing any of the fifeteene men living" (524). By this time White's company had also been informed by the pilot of their ship that they too would be left in Virginia and carried no farther than Roanoke.

Absorbing the Lost

The only material benefit associated with the Roanoke colony so far had been gained from privateering while sailing there and back; the settlement itself had produced nothing but disappointment, and interest in the endeavor was on the wane. White's settlement, which would be known as the City of Raleigh, was supposed to repair the damaged prospects for English Virginia. Its projected success lay in its differences from Lane's colony. The first difference was demographic. White's group was largely comprised of civilians and families instead of young soldiers, and the colony was to be a community rather than a military outpost. The administration of White's colony was also different. These were not soldiers working for wages but rather colonists granted land and a form of self-governance. Crucially the new group's destination also set it apart from earlier efforts. White's colony was headed to the richer lands and deeper ports of the Chesapeake Bay, not the storm-ridden Outer Banks that had proven all but fatal to English ships and hence to the confidence of English investors. However, when the ship's pilot, Simon Fernandez, announced that "he would land the planters in no other place" than Roanoke, and when every sailor aboard concurred with the plan, White, despite his desire to settle in the Chesapeake, capitulated, writing that "it booted not the Governor to contend with them" (523). The new settlers took up the old English outpost, cleared out the melons and deer that had already taken over the standing houses, and set the City of Raleigh upon the remnants of Roanoke.

By July 25 the company had taken up residence; by August 25 they had agreed that they were unlikely to survive unless John White quickly returned to London and mobilized financial backing. At the group's desperate urging, White finally consented to go back to London and act as the colony's agent, doing all he could to ensure that it would be remembered and supplied. On August 27 White boarded the homebound ship with Fernandez's departing crew. For all the speculation about the colonists' fate after White returned to England, far less attention has been paid to reading the historical record we do have of that colony or analyzing what happened *before* White's departure on August 27 and how that period is represented in his narrative. White writes a detailed account of this third colony (printed in Hakluyt's *Principall Navigations* in 1589), a direct, eyewitness record covering the period from the landing to just over a month later. Reading White's report, we find the instability that permeates Lane's report repeated. The hostilities between the Roanoke and their allies and the English settlers continue, but so do the patterns of misrecognition and inscrutability, of silence that turns into violence, and of being enclosed in a situation that defies understanding but also seems to demand action.

White's report of this third colony is not as structurally disordered as Lane's, but like Lane's, it is predominately a record of uncertainty. White records the events of only a single month, and yet even in that short period, in his narrative he spends a great deal of time backtracking in a futile attempt to clarify interactions with the Indians that are ominously mysterious or fatally misread by the settlers. White's alliance with Manteo is as key to his report as Lane's hostilities with Pemisapan are to his, but both men respond with violent action to the baffling silence they encounter from local tribes. As White steps out of the artist's role and into the governing role, he must decipher and represent information as a narrative of lived events, and not as a series of visual set-pieces about Algonquian life. In his written account, he confesses that he can no longer tell what he is looking at, can no longer recognize bodies from the very scenes of Native American life he once rendered with such scrupulous care. Holding White's report up against his pictorial representations, then, we can see how a narrative discourse of incursionary experience demonstrates a disordered epistemology that belies the colonial mastery of knowledge and form.

The resumption of Indian hostilities began within days of White's arrival. George Howe was the first casualty, and White offers a thick description of his death. He writes that on July 28, "diverse savages" came to Roanoke and kept cover in the tall reeds, either to hunt deer or to gather intelligence on the new arrivals:

> [Howe] was slaine by divers Savages, which were come over to Roanoake, either of purpose to espie our companie, and what number we were, or els to hunt Deere, whereof were many in the Island. These Savages being secretly hidden among high reedes, where often times they finde the Deere asleep, and so kill them, espied our man wading in the water alone, almost naked, without any weapon, save only a small forked stick, catching Crabs therewithal, and also being strayed

two miles from his company, and shot at him in the water, where they gave him sixteen wounds with their arrows: and after they had slaine him with their wooden swords, they beat his head in pieces, and fel over the water to the maine. (522)

Howe's position—alone, barely clothed, unarmed, astray, and concentrated on the single basic task of trying to feed himself—contrasts sharply with that of the Indians, who coordinate with each other, conceal themselves, attack suddenly, kill, mutilate, and flee. Phrase by phrase White's sentence narrows down to a single poor figure and then explodes into the violent killing. This jarring, telescope-and-detonate pattern is repeated often in colonial accounts. The tactics of Indian warfare, what the English later called "the skulking way of war," included ambush, concealment, and elements of surprise, as well as targeting specific individuals in order to send a message to the enemy group.[71] The way English colonists represent these attacks goes beyond describing or even disparaging those techniques. Rather, these accounts are structured around particularity, plucking single events from the context of an ongoing conflict so that mutual aggression between the two groups could be depicted as the slaying of an innocent man. This sacrificial stray then becomes a "first cause" for subsequent English attacks. The Howe murder, for example, would later become a banner cause for a second attack on Dasemunkepeuc. But here the detailed image of George Howe's slain body (White counts his sixteen wounds) is a gruesome reminder of the fatal costs of being unable to read one's surroundings.

After George Howe's death, White and the new group at Roanoke became intent on discovering the fate of Grenville's men. The discovery of the skeleton, the razed fort, and the brutal close-range killing of Howe—all within six days—scared them. As White puts it, "wee hoped to understand some newes of our fifteen men, but especially to learne the disposition of the people of the countrey towards us" (526). To find out, they went to Manteo's home village at Croatoan. White's account of this visit is rife with disquieting internal contradictions that he records but does not integrate into the larger claims of the narrative. Instead of strategically omitting parts of the visit or cleaning up inconsistencies, White leaves ample evidence that the alliance with the Croatoan is compromised by a new wariness; at the same time, he claims that the English and their most reliable allies are on exceedingly friendly terms. The initial encounter with the Croatoan is nerve-racking enough. In White's account, upon seeing the English, the Croatoan prepare to fight. The English then begin to march in with their guns raised, and the Indians start to flee. It is only after Manteo announces his presence by calling out to the Croatoan in their own language that the tension diffuses and the two groups gather to exchange the friendly welcome that the English first expected. Although the groups embrace and declare themselves brethren and friends, the mutual wariness persists. The Croatoan soon tell the Englishmen that they cannot spare their corn as they have but little for themselves. Next they bring forward a man who is gravely wounded as proof that "diverse of them were hurt the year before" by Lane's company (527). They do allow, however, that these injured parties may have been mistaken for Pemisapan's men; the Croatoan understand that they become even more illegible to the English when the settlers are in a fearful, violent state.

During his time in Lane's colony, White had tried to make Indians particularly legible to Englishmen. A de Bry engraving of one of White's paintings depicts "The marckes of Sundrye of the Chief mene of Virginia." It is a picture of a disarmed warrior drawn from the back, tattooed with a large diamond marking on his shoulder that identifies him as a Pomeiooc of high rank. Surrounding this figure, the identifying marks of seven other groups, including Wingina's, fill the page, "set downe," Harriot writes, so "that they might more easelye be discerned."[72] These Indian markers of identity and belonging could be schematized in pictorial and descriptive colonial documents, but the Croatoan rightly distrust that they will be read or recognized by English settlers, especially in the wake of Lane's company's violence. The Croatoan urge White to devise some other kind of token that the English could read in order to distinguish friend from foe, but if any such token was given, it ultimately proved insufficient. Not ten days later White would lead a near-fatal attack on Manteo's people, mistaking them once again for enemies.

At their meeting at Croatoan, Manteo's people tell White that it is common knowledge that the Roanoke and their allies (a coalition of "Winginoes men") killed both the skeleton colony and George Howe (527). Adding to the Roanoke threat is the news that Wanchese, the other Algonquian who had first gone to England with Manteo, was the chief operative of both the raid on the fort and the murder of Howe. White had heard Wanchese describe Indian battles at Raleigh's English estate three years earlier; now Wanchese himself was battling the English. Manteo translates the whole series of events to White, just as he and Wanchese had earlier translated the stories of the European shipwrecks to Barlowe. Judging from the careful account that White passes on to Hakluyt, Manteo is able to describe the raid on the skeleton colony in meticulous detail—from the moment two Indians approached the English fort, through the skirmish that began with an embrace and lasted "above an howre," to the last sight of several English survivors fleeing to a tiny island in the harbor, "where they remained a while, but afterward departed, whither, as yet we knowe not" (527).

The English soldiers are described as living carelessly. They guilelessly greet their assailants and when attacked, run around "without order," without weapons, and without a plan. The thirty Indians, who represented three tribes, are described as a superior force in every way: fast, nimble, equally skilled at attacking and defending, coordinated, resourceful, and finally victorious. The raid on Roanoke is an Indian story. As with the earlier tale of the castaways, Manteo's translation of native intelligence is the only way for the English to learn how white men disappeared in America. The one English casualty from the raid that White describes in detail is a man "shotte into the mouth with an arrowe," a concentrated symbol of being unable to tell what happened (528). Knowing that they are unable to repel a similar attack regardless of what precautions they take, White's group asks the Croatoan to speak on their behalf, to broker a peace for them, proposing that "all unfriendly dealings past on both partes, should be utterly forgiven, and forgotten" (527). The chief men of Croatoan reply that they would "doe the best they could" to organize a meeting in seven days. It is the last White hears of a détente.

Nine days into the silence, White "thought to differre revenging thereof no longer" (530). His group, which was expressly not a military deployment, had been in Roanoke for only fifteen days when a midnight crew of men, with Manteo as their guide, passed over the water into Dasemunkepeuc. It had been a little over a year since Lane's attack on the same town ended with the decapitation of Pemisapan. Like Lane's, White's report focuses most intently on those moments when Indians are least intelligible: "Having espied their fire, and some sitting about it, we presently sette on them: the miserable soules herewith amased, fledde into a place of thick reedes, growing fast by, where our men perceaving them, shotte one of them through the bodie with a bullet, and therewith we entered the reedes, among which wee hoped to acquite their evill doing toward us, but wee were deceaved, for those Savages were our friendes" (530). Seeking to avoid just this kind of revenge, "Wingina's remnant" had deserted Dasemunkepeuc directly after killing George Howe. The "miserable soules herewith amased" are those Croatoan who had come into the town to gather the unharvested crops the Roanoke left behind. White cannot distinguish friend from enemy; furthermore he claims that because the people sitting at the fire are "apparelled all so like others," no one even recognizes that women and children are among them (530).

There is no reason to doubt that White was genuinely mistaken about the Indians at the raid. What is compelling, however, is that the man who could not recognize them was also the man who had drawn their faces with such specificity. Not only did White have more experience among these native groups than anyone else in his colony, but the quality of his attention was richer than the average person's by far. One explanation for White's benighted state (literally and figuratively) is that for nine days he had been waiting in vain to hear how his offer of friendship had fared and was increasingly unsettled by the silence. In the attack, then, White and his crew plunged into both the darkness and the terrifying Indian silence with their imagined narratives reeling: perhaps the easy victory over Grenville's men had strengthened native alliances; perhaps the men who killed Howe were planning a full-scale assault; perhaps Wanchese's determination to eradicate settlers was all the more intense for having learned so much about the English colonial enterprise. For White as for Lane, as the state of not knowing intensified, so did the resolution to bring the crisis of meaning to an end with violent action. From the English perspective, the maddening effect of Indian silence was broken by the clamor of their own violent attack.

As the English loosed their assault, a Croatoan called out the name of an Englishman he recognized in order to shock them out of their ferocity. The English then spotted a child clinging to his mother's back. This sight must have especially struck White, for in his first year at Roanoke, he made a detailed portrait of a mother and her child in Dasemunkepeuc illustrating "the manner in which they carry their children": the child's arms wrapped around the mother's neck, its left leg tucked into her elbow, its right leg resting along the length of her back. It was a child-carrying technique White had never seen before. Another of his paintings depicts Indians sitting in a circle around a fire, their various postures precisely depicted. Some are naked, men and women are attired much alike, and one man's back is tattooed with the sign of his home village. In White's description of the raid, this careful visual record of Virginia comes to life, but chaotically so. The figures he once represented with such skill—from the variously clothed people sitting around the fire to the intertwined mother and child—become, in his fury, illegible to him. "Wee were deceaved," he writes.

In 1584 the document that chartered the first English settlements in the New World ended with an abandonment clause; in 1587 the first written compact drawn up and sealed by English people in America certified that John White was not abandoning his colony in Virginia. Before White left his people at Roanoke to plead for their support back in England, he insisted on creating this official document and reproduced it in whole in his narrative. It testified that the settlers needed "present and speedie supplie of certain our knowen, and apparent lackes, and needes"; that they most "earnestly intreated, and uncessantly requested" White to go back to England; that he repeatedly refused; and that his final acquiescence was "much against his will" (535). As a document, it was eminently readable, but at that point any remaining faith that words, dates, and seals could secure the settlement was infused with desperation and panic. These bonded words, addressed from the settlers to "her Majesties Subjects of England" at large, defended against an encroaching and unavoidable knowledge: Roanoke was a place where people were left behind and lost.

When John White finally returned to Roanoke in 1590, the English boats approached a silent shore. As White describes it, into the "exceeding darke" night, nineteen men on two anchored boats "sounded with a trumpet a Call, & afterwards many familiar English tunes of Songes, and called to them friendly; but we had no answere" (613). Despite the uncanny silence, White comes onto shore at daybreak to find two traces of human presence. The first is "in the sand the print of the Salvages feet 2 or 3 sorts troaden that night." The other is "upon a tree, in the very browe thereof were curiously careved these faire Romane letters CRO" (613). White follows these signs, entering a fort that has been abandoned for the fourth time: "[W]e passed toward the place where they were left in sundry houses, but we found the houses taken downe, and the place very strongly enclosed with a high palisado of great trees, with cortynes and flankers very Fort-like, and one of the cheife trees or postes at the right side of the entrance had the barke taken off, and 5 foote from the ground in fayre Capitall letters was graven CROATAN without any crosse or signe of distress" (614). Passing through the gate, White finds bars of iron and pieces of lead, guns, and light cannons "almost overgrown with grasse and weedes." Buried chests of valuables, most of them White's own, had been dug up and pilfered through, their contents scattered around the empty ditches: "about the place many of my things spoyled and broken, and my bookes torne from the covers, the frames of some of my pictures and Mappes rotten and spoyled with rayne, and my armour almost eaten through with rust" (615).

In 1590 the engravings of John White's paintings of Native America gave shape and form to European imaginings of the New World. That same year White returned to find the frames of those paintings rotted away and his company of English settlers gone. Littered about their abandoned fort were the tools of colonization—books, maps, armor, cannons—torn and spoiled, corroded, and tangled with weeds. White's words about the people he left behind are few and conflicting; he first rejoices that they must have found succor in Croatoan but later calls the colonial attempt "as lucklesse to many, as sinister to my selfe" (715). "Lucklesse" and "sinister" were not the terms upon which these missions had begun, when Elizabeth I granted these lands according to her "especial grace, certaine science, and meere motion," but they became the coda to a catastrophic history of incursion.

Despite continued claims to the contrary, the first narratives written by English colonists attested that it was not so that English people would arrive and, through their superior civilization, technology, and religion, control a savage world. Instead these narratives broke from a discourse of confidence and plentitude because they had to contend with representing events and contexts that even those on the ground could not comprehend. Although the Roanoke ventures resulted in the first authoritative English images and catalogs of the New World, they also produced the first colonial literature of settlement as a crisis of meaning. In Roanoke the places that the English tried to possess ended up being empty of colonists but full of colonial events both fateful and indecipherable. The soldiers, planters, and the hanging bodies and scattered bones; the wrecked houses and ships; the torn books and drawings; the dead men half living; the empty villages; the Indian leaders bound, beheaded, or watching from afar—indeterminacy around these happenings was finally absorbed into an insoluble mystery about what happened to the Lost Colony, a legend that shrouds the historical record of all that was left in Virginia.

CHAPTER 2

Jamestown: Things That Seemed Incredible

[N]otheinge was Spared to mainteyne Lyfe and to doe those things which
seame incredible.
—George Percy, *A Trewe Relacyon of the Procedeinges and Ocurrentes of
Momente Which Have Hapned in Virginia*

When James I issued a charter to the Virginia Company in 1606, the failure of the Roanoke colony was written between the lines. Unlike Elizabeth's
gloriously expansive 1584 patent to Walter Raleigh, the papers that authorized the Virginia Action, stated its intentions, and organized its institutional forms were detailed and circumspect. Jamestown's planners knew
more and feared more.[1] However, among the raft of instructions given to the
new group of settlers, one stipulation seemed simple enough to carry out:
"You Shall do well to Send a perfect relation by Captain Newport of all that
is Done."[2] Such relations were crucial to the colonizing mission. Good news
from Virginia was ready-made promotional material, convincing investors
to back England's "new" New World action and enticing English subjects
to risk starting life anew overseas. One of the first relations sent back from
Virginia was written by George Percy, who had this to report: "Our men
were destroyed with cruell diseases as Swellings, Fluxes, Burning Fevers,
and by warres, and some departed suddenly, but for the most part they died
of meere famine. There were never Englishmen left in a forreigne Countrey
in such miserie as wee were in this new discovered Virginia."[3] It was not the
perfect relation the Virginia Company had in mind.

While English bodies disappeared into the land at Roanoke, the mortal toll of the Jamestown venture was fully embodied and laid out to view. Any history of the settlement has to begin by stepping over these bodies, and the resulting discomfort is often palpable. Karen Kupperman observes, "Historians skip over Jamestown and early Virginia as if the subjects were faintly embarrassing"; and John Kukla writes, "Horror stories about the Starving Time at Jamestown in 1609–1610 have prejudiced the image of early Virginia in the minds of historians."[4] Perhaps the most blunt assessment comes from Edmund Morgan, who sees early Jamestown as a complete fiasco. He writes, "The adventurers who ventured their capital lost it. Most of the settlers who ventured their lives lost them. And so did most of the Indians who came near them. Measured by any of the objectives announced for it, the colony failed."[5] Thus, Virginia's first years are written as a precarious beginning, perilous for all, fatal for most, but not truly indicative of what colonial life was or was to be. While the intensities that shaped early Jamestown are widely acknowledged, they are often narrated as false starts. Historians note that the colony almost did not make it, or that it was on the verge of becoming another Roanoke, or that it was salvaged by some crucial shift—in agriculture, land rights, labor, population—that marks the "before" and "after" of Virginia's beginnings. In other words, studies of the settlement must always identify the turning point between the horror of the early years and the subsequent history of colonial development.

Accounts of those first disastrous years have generally followed a diagnostic model for the ailing Jamestown—cataloging symptoms, discerning causes, and sometimes retroactively proposing alternative scenarios. Jamestown's problems are certainly not hard to identify. The settlement was inundated with helpless newcomers, faulty intelligence, incompetent leaders, accidents, and arrogance. The colony's sense of mission was unclear, its priorities were confused, and its political structures were immediately weakened to the point of incoherence. The settlement was made up of people with no agrarian experience who had no intention of learning how to feed themselves. They established their fort in a swamp and neither knew about nor adjusted to local climate conditions. They neither anticipated nor understood the strong and organized Powhatan political culture into which they intruded. Though the consequences of these failings were brutal, they were not surprising. Early Jamestown was, to paraphrase Morgan only slightly, a horror show. But once the causal questions are answered, the material conditions accounted for, and the bodies stepped over, Virginia's miseries are made to become a sideline to its subsequent histories.

In this chapter I suggest that transition happens too quickly. When Virginia's early failures are reduced to material conditions and ascribed to the struggles of an "infant" colony in this way, a more complicated history of early settlement gets lost. The extremity of this history is explained and explained away; its catastrophes are contained through a narration of recovery. The dire scenarios are imagined, but that imagining does not extend to thinking about how suffering and its attendant violence operated during the "horror" years of Jamestown. In an explanatory model of early settlement, crisis marks failure, but I propose in this chapter that adopting a discursive model will demonstrate that crisis was a means of producing coloniality. In other words, rather than looking ahead to the future development these early setbacks forestalled, I focus instead on the function of unsettlement in colonial settlement.

Such an approach reveals a gap in many analyses of the Jamestown settlement. For example, older historical arguments that chart a movement from disorder to order—a movement from "chaotic factionalism," in Bernard Bailyn's words, to a developed "society," in Stuart Diamond's—summarily dismiss early Virginia as "a profoundly unsettled world."[6] John Kukla's work proposes an earlier date for Jamestown's social organization, but he still employs the chaos versus order paradigm; passing quickly over the early settlement, he is more concerned with "the emergence of social order within a few decades after [the first] catastrophic winter."[7] Atlantic studies, on the other hand, begin Virginia's history long before a sustainable colony took hold, looking to the late sixteenth-century articulation of Anglo-American colonial prospects and the influence of the Spanish model of colonization. In their search for broader patterns linking Virginia to other Atlantic colonial settlements, these treatments also tend to abbreviate early atrocities. For example, J. H. Elliott writes, "The settlers of Virginia originally proved to be 'recalcitrant' colonists because the Chesapeake Indians, in refusing to provide either tribute or labor, had upset their expectations of a Spanish colonial model. It was not until the 1630s that the settlers' desire for increased tobacco cultivation and their insistence on avenging the Indian massacre of 1622 impelled them to possess Indian lands by force." At that point, Elliott notes, Virginia was "still at best a minor player. But it had joined the game."[8] Charting when and how the Virginia colony cohered enough to "join the game," these historical approaches move from expectation to adaptation, from disorder to order, from confusion to organization. Plotted in a developmental sequence, the first terms are used to describe a set of conditions under which nothing lasting could be accomplished, and they are quickly subsumed into the second. In what follows, however, I posit

that disaster itself was a condition in which the first, fractured forms of coloniality emerged and that the catastrophes that nearly destroyed the settlement
in Virginia also in part created it.

This chapter argues that, especially in Jamestown, the terms that
George Percy used in his relation, *Englishmen left in misery*, began to characterize a new type of settlement writing, a discourse of catastrophe that
was as prevalent as map, catalog, survey, or any other form used by colonial writers to represent "all that was done" in the new settlement. This
settlement writing focused on material crises such as starvation, siege, and
massacres and *also* on representational crises such as faltering codes, lost
identifications, and the struggle to describe staggering events. Occurring
at such a radical remove from the home culture and always connected
to the struggle for physical survival, both material and representational
crises caused a breakdown in the way dislocated English settlers defined
themselves and the world around them. These crises opened a breach that
forced the settlers to confront and to represent their dreadful imperatives,
their extreme actions, and their colonial difference. As the wonder of the
New World became the misery of settlement, the colony was depicted as a
place that existed beyond the bounds of English norms or even English understanding, a place where settlers became colonial from within a state of
emergency, a theater of atrocity where, in states of both suffering and violence, settlers did things that seemed incredible. I have sought throughout
this chapter to expand a compressed historical account of early settlement
at Jamestown—a time and place that, despite its "shaky beginnings," has
been settled as "the birth of America"—in order to pursue an analysis of
what crisis produced there.[9] Reframing this history around its abjection,
its atrocities, and its terrible abandon, I want to trace a formulation of coloniality that emerged during its acute states of misery and violence, and
not after the colony was stabilized.

A Perfect Relation

In 1606 the plans for establishing English colonies in America were still in
an experimental stage, but the outlines of the venture seemed clear. Boats
would leave England with people and supplies, and they would return to England with riches and glory. Or in the more rapturous phrasing of Michael
Drayton's "Ode to the Virginian Voyage":

And cheerfully at sea
Success you still entice
To get the pearl and gold,
And ours to hold
Virginia,
Earth's only paradise![10]

But before Drayton's "brave heroic minds" could "Go and Subdue" Virginia, the colony had to exist on paper. Every aspect needed to be committed to writing—the justifications for colonial possession, the deed of land and distribution of powers, the official relations between and among the "purses and persons" of the Virginia Action, the detailed instructions for constructing a stable settlement—as part of what Michel de Certeau has called the "scriptural economy" that attends the imposition of social order.[11] A packet of preliminary documents drawn up in 1606 accomplished all of this. Though the goals for the colony still included imparting the Christian faith to "such people as yet live in darknesse," the document's first order of business was to impose strict social and legal control within the settlement. If native inhabitants were to be brought "in tyme . . . to humane civilitie and to a setled and quiet government," it would be through the example of a disciplined English colony.[12]

Extensive provisions for maintaining control within the colony were deemed necessary, given that a great many of the settlers sent to Virginia were considered unsavory and thus expendable. Indeed, addressing the problem of urban overcrowding was one of the action's selling points. For example, a 1603 order by James I decrees that the English residents of Virginia would include "incorrigable and dangerous rogues . . .banished and conveyed" overseas.[13] Even those settlers not drawn from the ranks of criminals were likened collectively to a swarm of bees forced to leave the busy hive of London before they destroyed it.[14] As one promotional pamphlet argued, "our land abounding with swarmes of idle persons, which having no meanes of labour to relieve their misery, doe likewise swarme in lewd and naughtie practises, so that if we seeke not some waies for their forreine employment, wee must provide shortly more prisons and corrections for their bad conditions."[15] "Our multitudes," in the words of another, "like too much bloud in the body, do infect our country with plague and povertie."[16] It was hoped that the infection could be bled out and that in America these thieves, vagabonds, and rogues would eventually become productive and useful subjects of the Crown. This transformation, however, would take time. Therefore, in addition to giving the colony's leaders license "to make a habitacion and plantacion," the preliminary documents empowered them to exercise a broad authority over the "Loving people willing to abide" there. The president and the council were authorized to deal with "all manner of excesse" and "all idle loytering and vagrant persons" however they saw fit and to punish them to the fullest extent of the law. For those who stirred "tumults, rebellion, Conspiracies, mutiny and seditions . . . murther, manslaughter, Incest, rapes, and adulteries," execution awaited.[17]

Although the first three documents of the 1606 preparatory parcel grant that circumstances might prove difficult to control, they counter that threat by invoking structures of authority: the king, his Crown, his privy seal; a plan for government; and the power to keep strict order both by dictum and by corpus. Ultimately these three documents convey a faith that English cultural systems would be transferable and that the New World could be disciplined into familiarity. By contrast, the final paper, entitled "Instructions Given by Way of Advice," sounds a different note entirely. Here the dangers of settlement are played out at the highest pitch. Cautionary advice quickly accelerates into a barrage of threats. Problems, especially with the Indians, will be inevitable, and their consequences will be severe: "[Y]ou must in no Case Suffer any of the natural people of the Country to inhabit between You and the Sea Coast for you Cannot Carry Your Selves so towards them but they will Grow Discontented with Your habitation and be ready to Guide and assist any Nation that Shall Come to invade You and if You neglect this You neglect Your Safety."[18] In this document the grammar shifts to the alarmingly confidential second-person "you" and to imperative verbal constructions ("you must," "you cannot," "you will"). Even the conditional "if" rings certain as a death knell: "if You neglect this You neglect Your Safety."

Regarding relations with the native inhabitants, the "Instructions" lift the veil to reveal what is behind the Englishmen's putatively benevolent motives for treating them gently and fairly. The action, it seemed, was less concerned with imparting notions of religious charity or English civility than with avoiding hostile engagement at all costs. After one colony was run out of Virginia and another disappeared into it, some lessons about the perils of Anglo-Indian interaction were learned: "In all Your Passages you must have Great Care not to Offend the naturals." Not you *should* take care but you *must*. The "Instructions" go on to warn that if settlers fail to stockpile corn before the natives realize that they are planning to stay, the settlement will surely face "the Danger of famine." But the document does not stop there; it sketches out other nightmare scenarios arising from Indian perfidy: colonists led into the woods and abandoned; stripped of guns and left defenseless; killed with a hail of arrows; or routed by allied native forces. Although inimical relations seem unavoidable—"you Cannot Carry Your Selves so towards them but they will Grow Discontented"[19]—the document does propose some practical strategies for mitigating the threat: "Above all things Do not advertize the killing of any of your men, that the Country people may know it; if they Perceive that there are but Common men . . . they will make many Adventures upon You. If the Country be populous you Shall Do well also not to Let them See or know of Your Sick men if you have any which may also Encourage them to many Enterprizes."[20]

The "Instructions" continue like this for pages, but their proposed solutions to the increasingly detailed catalog of potential perils would prove impossible for the English settlers to carry out as their colony devolved into anomie. Even so, the "Instructions" reveal a crucial detail about what the Virginia Action looked like at its outset. Though its preliminary objectives include plans for procuring commodities and establishing trade networks, as well as ambitions of discovering a northwest passage and mines of gold, there are sections of grim urgency in these documents that do not convey such optimistic expectations at all. Lurking amid the forward-looking preparations for the establishment of this new social body are fears of disaster and predictions of treachery.[21]

Although English interests in Virginia were diverse, they all relied on positive reports coming back from the early settlers. The conflicting demands of the requirement to "send a perfect relation . . . of all that is Done"— tell us everything and tell us good news—reveal the central but foreclosed role allotted to these reports. The Virginia Company, whose investors demanded a profit, especially needed to receive positive reports to stay in the black. The opening argument of Wesley Frank Craven's 1932 history of the Virginia Company emphasizes the importance of the corporation's bottom line: "Whatever else may have entered into the activities of the company, it was primarily a business organization with large sums of capital invested by adventurers whose chief interest lay in the returns expected from their investment."[22] From the investors' perspective, the main point of colonial relations was to shore up their balance sheets. Despite the low priority placed on settlers and their concerns by the broad assemblage that constructed the Virginia Action, and despite how quickly the settlers were isolated from it, the whole enterprise depended on these same settlers' total and disciplined obedience to its goals.

"Suffer no man . . . to write any Letter of any thing that may Discourage others," the "Instructions" commanded.[23] Yet despite the company's efforts to silence and censor, discouraging reports began to jeopardize the Virginia Action. Rumors circulated, letters were written home, and bad news leaked. As the experience of living in Jamestown became increasingly chaotic and challenging, the relations from Jamestown went well beyond what the Virginia Company considered it permissible to relate. Early warnings of colonial setbacks did not mitigate the urgency with which these conditions were reported and the hostile reactions with which they were received. Even before the settlement's most deadly episodes had transpired, the London damage control machine was up and running. Interested parties in London wrote their own tracts intending, in the words of Robert Johnson's 1609 *Nova Britannia*, "to rescue our enterprize from malicious ignorance" and to refute those "English natures, which laugh to scorne the name of Virginia."[24]

The settlers, beholden to a national enterprise even as they felt abandoned by it, quickly grasped the connection between colonial "persons" and London "purses," between their chances for survival and the action's financial returns.[25] Unable to send anything of value back to England and yet needing increased support, their letters are full of pleas and promises. The first official letter of the council in Virginia in 1607 begins, "We acknowledge our selves accomptable for our time here spent were it but to give you satisfaction of our industries and affeccions to this most honourable action." The council's letter aspires to "quicken" spirits and to "putt life into such dead understandings of beleefes that muste firste see and feele the wombe of our labor . . . before they will entertaine any good hope of us."[26] In other words, even before the first stirrings of English life in Virginia, leaders on the ground feared that the sense of expectancy might already be dead. The metaphor of the womb is generative, but the language of seeing and feeling life where there appears to be none is less so; this probing hints at the resurrection of something once dead rather than the gestation of something still living, evoking Thomas, who has to put his hands inside the wounds of Christ in order to believe that he has come back to life.

That the first letter already presents a discursive vacillation between living and dead states portends an unsteady future for the enterprise. The letter ends with an appeal that resounds throughout the early literature: "This noate doth make knowne where our necessities doe moste strike us, wee beseech your present releiffe accordinglie . . . otherwise to our greatest and laste greifes, wee shall against our willes, not will that which we moste willinglie would."²⁷ Though the clever phrasing plays with the idea that the will of the settlers hangs in the balance, it was apparent from the start that the settlement existed at the will of the Virginia Company. The deal was clear. The labor and lives of the settlers were entirely under obligation to the company. In return, the company would watch how events unfolded in Virginia, and do what it could. In the end it was the action that was to be protected at all costs and not the actors, who were considered necessary but expendable. Replacements could be found. Thus when settlers wrote back to the company, they had to resurrect dead understandings, protect damaged reputations, and plead for more help and more time, all the while knowing that the company's satisfaction came first—and that the duty to deliver good news from Virginia turned the idea of a perfect relation into a perfect fiction.

George Percy's Jamestown

John Smith and George Percy, the two men who produced the most comprehensive eyewitness accounts of the early Virginia settlement, approached the requirements of writing back to England very differently. Of the two, Smith is by far our preferred narrator. His actions in Virginia and his voluminous writings about the colony have made him a principal figure in the scholarship on early English colonialism.²⁸ Given Smith's historical role and literary output, many credit his works with inventing the character of colonial writing, and some even claim that his writings initiated American literature.²⁹ Smith's writings give detailed accounts of the first extensive Anglo-Indian relationships, map the ways and means of settler colonialism, and shape a historical memory of both. In word and deed Smith was central to the establishment of the first permanent English settlement in North America. While in Virginia he used his activities beyond the settlement's borders to distance himself from the colony's failures and to formulate a theory of colonization in action. Returned to England, he was, over the next twenty years, the most prolific writer about English colonization as the experiment of settlement turned into a program of empire. Smith's ability to invent new political and textual subject-positions for himself has made him a pivotal figure in the scholarship of early American contact zone activity and colonial discursivity. His vision that colonization could transform social organization was based on an unwavering belief in the powers of direct experience, industry, and self-actualization, leading several scholars to give Smith priority of place in constructing a "new model of identity and leadership that would assume archetypal proportions in American cultural consciousness."[30]

Smith was in Virginia only from 1607 to 1609, but within those two years he knew more about America than any Englishman alive. Smith realized that English settlers were *tassantassas*, strangers, and that the place the English called Virginia was simultaneously Tsenacommacah, an extensive territory of more than thirty tribes that made up the Powhatan confederacy. This confederacy was presided over by the paramount chief Wahunsonacock, known to the English as Chief Powhatan. Although Smith's ability to manipulate tribal politics is sometimes overstated, he did know that in order to consolidate power, he had to achieve a high status in both English and Indian spheres.[31] Eventually, Smith's aptitude for inserting himself into the dominant native systems while tenaciously holding on to his own English agenda won him that status in each camp. There was a direct connection between his adroit improvisations in the arenas of power and his ability to provision the colony with food. On a fundamental level, John Smith kept settlers, and thus the colony, alive. His famous dictum "He who will not work will not eat" encapsulates the brand of stern, pragmatic leadership that saved the colony from early ruin. Despite dissent that continued unabated among the fractious council members seeking to wrest control from him, Smith's presidency was a period in which the majority of men worked, ate, and reclaimed the will to live.[32]

Meanwhile, who was George Percy? George Percy was the eighth son of Henry, Earl of Northumberland, and one of the "gentlemen of note" who decided to join the settlement in Virginia at its start. He was twenty-seven, epileptic, and fully dependent on his brother Henry Percy, the current earl, for financial support. Once in Virginia, George Percy displayed no leadership skills and was often sick, ever inflexible, and certainly never a willing player in the dramatic theater of Anglo-Indian engagement that Smith had such a large hand in shaping. Surprisingly, Percy was installed as president of the colony after John Smith's departure, during which time, from October 1609 to May 1610, the colony collapsed. Within months the Powhatan confederacy cut off all food supplies to the settlers, causing a mass famine that came to be known as the "Starving Time." Of the five hundred colonists, only sixty survived.[33] By the time the next English ships came into Chesapeake Bay and entered what was left of the fort at Jamestown, it was clear that the colony was beyond saving. Twenty years after Roanoke, English settlers had no choice but to abandon their "permanent" settlement once again. Percy meekly relinquished what was left of his leadership, the ghastly survivors boarded the ships, and the whole colony headed back to England in failure.

Percy also occupies a lowly status in the historical and literary analyses of the Virginia settlement. Leading up to the four-hundredth anniversary of Jamestown's founding in 2007, Mark Nicholls published a scholarly edition of George Percy's work, the *Trewe Relacyon*, accompanied by a biography and critical analysis.[34] After the Nicholls edition appeared, Forrest K. Lehman wrote an article comparing Percy's text to Smith's *Generall Historie*.[35] But before the Nicholls edition, the most recent scholarly article published about George Percy was written in 1971 by Philip Barbour, the editor of John Smith's collected works and a leading historian of the Virginia settlement.[36] The next most recent treatment of Percy is a biographical sketch published in 1949.[37] Perhaps the reason we know so little about Percy—as this meager scholarly treatment indicates—is that we know so much about Smith, and so fully identify him with the Virginia settlement and the beginnings of English colonialism. If our Virginia is John Smith's Virginia, then Percy has no place in it.

However, like John Smith, Percy wrote. In 1607 he sent to London an important narrative that was circulated privately and then published by Samuel Purchas in 1625 as *Observations Gathered out of a Discourse*. Sometime after 1622 (probably around 1625), Percy composed his longer history of Jamestown, *A Trewe Relacyon of the Procedeings and Ocurrentes of Momente Which Have Hapned in Virginia from the Tyme Sir Thomas Gates Was Shippwrackte upon the Bermudes Anno 1609 untill My Departure owtt of the Cowntry Which Was in Anon Domini 1612*. This text was also privately circulated, maintained in family archives, and first printed in its entirety in 1922. The *Discourse* and the *Trewe Relacyon* are key primary sources on which every scholar of the Jamestown settlement depends. Philip Barbour, no fan of the man he once portrayed as a spoiled aristocrat, calls Percy's *Trewe Relacyon* "the most eloquent portrayal of the sufferings of the Jamestown colony which ever was written." Indeed, Barbour makes the case that Percy's literary style, his detailed observations, and his early "touches of lyricism" combine to make George Percy the author of "some of the most vivid passages in early American literature."[38] However, while both the *Discourse* and the *Trewe Relacyon* have long been absorbed and quoted, they are never interpreted within their own discursive structures. While Smith is read for his total colonial practice, Percy is picked through for vivid passages instead.

Clearly, George Percy was no John Smith. Yet if Smith's writings give us the full map of Virginia, Percy, I argue, is the key writer of Jamestown. When the audacious and unrestrained Smith pushes out of Jamestown, his writing expands. Reports of the land, geography, populations, and especially of his confrontations and negotiations with the Powhatan and other native groups energetically comprise a new kind of writing. However, Smith's relations also display a second, less celebrated mode. Whenever he returns to Jamestown, the writing contracts, contemptuously describing petty politics, conspiracies, grumbling, dissension, treason, sickness—in short, the life of most men in English Virginia. Given the critical attention to Smith's extraordinary journeys, it is this "meanwhile" that interests me—meanwhile, back in Jamestown. Undoubtedly, Percy writes from this "meanwhile" position. Despite his comparatively lackluster biography, he, not Smith, is the figure and the writer who best represents life and death, agony and atrocity in the Jamestown settlement, and who reveals most powerfully how Virginia's New World romance turned into a graveyard of meaning.

To put Percy and Smith into relation is to recognize why catastrophe, as well as possibility, was foundational to early settlement writing. Smith charts newly possible worlds, but Percy proves that a discourse of catastrophe was sometimes the only way to write Virginia. Reading the two writers side by side, a series of contrasts emerges. While Smith creates new subject positions, Percy writes from the wreckage of old ones. Smith lavishes attention on ritual spectacles full of signs and significance; Percy is absorbed by dystopic spectacles wherein signs and significance are vacated. Smith is always political, acutely aware of the operations of power and the engaged subjectivity of his opponents. Even in his fits of pique, Smith remains deeply rooted in the interpersonal world. Percy, in contrast, writes as an observer of disasters that he in part created. Narrating incredible things, he is a powerless witness. If Smith writes history as autobiography, Percy writes history as abjection.

However, the story of Jamestown is in large part about death, and it is Percy who gives us the death toll. Reading Percy's early *Discourse* allows us to understand the disaster of settlement as something more than a plotline of hazards and mistakes. Percy's alternative discourse, this "lecture of miserie," as he later calls it, is essential to settlement writing because it stays inside the catastrophe instead of seeking to move beyond it. The writing is engulfed by uncertainty and extremity, closing down the encyclopedic possibilities for inhabiting the New World and rendering the alienation and violence of colonial settlement clear. If, as Mary Fuller and James Egan have argued, John Smith provides the prime example of how autobiographical histories of settlement create authorized selves, I propose that the abject history of settlement creates a different kind of colonial self, one that is equally new but radically threatened, unknown, and displaced.[39] Neither fully subject nor object, the writer crosses over into the abject: jettisoned, drastically apart, and yet a witness to his own devolution.

Percy's text does not begin this way. His record of the transatlantic journey is something very like the perfect relation that the Virginia Company requested. He writes of the voyage in the manner of a sixteenth-century travel narrative, with thick descriptions full of wonder and strange sights, blazing stars and sweet smells, and nature that looks as if it "had beene set by Art." He describes a wild bull with horns four feet across, a field of grass so carpeted with eggs that "wee were not able to set our feet on the ground," and "savage Indians" who trade pineapples and tobacco for hatchets and copper jewels (922, 923). These are set pieces of the European voyager's wonder, a virtual museum tour of New World marvels and oddities narrated in a rhetorical tradition of aesthetic rapture and exotic fascination. As Stephen Greenblatt notes, catalogs of marvels were "inseparably bound up in rhetorical and pictorial tradition with voyages to the Indies," and Percy was surely writing in the wake of those travelers' tales.[40] Arriving in "the Land of Virginia," Percy sounds familiar notes, recording "faire meddowes and goodly tall Trees, with such Fresh-waters running through the woods, as I was almost ravished at the first sight thereof." The ravishing scene is interrupted by a shoreside encounter with a group of Paspahegh warriors on whose hunting grounds the settlers have landed: "At night, when wee were going aboard, there came the Savages creeping upon all foure, from the Hills like Beares, with their Bowes in their mouthes, charged us very desperately in the faces, hurt Captaine Gabrill Archer in both his hands, and a sayler in two place of the body very dangerous. After they had spent their Arrowes, and felt the sharpnesse of our shot, they retired into the Woods with a great noise, and so left us" (923–24). This is Percy's first description of the Paspahegh, the people who would define his experience with Native America. And yet even in this first hostile encounter, Percy depicts them much as he has the people of Dominico or Nevis earlier in his journey. At Paspahegh he describes the Indians' approach as animal-like, their attack as fierce, their language as "a great noise," but nothing in the writing particularly distinguishes these local natives from other indigenous people. That this is not just another stop on his journey but the site of his settlement does not yet register. Early in Percy's

Discourse, the people, hills, and woods of the New World are all exotic and all of a piece. Narrating the expedition's landfall in Virginia does not in itself require a discursive shift.

The *Discourse* continues in the same vein for some time. His written portraits of figures like the werowance of Rapahanna are as detailed and vivid as any we have, and he writes optimistically of the "great plentie" of the land. Percy's relation does not take the turn toward catastrophe until an event much more significant than the Virginia landfall: the flagship's return to England on June 22, 1607. It is the departure of this original ship, the *Susan Constant*, piloted by Captain Newport, that marks the beginning of colonial time, and it splits Percy's narrative in half:

> Munday the two and twentieth of June, in the morning, Captaine Newport in the Admirall departed from James Port for England.
>
> Captaine Newport being gone for England, leaving us (one hundred and foure persons) verie bare and scantie of victualls, furthermore in warress and in danger of the Savages. (932)

For Percy, Newport's departure is an event so profound that he can only bridge the paragraphs before and after it by repeating the news twice.

Soon thereafter the colony experienced the first of its mortality crises. The English population in Virginia plummeted from 104 men in late June to only 38 by that winter. In Percy's *Discourse*, the fading sight of the *Susan Constant* and a description of the rising death toll follow directly upon each other. By contrast, Smith, happy to see his rival leave, mentions Newport's departure only fleetingly and far more confidently: "Captaine Newport having set things in order, set saile for England the 22 of June, leaving provision for 13 or 14 weeks" (7). When Smith's *True Relation* narrates the later mortalities, Newport's leaving is not a factor. For Smith, the real problem is the one that has plagued the group since first landing: corruption and infighting on the council. In other words, the issue is not who left but who stayed: "through the hard dealing of our President, the rest of the counsell beeing diverslie affected through his audacious commaund . . . through which disorder God (being angrie with us) plagued us with such famin and sickness, that the living were scarce able to bury the dead" (8). Despite the providential invocation, Smith's take on the wasting colony is a story of greed and stupidity. According to Smith, the crisis began to abate with the impeachment of its instigator, the colony's president Edward Maria Wingfield, who had "ordred the afffaires in such sort that he was generally hated of all" (8). But even with so much misery in the fort, the council continued full of "mallice, grudging and muttering," while the settlers were "in such despaire, as they would rather starve and rot with idleness, then be perswaded to do anything for their own reliefe" (8–9). With only eighteen days' provisions left, Smith took it upon himself to go trading. Demanding or bargaining for food, he used his increasing skill and knowledge of the Powhatan world to sustain what was left of the English colony.

The rapid decline of the colony's political and physical life allows Smith to pursue his ambition to lead Virginia, but for Percy, whose primary connection is still to England, Newport's departure and the subsequent deterioration of social order have a different effect. Sentence by sentence his text falls apart. After reporting Newport's departure, Percy nervously recalls the promise of a supply ship. He implores his English readers to look after their own interests, assuring them that "if the beginners of this action doe carefully further us, the Country being so fruitfull, it would be as great a profit to the Realme of England, as the Indies to the King of Spaine." He then turns back to Virginia, describing a special offer of friendship from the "King of Rapahanna," who "lifted up his hand to the Sunne" for them and "laid his hand on his heart." Percy notes that "no Christian will keepe their Oath better upon this promise" (932). In this transition from imploring the help of the Old World to invoking the budding alliances of the New World, Percy attempts to substitute his faith in an English obligation he cannot fully trust with faith in a Native American gesture he cannot fully read. Neither conviction proves easy to hold. On the one hand, he is clearly writing to the Virginia Company as a mistrustful and potentially abandoned settler. On the other hand, although he wants to see reverence, habit, and order in the Native American oath, it soon turns "monstrous" in Percy's eyes: "These people have a great reverence to the Sunne above all other things at the rising and setting of the same, they sit downe lifting up their hands and eyes to the Sunne making a round Circle on the ground with dried Tobacco, then they begin to pray making many Devillish gestures with a Hellish noise foaming at the mouth, staring with their eyes, wagging their heads and hands in such a fashion and deformitie as it was monstrous to behold" (932).

During the initial English forays, Percy describes the Rapahanna werowance and his people as being "as goodly men as I have ever seene." He is especially impressed by the werowance's extraordinary regalia and stately bearing. The chief entertains them, Percy writes, "as though he had beene a Prince of civil government, holding his countenance without laughter or any such ill behavior; he caused his Mat to be spred on the ground, where hee sate down with a great Majestie, taking a pipe of Tabacco: the rest of his company standing about him" (926–27).[41] But with the initiation of colonial time, with Newport gone and this native "King" performing a substitutive bond in his place, the serene countenance, princely carriage, and royal court are all hideously transformed. What begins with reverence and order turns into a monstrous ritual in which eyes bulge, mouths foam, and heads and hands shake spasmodically.[42] This turn to the grotesque opens a chasm into which Percy's text then falls:

> The sixt of August there died John Ashbie of the bloudie Fluxe. The ninth day died George Flowre of the swelling. The tenth day died William Bruster Gentleman, of a wound given by the Savages, and was burried the eleventh day. The fourteenth day, Jerome Alikock Ancient died of a wounde, the same day Francis Midwinter and Edward Moris Corporall died suddenly." (932)

This is the fall into catastrophe. The *Discourse* proceeds with an incantation of twenty-five deaths, sometimes as many as three a day, uninterrupted by comment or narration.[43] It is unrelenting, and unlike anything preceding it in the literature.

When the text finally resumes its expository prose, its discourse is transformed. Gone are the fine paths, pleasant springs, and goodly cornfields. Percy's attention to detail, once trained on the outside world, constricts to shuddering glimpses of the conditions in the fort. He records three-night-long watches on the bare cold ground; a small can of soaked barley to split among five men; dirty, brackish water to drink; the river at low tide full of slime and filth; five full months of "miserable distresse" (933). Percy no longer narrates or describes but rather testifies: "There were never Englishmen left in a forreigne Countrey in such miserie as wee were in this new discovered Virginia."

Comparatively, Smith's description of this time gathers up the forces of the "I." Smith's expression of the singularity of his experience supports the theory that the combined cultural phenomena of unprecedented events in the colonies, changing structures of authority, and an increasing reliance on first-person forms of representation, along with the rapid growth of print culture, led to the emergence of an autobiographical "I" in the seventeenth-century colonial arena.[44] However, to posit this first-person singular "I" as the primary new form of writing coming from the colonies is to overlook colonial texts, such as Percy's, that occupy a vacated, first-person plural "we." The latter writing is as colonial as the former. As inherited principles that organized identity were disrupted in early settlement, new categories of self, experience, and presentation emerged. However, those categories were also destabilized by misery, absence, shock, and loss, so that at the same time that colonial authority was being claimed, catastrophic relations were also shaping colonial discourse. Possession existed alongside dispossession; a heightened role for writing existed alongside bodily suffering and rapacious mortality; maps were charted alongside records of necrology; a discourse of authority existed alongside a discourse of misery.

Abject Misery

In Jamestown, London's imagined protocols for colonization proved unworkable. The documents that inaugurated the Virginia Action could in no way sustain Virginia in action. The "Letters Patent" gave settlers the king's license to pursue a "noble" work and guaranteed them all the rights of Englishmen. The "Order for Government" dictated procedures to initiate a firm political structure. The "Instructions" told them where and how to settle and detailed their daily occupations down to the man.[45] However, these authorizing forces could not consolidate the territory they marked out. Of course, the colony was to be created and held by forces on the ground, but the preliminary documents soon became meaningless in dealing with local contingencies. The goal of colonization was territory formation, but the settlement in Virginia instead became deterritorialized, which is to say that the forms and codes for organizing colonization unraveled in such a way as to make their restitution impossible, rendering them useless to structure the English Action and irrelevant to the colonists.[46] The documents that authorized their presence could no longer provide a stable basis of meaning for settlers who struggled to represent their colonial condition.

From within the crisis, then, neither the discourse of New World exploration nor the discourse of fruitful habitation and possession was available, and there was no other collective language to substitute for these abandoned discourses. Therefore, when Percy compiles his roster of the dead, he writes of a growing absence to an absent audience. Describing "our men night and day groaning in every corner of the Fort most pittifull to heare," he laments that "if there were any conscience in men, it would make their harts to bleed to heare the pittiful murmurings & out-cries of our sick men without reliefe every night and day for the space of sixe weekes, some departing out of the World, many times three or fourre in a night, in the morning their bodies trailed out of their Cabines like Dogges to be buried: in this sort I did see the mortalitie of divers of our people" (933). In this passage Percy traces the alarming escalation of the crisis at Jamestown in a series of phrases that intensify as he moves from describing the human ("pittiful murmurings") to the inhuman ("like Dogges to be buried"). His "I did see" at the end of this outcry marks the evacuation of a corporate self even as there is not yet a recognizable individual self to take its place. His powerlessness registers alternately as a hyperbolic petition and as a recital of deadened facts.[47] Already the distant audience to this lamentation has become virtual, as Percy tries to conjure a sympathetic "conscience in men" that might compensate for the humanity stripped from the corpses dragged out "like Dogges."

However, the suffering is not and cannot be witnessed by the world as he knows it, which is part of the episode's uncontainable horror. The truth of this suffering can be denied from an oceanic remove. In this affective separation, the writing of catastrophe resembles the condition of coloniality itself, which also relied on a continued connection with a fatally distant England that could and did respond to catastrophe by turning its back. Formerly part of a "we" with a common purpose, settlers become the outcast "they," over in Virginia, not only distanced from the honorable Virginia Action, but in this case crying without relief and dragged out of the fort like dogs. As settlers deteriorate from authorized imperial agents to bodies in naked misery, their words lose the ability to reincorporate a lost commonality. The "we" that connects Virginia to London is gone, replaced at best by a wished-for, hypothetical community: only "if there were any conscience in men" might the "I" and "divers of our people" be imaginatively rearticulated into the whole.

As colonists were stripped of the collective signifiers and social forms that had defined them, the body became the primary site of disarticulation. Mortality crises provoked desperation and then abjection because as half the settlers turned into corpses, there was no recourse to stabilizing cultural institutions and collectives. The starving, moaning body was an abject thing, but I use the concept of abjection in a broader way. As Julia Kristeva argues, abjection is not only an extreme physical degradation; it is also a state of being caused by "what disturbs identity, system, order, [w]hat does not respect borders, positions, rules."[48] In the deteriorating colony, abjection expanded beyond physical states and beyond the experiences of individual persons. Settler abjection spread through the settlement as a pervasive sense of uncanniness, culminating in the collapse of a formerly meaningful corporate identity. The transgressive quality of abjection, the way it continually crosses between inside and outside, mirrors the horror with which the settlers saw what they had become both within and without: the most feeble wretches left in a foreign country. Beyond the individual psyche, then, the collective sense of Englishness transformed into a sense of settler self-otherness, one that disturbed "identity, system, order" and that did not respect "borders, positions, rules."

Out of this pervasive unsettlement, a colonial condition emerged, one with a new relationship to the physical form. As this new colonial body was losing the battle for survival, it prompted not only disgust but also self-alienation that could not be repaired by the surrounding world. There were, after all, no external features in the landscape, built or natural, to support a culturally defined self, and the consensus "commonsense world" of habitus that might have sustained a social self was also gone.[49] The slow dispossession of the body through disease and starvation in colonial space therefore represented more than a physical breakdown. This physical deterioration and abject jettisoning of the self was happening in the absence of markers of English identity and belonging. The settler's body was dissociated from the corporate body of Englishness, and so something else became its identifying principle. Colonists understood themselves as becoming colonial through a confrontation with, and eventually through identification with, their misery.

Witnessing "the mortalitie . . . of our people" and seeking "any conscience in men," Percy's colonial writing position defines a new reality that, because the settlement existed at such a vast remove and in such a radically unknown place, became totally engrossing. The question "Who am I?" was directly linked to the question "Where am I?"—for in what way could Jamestown be compared to London? Everything in the New World bore the signs of difference and of the increasingly harrowing conditions of colonial settlement. Lost markers of Englishness were replaced by an abjected "not I" and "not us" that made settlers barely recognizable to themselves, represented in the canceled form of identity: "There were never Englishmen." Kristeva describes the abject as "a massive and sudden emergence of uncanniness . . . [that] now harries me as radically separate, loathsome. *Not me. Not that. But not nothing either.*"[50] This "me/not me" was the daily, material reality of settlement, and it is also central to the discourse of misery. In turn, the "me/not me" became the very formulation through which the settler identified, the uncanny disconsolidation through which coloniality took shape.

In the early years, then, the attribution of otherness was not only directed by English people toward native peoples; there was also a powerful sense of self-otherness within the settlement community. After all, in the first seasons at Jamestown, the greatest scorn was directed toward the failing forts. Native power was articulated, while every English structure broke down. Indians raided when they wanted to, gave or withheld food when they wanted to, and realized that the settlers were starving only months after the first ships left Englishmen in Virginia. In the context of these power relations, the distancing "not me, not that" often flew back to its source in the settler himself: in Kristeva's words, "[u]nflaggingly, like an inescapable boomerang."[51] The settlement out of which Percy wrote, especially as it dissolved in extremis, was othered from both inside and out.

One might assume that colonial writers wrote to give meaning to horrible events, but I suggest that this is not the case. As the place where meaning collapses, abject misery is less an event from which one recovers than a lingering state and structure of otherness. In other words, the discourse of misery in settlement is primarily motived not by a desire to resolve meaning around horrific events but rather by a desire to name them. Cause, effect, interpretation, motivation—these are muted at best. For instance, when Percy reports that the settlers are rescued from utter starvation by their "mortall enemies" the Powhatan, the passage reads as providential: "It pleased God, after a while, to send those people which were our mortall enemies to releeve us with victuals, as Bread, Corne, Fish, and Flesh in great plentie, which was the setting up of our feeble men, otherwise wee had all perished. Also we were frequented by divers Kings in the Countrie, bringing us store of provision to our great comfort" (934). But while food saves the feeble men, the intervention does nothing to change the narrative direction of Percy's relation. A retinue sent by God ("Kings" bearing gifts) may counteract dehumanization (corpses dragged like dogs), but it does not mitigate the scene of catastrophe into which the fort has fallen and within which the written relation persists. Instead of moving from this "great comfort" to any renewed purpose or action, Percy returns to the business at hand—lining up the dead: "The eighteenth day, died one Ellise Kinistone which was starved to death with cold. The same day at night, died one Richard Simmons. The nineteenth day, there died one Thomas Mouton" (934). As significance disappears in Virginia, Percy sinks into the passive and terrible task of naming the corpses who surround him and who, in their rapid degeneration from identifiable people to colonial waste, also threaten to annihilate him. The representational form of the roster may seek to contain the deaths, but the effect of listing name after name, day after day, also communicates a seeming endlessness, a steady accretion of bodies that sinks the narrative under their increasing dead weight.

There is no knowing if or how Percy's *Discourse* recovers from this scene. Samuel Purchas, publishing the *Observations Gathered out of a Discourse* in 1625, ends the account abruptly, noting, "The rest is omitted, being more fully set downe in Cap. Smith's Relations."[52] Indeed it was. In most of our histories of early Jamestown, what occupied Percy's writing during this season of misery becomes a background to a story whose chief teller was John Smith. All the problems at the fort—the infighting, the instability, the ineptitude, the general lack of wherewithal—become the bad situation that just keeps getting worse as Smith and his allies push up the rivers and into the country. Mapping Virginia was representational, a complex colonial practice. Mortality in Virginia was material, a register of helplessness and decay. George Percy's text operates in the space between, registering the disintegration of both the fort and the means of representing it.

I have treated the *Discourse* at some length because the colonial turn from New World wonder to settlement misery coincides with the critical moment when the negation of Englishness is expressed in terms of abandonment and abjection. The "I" becomes colonial by default: *not that, but not nothing either.* Percy's "necrology" is sometimes plucked out from the rest of his text and inserted into a larger narrative of false starts and fatal flaws, futile plans and ill will, do-nothing colonists drinking tainted water. And yet in the colony's first year when it seemed it would be destroyed, a dark and metamorphic discourse emerged in colonial writing. Writing settlement as catastrophe not only defied the primary role set for colonial "perfect relations"; it also became a means through which settlers witnessed themselves and registered their shock at the unprecedented circumstances that they could neither absorb nor defend against. Through canceled forms of Englishness, it marked the threshold between an old identity and a new one as a site of abjection, at which what collectively disturbed "identity, system, [and] order" came to express the inescapable condition of becoming colonial.

A Planter's Manifest

Only 38 of the original 104 settlers survived Jamestown's first mortality crisis, but the worst was yet to come. In the winter of 1610, the settlers at Jamestown again ran out of food and were forced to barricade themselves inside their ruined fort. Then a whole "worlde of miseries ensewed" (1099). They ate dogs, cats, and rats; sucked on leather boots and shoes; and licked the blood off dying men. They dug up corpses from the ground and ate them. Most of what we know about Virginia's Starving Time comes from Percy's later history, *A Trewe Relacyon*, a text that brings into sharp focus the nearly unimaginable situation inside the walls of the Jamestown Fort. No other colonial author describes that time with anything like his intensity. Many historians use Percy's words to convey in human terms the experience of having nearly 85 percent of the settler population die within six months and to emphasize how unlikely it was that the colony would ever recover.[53]

What is less noticed about this text, and what I argue is more instructive, is the broader role that atrocity played before, during, and after this particular season of misery. Citing the most awful depictions of the Starving Time helps to construct vivid accounts of the colony's nadir. However, continually extracting those "vivid passages" from their surrounding discourse obscures the deeper relationship between the suffering of the Starving Time and the widespread violence in the early years of settlement in Virginia. George Percy offers the most wretched description of Jamestown Fort as it became, in David Quinn's words, "a death-ridden outpost."[54] George Percy also threw Indian children into the James River and shot their brains out as they were trying to swim ashore. While the Starving Time unleashed the worst misery known in England's early American settlements, this indiscriminate destruction and murder of innocents unleashed their first total war. In the telling, however, catastrophic discourse effectively collapses the boundary between misery and brutality. To characterize events as unaccountable and then to write a harrowing, detailed report of them, as Percy did, is to erode meaningful difference between types of violence amid an onslaught of shocking specificities. This creates equivalency between deprivation and overkill because now the whole act of settlement has become a theater of atrocity. Once the rendering of catastrophe has created an atmosphere of total hazard, and one that does not admit an alternative vision, the horror of the fort can turn into terror beyond the fort's walls. Because these outposts became places where centers did not hold, they also became places where no holds were barred.

Again, we turn to Percy because he gives the most extensive and intensive account of the years between 1609 and 1612. His *Trewe Relacyon*, so often read in fragments, is unique in its totality. Before describing the Starving Time, Percy narrates a series of assaults that lead up to the forced enclosure of Jamestown. He then provides the most detailed account available of the protracted combat that follows. The *Trewe Relacyon* is the only settler's account structured in this way around the buildup to and waging of the first Anglo-Powhatan war—England's first major, extended combat in America, and the one that set the terms for subsequent colonial-Indian warfare.[55] Of the three other main chroniclers of these years, John Smith left Virginia just as the conflict germinated, and William Strachey and Ralph Hamor arrived after it was well under way; none of the three was in Virginia during the Starving Time. Other accounts by those who were in Virginia include one from an English boy living with the Powhatan, Henry Spelman, who focuses mostly on Powhatan religion and society, and one section of *The Proceedings of the Colony in Virginia*, whose joint authors note cryptically, "It were too vile to say what we endured" (157).[56] Not only was Percy residing in the settlement during the tumultuous period, but he was also central to it—first as president of the colony, then as chief commander under De La Warr, then as deputy governor before the arrival of Sir Thomas Dale. But in addition to providing an eyewitness account of events, Percy's narrative uniquely allows us to connect the settlement's "woes & miseries" to the "Revendge upon the Indyans."[57]

Given the spectacular failure of the colony, it is easy to read the *Trewe Relacyon* as Percy's bid for self-justification. After all, Percy was the president during the colony's worst period, from John Smith's humiliating departure in October 1609 to the abandonment of Jamestown in May 1610. If anyone were to bear the brunt of the blame, it would logically be Percy. For example, Mark Nicholls argues, "Percy decided to concentrate specifically on protecting his own reputation, so producing a work that is more defensive than offensive, more concerned with exonerating George Percy than with advancing any sustained and painstaking critique of John Smith."[58] Forrest K. Lehman contends that Percy wrote "as a way of excusing his own failings" during his tenure as the colony's president and to "defend himself by laying blame on everyone else."[59] On one level this is true. In the "Dedication" to his nephew, Lord Algernon Percy, Percy admits that part of his purpose is to clear his name. He adopts a posture familiar in Virginian settlement apologias: everyone (and especially John Smith) is telling lies, but now I will come forward and tell the truth, not only for the good of my name but also for the good of Virginia.[60] Percy writes that "all which I ayme att is to manyfeste my selfe" and "to delyver thatt trewly which my selfe and many others have had bitter experyense of" (1093–94). In the body of the text, however, such defensiveness is absent, and the exculpatory motive for writing becomes more complicated. Percy's aim to "manyfeste" himself also includes the sense of making manifest: representing that "bitter experyense" and making himself and others manifest amid the colony's increasingly disastrous implosion.

At the outset A Trewe Relacyon faces two kinds of unreality: first, the public record of lies, exaggeration, and spin surrounding these events; and second, the cognitive unreality of living and acting in a world beyond thresholds. Percy writes against those who blame the settlers for the failure of the settlement, but his account does not take the form of an argument. He struggles instead to relate the increasingly unimaginable world that the settlement became, and how meaning was suspended there. What is at stake, therefore, is more a naming than a name. Percy's text does something far beyond excusing his own failings. Through both its structure and its detailed particulars, Percy's Trewe Relacyon demonstrates, or makes manifest, how incremental alienation from stable forms of meaning created a condition of possibility for the violent entrenchment of the colony.

Although Percy strove to maintain his Old World aristocratic bearings while in Virginia, he opens his narrative by acknowledging that Jamestown made him more of a planter than a Percy. Rather than deflecting accounts of the colony's failure, he dives right into Virginia's miseries, linking them to a long history of colonial horrors: "If we Trewly Consider the diversety of miseries mutenies and famishmentts which have attended upon discoveries and plantacyons in this our moderne Tymes we shall nott fynde our plantacyon in Virginia to have Suffered aloane" (1093). The French were starved in Florida; the Spanish ate their horses on the straits of Magellan. Elsewhere men were "inforced to eat Toades Snakes and sutche lyke venemous wormes," and bodies of mutineers were cut down from the gallows and "bur[ied] . . . in hungry Bowelles" (1094). Thus while the bitter Jamestown experience may separate those who have tasted it in Virginia from those who would stand in judgment in England, it also connects the colonists to a common tribe of planters who have suffered misery and committed atrocities at a similar remove from, and in similar service to, their empire. Though their experiences are beyond understanding, "beyond" becomes a category of being for these men. Although we suffered alone, we have not been the only ones to suffer; although we became a thing apart, what we became *is* a thing, and it is called "a planter." Separated as Percy is from the English at home, the first goal of his text is to formulate some other imagined grouping beyond the time and place of Virginia, to join with another band subjected to misery, mutiny, and famishment: the planters.

While the argument that all plantations suffer was not unique to settlers, it was put to a very different use in London's official responses to Virginia's problems. In those texts similar cases of misery were invoked, but these were meant to minimize the centrality of disaster in the settlement, not to affirm it. For example, the furiously backpedaling London Council for the Virginia Company reminded investors that the Spanish had endured far worse but persisted and won: "If we cast our eye upon the Spanish Conquest of the Indyes, how aboundant their stories are of Fleets, Battailes, and Armies lost: eighteen upon the attempt of Guiana, and more than seventy in both the Indyes, and yet with how indefatigable industry, and prosperous fate, they have pursued and vanquished all these."[61] The beginnings of the Spanish Empire, they argued, "were meaner than ours, and subject to all the same and much more uncertainty," and yet look at the results: "[h]ow farre hath she sent out her Apostles and thorough how glorious dangers?"[62]

Ultimately the Virginia Company sought ways to deny its accountability for what was happening in Virginia. If the voyage "went out smilling on her lovers with pleasant lookes" and returned "with a rent and disfigured face," it was the fault of those "wicked Impes," the settlers themselves. "[L]et the imputation of miserie be to their idleness," one promoter writes, "and the blood that was spilt upon their own heads that caused it."[63] In the company's extensive propaganda campaign, corporeal metaphors helped to imagine a collective, widespread crisis as an individual, recuperable body. Although the settlement had become infected, its diseased past could be quarantined off from the healthy future still to come. If only investors would stay the course, a hale body of leaders, laws, and settlers would replace the current decrepit body. The "disfortified fort" and its "desperate condition" were "things already done and past," they promised; the "ill and odious wound of Virginia" was as good as healed. In their publications, the organizers of the Virginia Action washed their hands of the colony's failures. The rhetoric might be summed up in their blunt but memorable question "Who would have expected this?"[64]

In theory the plan was for the company to provision the colony from London while the settlers extracted wealth from Virginia, but each supply mission turned out to be a small disaster. The first supply brought men and food to the colony. Five days later someone accidentally set fire to the fort and destroyed both the new supplies and whatever old stock remained. The second supply was ineffective as well; its stores were quickly consumed, and its men devoted their time, material, and labor to feckless pursuits. By the time this second round of ships headed back to London, they had left behind more mouths to feed and only a few weeks worth of food. John Smith, typically contemptuous of this sort of incompetence, writes that these new men "were all sicke, the rest some lame, some bruised, all unable to doe any thing but complaine" (341). The third supply simply did not arrive in Virginia. Famously, a three-day hurricane broke the fleet at sea, wrecked the flagship *Sea Venture* on Bermuda, and stranded its survivors there for ten months. The lost flagship carried the mission's most significant cargo: a new set of leaders for the colony and a commission for a change in government. The colonists did not learn what had happened until the other ships from this third fleet straggled into Jamestown in August 1609, once more bringing more people and few provisions. While the leaders—the missing "heads"— of the third supply were marooned in Bermuda, the "headless residue" that did arrive soon wreaked havoc in what had become John Smith's Virginia.[65] An expedition that was designed to impose an official, centralized order instead led to the most serious fragmentation of power yet. Even by the fledgling colony's standards, it was chaotic. As Philip Barbour describes it, there were "no orders, no charter, and no one in undisputed command."[66] In *The Proceedings of the Colony in Virginia*, Smith writes, "Happy had we bin had they never arrived; and we forever abandoned, and (as we were) left to our fortunes, for on earth there was never more confusion, or miserie, that their factions occasioned" (107). The partial arrival of the third supply led to the end of Smith's government, the end of his considerable influence among the Powhatan, and the start of the buildup to the first Anglo-Powhatan war. It is in this mutinous season that Percy's *Trewe Relacyon* begins.

Smith dealt with the arrival of over 300 ungovernable men by distributing the rowdies and ringleaders throughout the smaller forts around Jamestown. Realizing that he could neither feed nor control them, Smith spread the unfamiliar, undisciplined, and armed men into the country. This strategy did nothing to avoid the overthrowing of his newly established political order among the English. Worse, it effectively broke the temporary truce called by Wahunsonacock because of the "1000 mischiefes those lewd captains led this lewd company" (107). In one act of dispersal, Smith sent the newly arrived gentleman Francis West out with 160 men and six months' worth of food to erect a fort up the James River at a place called the Falls. Completely inexperienced and lacking discipline, West insisted on defying Smith's order and choosing his own spot in which to settle. The men adapted to their new locale by stealing food, burning houses, and randomly attacking people in the surrounding villages. Responding to these outrages, local warriors killed nearly half of the fort's occupants until any Englishman who attempted to move beyond the palisade would either come back gravely injured or not come back at all. According to Percy, when Smith went to evaluate West's purported command, "a greate devisyon did growe," each man taking umbrage that his authority was unrecognized by the other. During the conflict Smith was rumored to be so anxious to be rid of West and his crew that he would have killed them himself if he could. Another view held that Smith "animated the Salvages ageinste Capteyne West" by confiding to them that the English "had noe more powder lefte them then wolde serve for one volley of shott" (1096).

On Smith's return trip to Jamestown, a match ignited the gunpowder in his pocket, which exploded in his lap and grievously injured both Smith's body and his command over the colony.[67] He was denied any further authority and was forced to return to England, and Percy was made president in his place. During Smith's presidency, only eight settlers died; Percy would preside over the deaths of more than four hundred. When Percy wrote that catastrophic history, the "ill and odious wound" of Virginia was manifestly opened.[68]

Dead Messengers

Percy narrates several acts of violence that occur before the worst of the starvation sets in: a land grab gone very wrong at Nansemond; a truant group and its pursuing officer killed in the village of Kecoughtan; and a trading party ambushed and tortured at Orapakes. These violent incidents are significant in two senses. First, they depict the rapidly deteriorating situation between Indians and English leading up to the first Anglo-Powhatan war. Second, the incidents themselves produce forms of signification, enacting a system of representation and communication when all others were collapsing. The men killed in this series of brutal clashes were often messengers sent from the English to the Indians, but once they were killed, the bodies of dead Englishmen were used by the Powhatan to send horrific messages back to the settlement. In Percy's relation, the path to the Starving Time is strewn with these dead messengers. Indians kill English envoys and then use mussel shells to scrape out their brains. When a group of settlers come begging to the Indians for food, they are not only killed, but their corpses are propped up in the forest like scarecrows with their mouths stuffed with bread. An English captain is burned alive while his skin is scraped off and thrown into the fire before his face.

These scenes progressively represent not only the breakdown of Anglo-Powhatan relationships but also the inexorable movement of English settlers from subjects to bodies to things. The destruction of each messenger accelerates the loss of the settlers' ability to make and control meaning in the hostile world their actions have created. Instead, the maimed figures mark the settlement as a place where unthinkable events are frighteningly compacted into disfigured English bodies. By playing out these episodes one by one, and especially by concentrating on descriptions of torture and corpses, Percy's text incrementally and radically defamiliarizes English bodies in Virginia. This defamiliarization is a necessary precondition for representing later horrors both inside and outside the Jamestown Fort. The liminal state between death and life represented by these tortured bodies, the subsequent abandonment of the various forts, and the concentration of the English population in Jamestown all have a discursive as well as a material function in Percy's prelude to the Starving Time. It is to compress the presence of the English settlers, to empty them as volitional subjects, and to make the vitiated version of Englishness that survives, inasmuch as it survives, into a spectacle, a thing deeply alienated and uncanny.

The first violent episode Percy describes takes place at Nansemond. While dispersing the new arrivals of the third supply, Smith sends John Martin, Percy, and sixty other men to stake an outpost in an Indian territory to the north. Martin, in turn, sends two of his men as envoys to the Nansemond werowance to try to trade copper hatchets for a nearby island. When the messengers do not return at the appointed time, the English decide to take the island by force, with Percy in charge of the raid. As Percy crosses the water, he thinks he sees the English messengers being carried away in a canoe: "[W]e espied a Canoe wherein we weare perswaded our messengers to be, but they perceaveinge us Retourned backe from whense they came and we never sett eye upon our messengers after" (1096). It is a small but eerie scene. For a moment Percy's eyes catch sight of the messengers vanishing from view, gliding off in the opposite direction from men already keen to avenge their disappearance. The sentence continues, "and we never sett eye upon our messengers after, Butt understood from the Indyans themselves thatt they weare sacrifysed and thatt their Braynes weare Cutt and skraped outt of their heades with Mussell shelles." Now the vanishing sight of the English messengers is replaced by vivid news of their torturous deaths. The messengers devolve from valued representatives to silent bodies secreted away in a canoe to dismembered and discarded brains.

If this scene of sacrifice is purposely "savage" in its details, Percy's description of the subsequent English raid of the island is just as culturally bound in a European tradition of violence. The atrocity committed against the English messengers is answered by a wholesale destruction of the Indian village: assault, arson, desecration, and pillage. "We Beate the Salvages outt of the Island," Percy writes, and "burned their howses ransaked their Temples, Tooke downe the Corpes of their deade kings from their Toambes, and Caryed away their pearles Copper and bracelets wherewith they doe decore their kings funeralles" (1096). The small detail at the end sits strangely alongside the narration of the unmitigated destruction of the village, as if the ethnographic impulse to observe and record remains even as cultural artifacts become pure loot. But upon closer reading, Percy does not represent the raid indiscriminately. The houses, temples, tombs, and funerary goods Percy chooses to include are the very markers of culture that the settlers have lost in moving to Virginia.

Fearing the fallout from the raid, Percy and his men also capture the "Kings sonne" to hold hostage. En route back to camp, a gun is "suddenly fyered," shooting the werowance's son in the chest at close range. Remarkably the captive does not collapse but instead, "with his passyon and feare," jumps up, breaks his ropes, leaps out of the boat, and swims back to the main, his wound leaving a trail of blood in the water behind him. Unlike the English envoys, the son returns to his father as a living messenger. Returning to their own fort without their valuable captive as a bargaining tool, Percy tries to convince Martin to launch a preemptive attack on the mainland town of Nansemond. Martin refuses, "pretendinge that he wolde nott putt his men into hassard," and decides to hunker down while Percy returns to Jamestown. Soon after, Martin comes to Jamestown on the flimsiest of pretexts, leaving the rest of his men garrisoned in the makeshift fort and abandoning them to the inevitable Indian reprisal (1096).

The second episode of violence describes the fall of the fort at Nanse-mond and leaves a haunting spectacle in its wake: English corpses displayed as tokens of Indian power. After Martin's departure, seventeen men escape the abandoned garrison and sail to nearby Kecoughtan, "pretendinge they wolde trade there for victwelles." Percy reports that these men also disap-pear ("nott any of them weare heard of after") and are "in all lykelyhood" killed (1097–98). Within days their commanding lieutenant and others go out in search of them and are also killed. This second group is later found, "with their mowthes stopped full of Breade, being donn as itt seamethe in Contempte and skorne, thatt others mighte expectt the Lyke when they shold come to seeke for breade and reliefe amongste them" (1098).

Here, Percy pauses to reference the legendary death of the Spanish con-quistador Baldivia, who was captured, feasted lavishly, and then was killed by his captors pouring molten gold down his throat and taunting, "Now glut thyself with gold, Baldivia."[69] The Spanish general's throat choked with gold and the English lieutenant's mouth stuffed with bread powerfully mark them as instructional corpses, concentrated symbols of native resistance to insatiable colonial greed. The difference between Spanish gold lust and En-glish land lust is collapsed by parallel modes of retaliation; in both cases the products that Europeans demand are literally shoved down the throats of dead men. The mutilated corpses that carry the Indians' message represent what José Rabasa has called *"speech as a bodily act,"* which "effects violence in the process of its inscription as well as its reception."[70] The English bodies still act as messengers, but the message they now bear is not only about food but also about power. Although Rabasa has in mind the violence that colo-nizers inscribed by mutilating Indian bodies and sending them out to herald a new regime, in Percy's relation Indians enforce the message that what they possess will remain theirs.[71]

In the third incident, a panicked Percy sends perhaps the most impudent man in Virginia, John Ratcliffe, with fifty men to trade for corn at Wahun-sonacock's new inland seat at Orapakes. Even under these dire circum-stances in Anglo-Indian relations, Ratcliffe has no particular plan. He does not keep a guard; he allows high-ranking Indians to survey his situation; he lets his men wander into the woods, into the village, and into Indian houses. The Powhatan, having time to plan a concerted attack, "at a fitting time" and upon a signal, kill every Englishman in sight and take Ratcliffe captive. Percy then describes the actions of that "slye owlde kinge": "[H]e caused [Ratcliffe] to be bownd unto a tree naked with a fyer before, and by woemen his fleshe was skraped from his bones with Mussel shelles and before his face throwne into the fyer" (1098–99). Ratcliffe is literally flayed alive. He is put in the almost unfathomable position of witnessing his own metamorphosis from person to thing. "The Tragaedie of Capteyne Ratliefe" is brought back to Jamestown by the few survivors of the mission, but that is all they bring back (1099). Like other food-scouting parties sent out by Percy, this remnant comes back in defeat, having procured nothing but stories of settlers mutilated and destroyed and leaving newly incensed or triumphant enemies behind.

Percy's tableaux are important to recount because in their individual forms and overall structure, their series of dead messengers brings violence against English bodies ever closer to a living, but barely surviving, core. First, brains are scraped out of men who are already dead, materializing the metaphorical headlessness that characterized these new arrivals from the start. Then, corpses are erected in the woods with manipulated death masks; in rigor mortis, their dead mouths are made to speak the stern message of their enemies. Finally, as Ratcliffe's body is scraped off and burned "before his face," the man who had most conceitedly vaunted his Englishness watches himself literally disintegrate and be consumed in flames. The brains, the mouth, the living/dying face: these scenes intensify as the figure of the colonial grows more and more distorted and what is left of the faltering settlement's coherence disintegrates.

After Ratcliffe's disastrous corn-trading mission, Percy sends Francis West (formerly stationed at the Falls) to Potomac with three dozen men to seek food there. Potomac was located on the far border of the Powhatan confederacy, and its people were more willing to defy Wahunsonacock and enter into trade relations with the English. West succeeds in filling his boat with grain but afterward "used some harshe and Crewell dealinge by Cutteinge of towe of the Salvages heads and other extremetyes" (1099). After decapitating members of the only tribe who would consider trading with the starving colony, West and his mutinous crew commit what is clearly in English eyes a worse crime: they refuse to relieve the Englishmen who are already on starvation rations at Jamestown. West and his men abscond with the boat, and its freight of corn, and head home for England. Once abandoned by the Virginia Action back in England, now the colony is abandoned by its own. In the last sentence Percy writes before fully entering the Starving Time, he

registers the impact of this final desertion: "Capteyne Weste by the perswa-
sion or rather by the inforcement of his company hoysed upp Sayles and
shaped their Course directtly for England and lefte us in thatt extreme misery and wantte" (1099).[72] This scandal marks a finale to the series of raids,
abandonments, and murders because West's flight severs the last shred of a
social contract among the settlers. The violence depicted before the *Trewe
Relacyon* reaches the Starving Time—the first dead messengers, the corpses
with bread-stuffed mouths, Ratcliffe's flaying, and West's reprehensible desertion—paints Percy's Virginia as an abject world that not only is in a constant state of want, but also is terrifying, hopeless, and appalling.

Anatomies

When Percy's text enters the charnel house of Starving Time, its operative
word becomes "now"[73]: "Now all of us att James Town beginneinge to feele
the sharpe pricke of hunger which noe man trewly descrybe butt he which
hathe Tasted the bitternesse thereof. A worlde of miseries ensewed" (1099).
Percy puts the "now" of starvation, a suffering that no man but he can "trewly
describe," at the center of his relation, where, like a black hole, it effectively
draws all violence and suffering in to a totalizing catastrophe, a "worlde of
miseries" in which all things seem incredible.[74] In Percy's *Trewe Relacyon*,
the convergence of extreme suffering and extreme violence transforms the
act of settlement into a theater of atrocity. The text represents settlers acting in ways far outside anyone's expectations, which at once separates them
from cultural norms, merges the acute states of anguish and aggression, and
creates the violent imperatives around which the colony takes shape. Coloniality emerges out of catastrophe when these men, who now know what
others cannot know, also know themselves to have become forever different
in a world they already define by its total difference. "All of us at Jamestown"
is not only a description of a colonial site but also a categorical contradis-
tinction to the settlers' former Englishness.

In the "now" of the Starving Time, settler subjects lived (if they survived)
without a shred of superiority or power. Nothing defined them as much as
hunger. Hunger was always a threat in Jamestown; insufficient food supplies
had been a major problem from the start. As Seth Mallios has amply demonstrated, the effort to feed the colony formed the basis of almost all Anglo-
Powhatan trade.[75] Michael LaCombe has argued that food, in addition to its

physical and economic aspects, was closely linked to authority within the settlement, the methods of its distribution certifying both social and political status.[76] But as allied tribes in the Powhatan confederacy kept the fort in a state of siege, it was the forced aspect of starvation that made the Starving Time a turning point in this pervasive atmosphere of shortage. While in some ways Percy's descriptions echo conventional images of starvation, the threat to order and degradation of humanity in Jamestown does not map neatly onto other European histories of famine. John Aberth, Paul Slack, and Earnest B. Gilman have all documented historical responses to these extreme mortality crises in early modern England, which, Slack writes, were experienced both as "a personal affliction and a social calamity."[77] However, the colonial context did not allow for customary methods of dealing with mass calamity, thus ensuring a grimmer outcome.[78]

The social calamity of starvation, already intense, was further intensified within the already nearly destroyed colonial settlement for several reasons. First, this starvation was a direct result of disastrous relations with the Indians, who now actively withheld food and pinned the settlers inside their fort. The sense of social calamity was magnified by a state of siege mentality. Second, a recognizably English social world had not yet been built in Virginia. The extreme situation inside the catastrophe was not contrasted to any prior state of equilibrium from which the disaster departed and to which it would eventually return. English famine, plague, and war were blights on the landscape, but even those ordeals occurred on common ground and among fellow countrymen. The still-imaginary entity of English America was at this point not a common ground but rather was a place of fatality and failure. Third, the settlers numbered only in the hundreds and were over three thousand miles away from home. In London as many as one in five died during the worst plague years, but there was never a question of London becoming deserted; in Virginia the entire colonial settlement could be extinguished, exacerbating the settlers' already fragile colonial condition.

Percy's *Trewe Relacyon* takes us into the walls of the fort and anatomizes the feeble social body. The men quickly transgress a series of legal, cultural, tribal, and human boundaries by thieving, breaking food taboos, escaping to Indian villages, and finally by becoming feral. As with the series of dead messengers, the civil transgressions Percy describes proceed incrementally, breaking what social strictures remain by degrees and preparing the way for the more elemental anarchy that follows. The first transgression was breaking the law. Percy reports that "some to satisfye their hunger have Robbed the store for the which I Caused them to be executed" (1099). What temporary relief the men gained by stealing food was countered by the lasting satisfaction of the law, whose power Percy was still able to enact.[79]

The second level of transgression occurred when cultural definitions of "food" were lost. The men ate every last animal down to the rats and then began on the leather. For early seventeenth-century settlers, ingesting and digesting food had a profound array of medical, ethical, and religious meanings. If, as Michael Schoenfeldt writes, even in everyday life "[t]he stomach [was] at the center of a system demanding perpetual, anxious osmosis with the outside world," then the kind of osmosis happening at the fort was of a most dangerous kind.[80] Ruled by the tyrannous regime of hunger, men could no longer make choices about what to bring into the body's incorporative system. The fort cleared of consumables, many men were eager to forgo English loyalties permanently and flee to Indian villages, and some already had, figuring it was far better to be a servant to Indians than a dead man among the English. This was a third level of transgression. However, once the Powhatan confederacy resolved that the best way to expel the colony was to force the settlers into the fort and leave them to their own devices, Indian groups ceased absorbing English escapees. At that juncture, venturing into the woods was no longer the prelude to joining native society but rather was the entry into a wandering, hunted existence: "[S]ome weare inforced to searche the woodes and to feede upon Serpentts and snakes and to digge the earth for wylde and unknowne Rootes, where many of our men weare Cutt of and slayne by the Salvages" (1099–1100). Searching and digging for serpents and snakes was no way for the settlers to maintain their Englishness. Besieged settlers scratching out sustenance in their own killing fields, they were already lost by the time arrows cut them down.

Meanwhile, in the garrison, famine began "to Looke gastely and pale in every face" (1100). In the final transgression, the colonial binary between civilized and savage was disrupted by a third category, neither English nor Indian but feral.[81] This third term seems more apt than what some historians have characterized as an inversion of the civilized subject. For example, James Horn writes that "[e]xtreme deprivation had brought about a hideous inversion: the English, not the Indians, had become savages."[82] Becoming "savage" was a fear, but "becoming feral" better captures the more frightening and uncanny collective alienation from Englishness and the specificity of that rupture in the catastrophe of settlement. Settlers inhabited neither English nor native cultures but became merely bodies: altered, aggressive, bestial. Percy reports that corpses, English and Indian alike, were dug from the ground and eaten. Even the living were used as food sources, as some "Licked upp the Bloode which hathe fallen from their weake fellowes" (1100). This kind of "constraint" cannibalism had nothing to do with the idea of "ritual" cannibalism that fascinated Europeans in their encounter with the Americas (1100).[83] Although cannibalism was represented as the very essence of savagery, Michel de Montaigne famously wrote that the warrior who triumphed over his enemy by ritually consuming him ultimately proved nobler than rapacious Europeans who destroyed each other body and soul, driven by "treachery, disloyalty, tyranny and cruelty."[84] Although the desperate conditions might seem to excuse the broken taboo, the starvation context only increased the settlers' identification with the term "feral." Unlike ceremonial cannibalism, the survival cannibalism practiced by the settlers indicated a descent into purely animal drives.

At this point in the *Trewe Relacyon*, how does Percy handle his readers' disgust? He isolates the extreme actions of a few figures and blames the degeneration of the community and its atrocities on them. Again, Percy works in an incremental form. Like the series of dead messengers and civil transgressors, the isolated, degenerate figures that Percy singles out form another series that, progressing by degrees of intensity, fully expresses the material and metaphysical collapse of English Virginia. During a time in which many men were barely kept "from killeinge one of an other To eate," Percy confronts the first figure, writing that "amongste the reste this was moste lamentable": "[O]ne of our Colline [colony] murdered his wyfe Ripped the Childe outt of her wombe and threwe itt into the River and after Chopped the Mother in pieces and sallted her for his foode" (1100). Percy orders that the husband be executed and burned, but the crime carried so much cultural weight that execution was not sufficient to put it down.[85] The scandal of the cannibal husband was widely circulated well beyond Jamestown.[86] The London Council's *True Declaration* charges that it was only the "scum of men" who "roared out the tragicall historie of the man eating of his dead wife in Virginia." It admits that the man hated his wife, killing and dismembering her, but claims that it resulted from a personal grievance, not famine. In fact, upon investigation, the London Council lies, his house was found stored with "a good quantitie of meale, oatemeale, beanes and pease."[87] Later, John Smith in his *Generall Historie* uses black humor to discuss the case, musing, "whether shee was better roasted, boyled or carbonado'd [barbequed], I know not, but of such a dish as powdered wife I never heard of" (411). In

1705, almost a century after the fact, Robert Beverley laments that the event still "brought such an infamy upon the country, that to this day it cannot be wiped away."[88]

Controversy over the facts of the story persists, but in a larger cultural context, the textual traces of the cannibal husband haunt the Jamestown history as what René Girard calls a monstrous double: a figure who emerges at the height of crisis as other subjects "watch monstrosity take shape within [them] and outside [them] simultaneously."[89] Girard argues that monstrous doubles, who absorb the dangerous excesses of the community, belong both inside and outside of it: "They thus occupy the equivocal middle ground between difference and unity that is indispensable to the process of sacrificial substitutions—to the polarization of violence onto a single victim who substitutes for all others."[90] These monstrous doubles must be destroyed as sacrificial victims, but they are then displayed and destroyed over and over again. Over time the recirculative condemnation of the monstrous cannibal husband substitutes for a more thorough engagement with the crisis within the Jamestown fort. This is precisely what the husband's sacrificial killing guarantees. Therefore, while this figure "stands in for" the worst of the Starving Time, he effectively distracts us from it as well, allowing us to resist a broader analysis of catastrophe in the settlement and focus instead on its most extravagant, and punishable, example.

In the second tableau of colonial degradation, we might say that monstrosity shifts from the material to the phantasmal as the living become almost ghostly: "And those which weare Liveinge were so maugre and Leane thatt itt was Lamentable to behowlde them, for many throwe extreme hunger have Runne outt of their naked bedds beinge so Leane thatt they Looked lyke anotannes [anatomies], Cryeinge owtt we are starved. We are starved" (1101). The image of skeletal men crying "we are starved" is so disturbing precisely because its human forms are still recognizable: the social space; the urge to declaim; the first-person plural "we"; the ghostly form of the human body being chased by its own frenetic functions. Earlier in Jamestown's history, John Smith had tried to make Englishmen speak an incomprehensible language by teaching them the words "*Mowchick woyawgh tawgh noeragh kaquere mecher*," which meant, "I am very hungry. What shall I eate?" (302). No matter how foreign those Algonquian words may have sounded in settlers' mouths, they could not have been as alien as this cry in their native English: "We are starved! We are starved!" issued from the mouths of skeletons and released into the foul air. Percy's anatomies are not just starved men; they are men who have been so thoroughly wasted that their elemental structures are revealed. Because their emaciated forms communicate their pitiable state, their speech might seem superfluous, but it is precisely their speech that makes them grotesque instead of merely "lamentable." They are a frantic, phantasmic brigade that distorts the fort's sense of reality simply by telling its truth.

The drama of the fort ultimately comes to rest on the body of Hugh Pryce. Pryce—whose name is an anagram of Percy—is also a monstrous double, chosen by Percy as another sacrificial substitute and expelled from the community whose internal breakdown he represents. Percy textually resuscitates him in order to repeat both his profanity and his expulsion. Percy recalls how Pryce "in a furious distracted moode did Come openly into the markett place Blaspheameinge exclameinge and Creyinge outt thatt there was noe god." If there was a God, Pryce wailed, "he wolde not Suffer his Creatures whome he had made and framed to indure those miseries And to perishe for wante of foods and sustenance" (1002). Pryce, destroyed inside and out, rages because the divinely ordered Chain of Being has broken.[91] In response to earlier crimes, Percy meted out punishment as the representative of the state. However, Hugh Pryce's blasphemous fury goes beyond Percy's ability to punish or contain. When Pryce goes out into the woods with a "Corpulentt fatt man," a butcher, to search for food, both are immediately killed: "And after beinge fownde gods Indignacyon was sheowed upon Pryses Corpes which was Rente in pieces with wolves or other wylde Beasts and his Bowles Torne outt of his boddy beinge a Leane spare man. And the fatt Butcher nott lyeinge above six yards from him was fownd altogether untoutched onely by the salvages arrowes whereby he Receaved his deathe" (1102). As Percy's details insist, surely the incredible has taken over when wild animals disembowel Englishmen and shred their corpses to pieces in the woods of America. Like the Kecoughtan who stuffed the mouths of the dead settlers with bread, God in his indignation serves out death with poetic justice. The lean blasphemer's body is consumed while the fat butcher's body is left untouched. In the world of Jamestown, there are many crimes that do not call down divine retribution. Such instant and exacting holy wrath is reserved for the crime of descent into meaninglessness itself.

Hugh Pryce flouts any hope for meaning beyond the present horror. Even worse than cannibalism, Pryce's heresy crosses a line beyond which survival has no significance. His corpse therefore has to be pulled back into meaning as a symbol of Almighty vengeance, or else his and all the other

corpses would merely constitute a ghastly spectacle of waste. The fat butcher's corpse could be marked by Indian arrows, but Hugh Pryce's corpse had
to be marked by both beasts and God. Even so, it was clear the settlement
had become no more than death infecting life without meaning.[92] Turning
again, as he did in his *Discourse*, to the death toll, Percy does the grim math
of the Starving Time's final days: "of five hundrethe men we had onely Left
about sixty, The rest being either stearved throwe famin or Cutt off by the
salvages" (1101). The settlement was beyond saving; its only hope was to find
a witness.

On May 23, 1610, two small ships came into Chesapeake Bay. Sir Thomas
Gates, Sir George Somers, and the shipwrecked men from Bermuda rode in
on boats built from the wreckage of the *Sea Venture*. The encounter shocked
both parties: the settlers in seeing the miraculous return of the long-
marooned "head" of the colony, and the commanders in seeing what had
become of the rest of the body. Arriving at Jamestown, William Strachey
describes what they saw: "[V]iewing the Fort, we found the Pallisadoes torne
downe, the Ports open, the Gates from off the hinges, and emptie houses
(which Owners death had taken from them) rent up and burnt, rather then
the dwellers would step into the Woods a stones cast off from them, to fetch
other fire-wood: and it is true, the Indians killed as fast without, if our men
stirred by beyond the bounds of their block-house, as Famine and Pestilence
did within" (1014). In this material expression of disintegrated boundaries,
the fort's physical thresholds are destroyed, consumed, unhinged. There is
no base upon which Gates can build his command. When Strachey tries to
describe the survivors among these ruins, words fail him. General phrases
such as "misery and misgovernment," "particularities of the sufferances,"
"their own disorders," and "desolation and misery" contrast with the specificity of Percy's narrative. While Strachey elides the details of suffering by
writing simply that it is more "then I have heart to expresse" (1014), Percy
writes that Gates, Somers, and the others had to "read a lecture of miserie in
our peoples faces" (1101).

This difference between passing in silence and delivering the lecture of
misery emphasizes both Percy's testimonial imperative and its resistant audience. Percy's drive to tell what "no man can know" is also a story that no
one wants to hear. While Percy structures the Starving Time around several
painstaking episodes of human degeneration—the cannibal husband, the
running skeletons, the blasphemous Pryce—Strachey reports on the ruined
physical environment instead: the empty houses, the broken fishing weirs,

the unhinged gate. He then quickly moves from this bird's-eye view to the familiar rhetorical ground of blaming Jamestown's disreputable settlers: "Unto such calamity can sloathe, riot, and vanity bring the most settled and plentifull estate. . . . No story can remember unto us, more woes and anguishes, then these people, thus governed, have both suffered and pull'd upon their own heads" (1016). Again, the idle, "headless multitude" is excoriated and blamed for its own "wantes and wretchedness." Rehearsing over and over again in print how the settlers' woes and anguish were purely self-inflicted allowed for the continuation of a fantasy that there might have been a settled settlement honoring God, honorable to England, and honored by Indians, instead of one where every threshold was crossed.

The Drum of War

Gates and his Bermuda crew had seen enough: "[T]heir miseries considered itt was Resolved upon by Sir Thomas Gates and the whole colonie with all Spede to returne for England." When the "much grieved Governor" announced his decision to transport everyone back to England, the air, thick with unspeakable things, was pierced by "a generall acclamation and shout of joy" (1015). Gates kept strict order during the evacuation by forcing them to march to the beat of a drum. It was everything he could do to keep the ravaged men from burning Jamestown to the ground. In fact, Gates made sure he was the last Englishman on land specifically to prevent the hated place's immolation.

Gates was supposed to have beaten the drum of war, not retreat, in Virginia. He was sent there as the front-line commander of the church militant, with sanction to possess the land by any means necessary. The sermon "A Good Speed to Virginia," preached by Robert Gray in 1609 to consecrate the mission, took its text from the genocidal book of Joshua: "And Joshua Spake unto the house of Joseph, to Ephraim, and Manasseh, saying, Thou art a great people, and hast great power, and shalt not have [only] one lot. Therefore the Mountain shall be thine, for it is a wood, and thou shalt cut it downe, and the ends of it shall be thine, & thou shalt cast out the Canaanites though they have Iron Charets, and though they be strong."[93] Crossing the Jordan, Joshua's army destroyed anything that breathed—man or woman, young or old, person or beast. Entering Jamestown, Gates found the biblical precedent invoked by the sermon fully reversed. Instead of felling the woods to master the land, settlers had ripped wood from their own houses to survive. Instead of taking the walled city of Jericho, the English were confined to their crumbling fort, besieged by mocking enemies. Instead of triumphing over heathen victims, Englishmen ate vermin in abject misery. Contrary to every expectation, the land remained, in Gray's words, "possessed and wrongfully usurped by wild beasts, and unreasonable creatures, or by brutish savages . . . worse than those beasts."[94] The book of Joshua progresses from God's commission, to the conquest of Canaan, to the expropriation and redistribution of the land. This was the model for the English colonial program, except that Jamestown foundered in its settlement stage between the colony's commission and the conquest of the New World. Gates held a new commission for the colony, but by the time he arrived at the settlement, there was no hope of mustering a Joshua-like army. According to Strachey, even if the new provisions were "rackt to the uttermost," they would last only sixteen days; there was "not now a Fish to be seene" in the river, and no chance of trade with the Indians (1021). Although the Indians "well deserved" the use of force, men must be fed to fight. And so the drum of war instead beat the English retreat.

Incredibly, as the defeated English headed out to sea, their departing ships were met by the incoming ships of Thomas West, Lord De La Warr, who was plowing into Jamestown with a new charter, new provisions, new armaments, military reinforcements, and a license for total control over the colony. Encountering Gates and his evacuees, De La Warr turned all the ships around, sailed them back to Jamestown, and reoccupied the fort with a vengeance. It was later described as an act of God. From England, William Crashaw wrote, "If ever the hand of God appeared in action of man, it was heere most evident: for when man had forsaken this businesse, God tooke it in hand; and when men said, now hath all the earth cast off the care of this Plantation, the hand of heaven hath taken hold of it."[95] But the resupply can be considered as a deliverance only if one assigns a closed narrative arc to the colony: De La Warr came and the settlement was saved.[96] In fact, the state of acute crisis in which the starving settlement existed continued on as a state of emergency in which De La Warr, with all the imported power of the state, enacted total war outside the fort and martial law within.[97] As imported powers marshaled both the starved men and the new arrivals into a "just war" against their Indian aggressors, the death-ridden old regime was replaced by one with unlimited power. The settlement was reterritorialized in the most rigid and brutal way. If Gates could not be an English Joshua, then De La Warr would.

The newly instituted "Lawes divine, morall and martiall" put the settlement in lockdown; any actions beyond those ordered and enforced by the military command were punishable, mostly by pain of death.[98] The purpose of prohibition and extreme punishment was not only to quell chaos but also to replace it with a forbidding new order. De La Warr's crackdown replaced the breakdown by combating the unspeakable extremity of abjection with the articulated extremity of the law. And yet while the very form of the martial laws—the exhaustive enumeration of crimes, the endless proliferation of verbs, the compendiums of things verboten—seemed to close off catastrophe by imposing order, it also expressed the extent of the colony's disorder by articulating every possible transgression that could occur in a place that had already transgressed all boundaries. Many of the civil laws had to do with the strict regulation of transactions, and speech was deemed one of the most dangerous transactions of all. Of the first fourteen laws, ten regulated speech. Speech against God or the king or any royal authority was punishable by death. Bearing false witness carried a death sentence, while cursing was punishable by a dagger through the tongue and execution for repeat offenders. Anyone who would "detract, slander, calumniate, murmur, mutenie, resist, disobey or neglect" any command or commander was killed on the third offense. To speak ill of Virginia was fatal:

> No manner of person whatsoever, shall dare to detract, slander, calumniate, or utter unseemely, and unfitting speeches, either against his Majesties Honourable Councell for this Colony, resident in England, or against the Committies, Assistants unto the said Councell, or against the zealous indeavors, & intentions of the whole body of Adventurers for this pious and Christian Plantation, or against any publique booke, or bookes, which by their mature advise, and grave wisedomes, shall be thought fit, to be set foorth and publisht, for the advancement of the good of this Colony, and the felicity thereof.[99]

Clearly the advancement and felicity of the colony would rely on denial; the new kind of "perfect relation" would have little relation to Virginia at all. The violence that backed the settlers into the fort, the anarchy of the Starving Time, the spectacle of the wasted garrison, the "rescue" that stopped them from leaving, the draconian order and furious combat that followed—none was to be spoken of in the locked-down settlement.

The laws also militarized the colony: policing the boundaries around the forts; organizing men into rank and file; and strictly forbidding unauthorized movement, especially among the Powhatan. One law dictated, "No woman or man (upon paine of death) shall runne away from the colonie, to Powhatan, or any savage weroance else whatsoever." Another required that explorers and tradesmen in Indian country be hypervigilant, never stray from their commissioned route, and when their business was concluded, "make hast with all speed . . . to James Town again."[100] When colonists did go out among the Indians, the laws required that they do so in brigades, wearing their arms and colors and marching in strict order to the beat of a drum. Any who would "dare to absent himselfe or stray and straggle from his ranke without leave granted from the cheefe Officer" would do so "upon paine of death." Likewise for any person who ran from or yielded to Indian attacks, or for any who even spoke to an Indian without permission. Official communications were no less deadly. When De La Warr issued Wahunsonacock an ultimatum, the chief refused, saying that if the settlers did not confine themselves to Jamestown, he would command that they be killed. In response the English took Indian hostages and sent them back with their hands cut off.

Well supplied and taking their revenge for previous defeats, the English were waging what Strachey called a "warre well-managed," viciously and sadistically.[101] J. Frederick Fausz describes a torrent of English "*ad terrorem* tactics*": "deception, ambush, and surprise, the random slaughter of both sexes and all ages, the calculated murder of innocent captives, and the destruction of entire villages."[102] The violence that began before the Starving Time rapidly escalated as the English fought to take more land and the Indians fought to expel them. Fausz details nineteen military engagements between August 1609 and December 1611, thirteen of them following the siege of Jamestown. But it was the drum of war at Paspahegh that made especially clear how the settlement, despite its extreme regimentation, remained the site of atrocity.

The Echoing Air

Shortly after the reoccupation of Jamestown, an enraged De La Warr sent Percy and a troop of seventy men "to take Revendge upon the Paspaheans"

(1103). By the time he was put in charge of this battalion, Percy was one of the few men to have been in Virginia throughout the whole of its short, brutal existence. Consider just the events of the summer of 1610. On May 24 Percy led Gates into a deadly and decimated Jamestown. On June 7 Percy and every other English person turned their backs on the failed colony and sailed away. On June 8 they were all forcibly returned. Now on August 9 Percy was back in active service, leading a regiment that was larger in number than the survivors of the Starving Time and on a mission to exterminate the Englishmen's nearest and most hostile enemies.

On Percy's signal, the attack on Paspahegh began. Its werowance was absent, but the people present were murdered or put to flight, their crops destroyed, their houses burned, and their temples ransacked. The damage done, Percy called off his soldiers, at which point a lieutenant presented Percy with a group of captives: a warrior, the "Quene" of Paspahegh, and her children. Percy admonished the lieutenant for sparing their lives, which were now put in his custody, so "that . . . [he] mighte doe with them whatt [he] pleased" (1104). Percy ordered immediate decapitation for the warrior, but the queen and her children presented a more difficult problem. Percy knew her.

Percy's texts must be culled to extract the story of Paspahegh, to assemble dispersed facts, unravel a tightly wound time line, and restore individual people to light. This reading seeks to connect textually scattered episodes in order to construct a sustained narrative that the texts hold but do not tell outright, a narrative that demonstrates the violence of colonization through its human particulars and that resists the closures of a summary or chronological leveling of events. While the grand narrative of Jamestown may close with the established permanence of the settlement, the writing of Jamestown does not.

We must remember that for most of the people involved, the place the English came to claim was not Jamestown but Paspahegh. In his first account of settlement, the *Discourse* of 1607, Percy describes how in early May, even before the English seated their fort, they "came to the King or Werowance of Paspihe: where they entertained us with much welcome." An old man made a long oration to the visitors on behalf of the werowance, Wowinchopunck. Although the English "knew little what they meant," Percy remembers the speech for its "foule noise" and "vehement action" (926). Two weeks later the English began to build their fort on the seasonal hunting grounds of the Paspahegh, which explains why the marshy land they occupied was not populated and why the fort was subject to intensive surveillance and attack by the Paspahegh from the very beginning. Four days later, according to Percy, "the Werowance of Paspihae came himself to our quarter, with one hundred Savages armed, which garded him in a very warlike manner with Bowes and Arrowes, thinking at that time to execute their villainy." It was an aggressive face-off, but when the English raised their guns, Wowincho-punck "went suddenly away with all his company in great anger" (928).

This confrontation with a hundred warriors notwithstanding, the next day Percy and some companions meandered through the woods along a path of "the pleasantest Suckles" and "faire flowers." "[W]ee kept on our way in this Paradise," he recounts, until they wandered into a Paspahegh town and learned that most of the men "were gone a hunting with the Werowance of Paspiha." Percy and his friends were hosted in a more intimate manner this time and "stayed there a while," keeping company with the women and children and feasting happily on the "fine and beautifull" strawberries that had so delighted Percy since his arrival (929). Percy, who noticed everything, would later write in detail about the local women: their way of baking bread; the length and arrangement of their hair; their elaborate tattoos of "Fowles, Fish, or Beasts" (924, 931). Surely he had seen these things up close in Paspahegh.

Meanwhile, Paspahegh attacks on the fort continued, including a co-ordinated, multitribal assault by an estimated four hundred warriors that lasted seven days in early June 1607.[103] In December of that year, the group that helped capture John Smith and deliver him to Wahunsonacock included many Paspahegh men. By the spring of 1608 the English and the Paspahegh were raiding each other's towns and taking captives. And yet as hostilities with Wowinchopunck and his warriors continued, so did Percy's encounters with the werowance's wife. In the spring of 1609 John Smith took Wowinchopunck prisoner. Gifts and people began to flow into Jamestown from Paspahegh. Smith describes how "daily this kings wives, children, and people, came to visit him with presents" and to urge the werowance's release (98). In the end it was an English guard's negligence that allowed Wowinchopunck to escape, which he neatly did, fetters and all, and returned to his people.

As "the Quene" stood before him in the aftermath of the raid on Paspa-hegh, Percy surely remembered this woman who had first welcomed him and his handful of friends to her town, who had come with gifts and an entourage to the fort daily over several weeks, and who now was delivered to him, along with her children, as a prisoner. She must have recognized him too; presumably he was one of the first Englishmen she had ever seen. Only three years earlier she had hosted him, offering him strawberries while the men hunted and the children played. On August 9, 1610, Wowinchopunck's wife and children stood by while Percy's militia burned their town to the ground. They were then marched to the waiting English boats, where the men, still inflamed by the attack, began "to murmur becawse the queen and her Children were spared." What happened next changed the course of the war: "[A] Cowncell beinge called itt was agreed upon to putt the children to deathe the which was effected by Throweinge them overboard and shoteinge owtt their Braynes in the Water" (1104). The murder of these children went against every rule of Indian warfare, as Percy well knew. While English reports from the period described the Powhatan's means of tormenting their enemies, they also noted that "women or Children they put not to death, but keep them captives . . . their wives and Children should be a prize for the Conquerers."[104] Frederick Fausz writes that "[t]he Powhatans, who had rarely, if ever, slain women or children in their wars before 1607, were appalled by the atrocities done in James I's name." Helen Rountree designates this act as the one that finally put the Powhatan "fully at war."[105] The Paspahegh town was destroyed in a rampage, but the children were killed in cold blood.

Two miles downriver the troops went ashore again, marching fourteen miles into the country, cutting down corn, burning houses, destroying temples, and "perform[ing] all the spoyle" they could. Meanwhile, although Percy does not say so directly, it is clear that he stayed behind in the boat with the stunned and utterly bereft queen, her own life spared by her children's murderer: "I sent Capteyne Davis ashore with most of my Sowldiers my selfe beinge wearyed" (1104). After having wasted her town, killed her children, and yet argued "[t]o save the queens lyfe," Percy's exertions had left him "wearyed." As the two waited for the rampaging soldiers to return, something different from the battle for possession of the land was between them. Instead of nameless Indians shooting arrows and nameless settlers setting fires, here was the knowledge of a foul and personal assault, a silent stretch of time buried within the text—marked and yet forbidden to narrate—during which *this* English captain and *this* Indian mother sat in the aftermath of atrocity.

When De La Warr received the report of Percy's Paspahegh mission, he demanded that the queen be killed immediately, preferably by burning.

Percy offered only feeble protest: "I replyed thatt haveinge seene so mutche Blood shedd thatt day, now in my Cowld bloode I desyred to see noe more, and for to Burne her I did nott howlde itt fitteinge butt either by shott or Sworde to give her a quicker dispatche. So Turninge my selfe from Capteyne Davis he did take the quene with towe sowldiers a shoare and in the woods putt her to the Sworde" (1105). Percy is both passive and complicit, no longer arguing for her life but only that she receive a quick death. Weary, cold-blooded, and desiring to see no more, Percy becomes a cipher, dissociated from the events around him not because he has absorbed their meaning but because he has become absorbed into their atrocities, which refuse meaning. In his "Cowld bloode," Percy is past seeking to absolve himself. Instead he has represented both the horror of suffering and the terror of retribution through the discourse of catastrophe. The blood licked off dead men in the fort and "Blood shedd thatt day" at Paspahegh exist at opposite ends of colonial power, but they also exist together in a matrix of anguish and atrocity. Because both have become part of "those things which seame incredible," both have also become spectacles in a catastrophic space where bodies and boundaries are wasted.

With his writing located within that space, Percy is uniquely placed to offer the materials for what we might call the inner history of this war. Other sources briefly mention a raid on Paspahegh town, but only Percy narrates it.[106] Because he does so in retrospect, there are ways in which the murder of the Paspahegh children haunts the *Trewe Relacyon*. The images of dead or wounded children appear throughout. Recall Percy's description of the cannibal husband. Whereas others report the wife's death, only Percy's narrative includes how the husband "ripped the Childe outt of her wombe and threwe itt into the River." Recall also that in Percy's description of the Nansemond raid, the werowance's captive son is shot in the boat but escapes. The son swims to safety, but Percy remembers the trail of blood he leaves in the water. None of these events was supposed to happen—the captive should have been held, the womb should have been inviolate, the children should have been spared—but happen they did. In all three cases the children's blood spreading in the water marks the unchecked spread and contamination of violence. Percy structures his *Trewe Relacyon* as a before, during, and after narrative with the Starving Time at its center: that season of misery about which so many "falseties and malicyous detractyons" had been spread (1093). However, these images of blood in the water are vivid examples of the disturbing recurrences throughout the three sections, revealing how entangled they are.

Percy's *Trewe Relacyon* begins by saying that woe, misery, mutinies, and famishments define plantation, but the truth of his relation revolves around the fact that terror and atrocity are the works of plantation too. The boundary between experiencing suffering and inflicting violence dissolves because the narrative incrementally but insistently locates settlement as a place beyond thresholds. These first colonizing years are traditionally treated as a time of disorder and anomaly, a "seasoning" that the colony survived against all odds. In the writing of settlement, however, the horror and terror of this "seasoning" are the conditions under which coloniality emerged. The acute states effected through the settlers' suffering and violence rendered the provisional protocols of the colonizing mission useless. The bitter experience "which noe man trewly descrybe butt he which hathe Tasted the bitternesse thereof" is what separated colonists from Englishmen. Even if individuals came and went, the miasma of suffering, violence, and abjection belonged to coloniality itself. And even after these things that seemed incredible have been buried in a history of social, economic, and institutional consolidation, they continue to trouble that history as a season of misery that can never be fully cordoned off.

A final note: the deaths of Wowinchopunck's wife and children were avenged. The colony's new leaders were soon sick, dead, or sent back to England, and Percy was put back in charge. On February 9, 1611, six months after his raid on Paspahegh, what looked like "a small Troope" of Paspahegh men came around Jamestown's blockhouse. Percy sent out a small detail of soldiers to investigate, ordering that if they were to encounter Wowinchopunck, they must take him in alive. As the soldiers left the fort, Wowinchopunck made himself conspicuous, standing alone on the edge of a rise, seemingly unaware of the Englishmen sneaking up on him. There was no mistaking the man Strachey had once described as "one of the mightiest and strongest Salvadges that Powhatan had under him."[107] As one settler seized the werowance, a large group of Indians suddenly appeared and ambushed the settlers, sending their arrows freely among them. Meanwhile, Wowinchopunck struggled free of his opponent's grasp. Another captain, seeing that there was no way the werowance would allow himself to be taken alive, thrust his sword through Wowinchopunck's body, twice. "[F]or all thatt," Percy reports incredulously, "the stowte Indyan Lived and was Caryed away upon Rafters by the Salvages" (1107). Weeks later, "the Indyans did fall into their wonted practyses ageine, Comeinge one eaveninge Late, and Called att our blocke howse." Once again the men Percy sent to monitor the situation were led into an ambush, but this time the consequences were more severe.

Percy describes the battle in almost mythic terms. Although throughout this period the fighting force of the Paspahegh was numbered at forty warriors, Percy saw the blockhouse attacked by an army of "fyve or sixe hundrethe."[108] Arrows flew "as thicke as hayle" from the sky, killing all the Englishmen outside the fort "in a moment." In the aftermath the ground was almost hidden by the arrows and slain bodies. The space all around rang with the unmistakable sound of natives' triumph. Percy reports, "the Salvages did so aclamate, Showte and hallowe in Tryumphe of their gayned victory thatt the Ecchoe thereof made bothe the ayere and woods to Ringe." The sound spread through the fort. When more colonists armed themselves, the shouting dramatically changed. As Percy describes it, "They then changeinge their noate Cryeinge Paspahe. Paspahe. Thereby importeinge as mutch as thatt they had Revendged his wrongs" (1108–9). This chant surrounded the fort—"Paspahegh, Paspahegh"—permeating the "ayere and woods" of Jamestown with the sound of its original name.[109] It was a censure and a claim, an echoing memory of the atrocities that later histories would suppress. What is unimaginable in Jamestown sounds like "We are starved," but it also sounds like "Paspahegh." Both cries survive in the writing of that settlement.

CHAPTER 3

Plymouth: Scarce Able to Bury Their Dead

> But it pleased God to visit us then with death daily, and with so general a
> disease that the living were scarce able to bury the dead, and the well not
> in any measure sufficient to tend the sick.
> —William Bradford, *Of Plymouth Plantation*

Although William Bradford's *Of Plymouth Plantation* covers almost fifty years of the Separatist group's history, its most iconic passages refer to the hardships of the group's first two years in the New World.[1] This is a time so deeply enshrined in the national mythos as to constitute the public meaning of the word "Pilgrim." What did Pilgrims do? They suffered and persevered. They came to a howling wilderness in search of religious freedom and, once there, passed through trial and peril but never lost faith in each other or in their God. Pilgrims survived. The mythic aura around Pilgrim suffering always includes a pause for their dead, but only to resurrect those spirits as part of the promise for the American future. In this story the plight of the Pilgrims, their sacrifice and endurance, planted the first seeds of liberty and self-determination in America. Indeed, Bradford's history of those early years is shaped by a pattern of hardship and succor, loss and recovery, affliction and affection regulated by a God whose providential protection ultimately allowed for the plantation of his faithful people in a New World.

Of Plymouth Plantation eventually tapers off into silence, the annals that make up the second book ending in blank pages, but the national imaginary of Plymouth is projected toward a different end. It follows a pattern that Mitchell Breitwieser has identified with an ideological operation that "alternates tones of suffering with images of glory" and thus uses the losses of the past to propel a vision of, and desire for, the futurity of a perfect nation.[2] The Pilgrims suffered in the wilderness, and each time that suffering is recalled as an originary sacrifice, it generates the promise of national triumph. Even traditional treatments of *Of Plymouth Plantation* as a declension narrative subtly participate in this pattern, casting Bradford finally as a figure of loss whose elegiac history implores a rising but wayward generation to remember the sacrifices of the past.[3] Bradford writes his history so "that their children may see with what difficulties their fathers wrestled in going through these things in their first beginnings, and how God brought them along notwithstanding all their weaknesses and infirmities."[4] The declension narrative suggests that while the binding ties of collective hardship did not prevent the colony's dissolution, they did define the history of its origins.

Recent scholarship on *Of Plymouth Plantation* decidedly puts this concentration on the suffering yet stalwart community aside and attends instead to the abundant material such a focus on hardship eclipses. For example, analyses of Bradford's colonial mercantilism by Michelle Burnham and of his scribal world by Douglas Anderson have avoided a national literary frame for the narrative by restoring it to its contemporary transatlantic context.[5] In these accounts Bradford is fully engaged in a world of transaction and exchange that reaches well beyond his colonial site. In addition, though he claims that the "mighty ocean" was "a main bar and gulf to separate them from all civil parts of the world," these studies demonstrate that continued economic and textual circulation in that world in fact defined his discourse.[6] While such reframing of the text is necessary, I want to risk reentering that space of suffering in the first years of the Plymouth colony by returning to losses that have been either popularly mythologized or critically resolved through a framework of providential recovery. At the center of my return is an attempt to open up one of Bradford's famous quotations whose affective power seems to trump any critical analysis: "the living were scarce able to bury the dead."[7] Talking back to this phrase opens several historical problems about implanting and inscribing the colony that ideological responses to loss and suffering, beginning with Bradford's own, have sought to close off. Looking at these dead first forces us to confront their emphatic materiality, and then exposes an uneasy relationship: the demands the dead put on the living and the uses to which the living put the dead. The dead in and around Plymouth needed to be buried twice: once in fact and then in history. In both cases, however, they come into and go out of view in ways that bear upon the meaning of settlement. This chapter attends closely to the presence of the dead in the early settlement and traces the ways they were either figured or occluded in written accounts of the colony.

During the desperate mortality crises that defined the period from 1616 to 1622, both Indians and English struggled with the daunting task of burying the dead. Between 1616 and 1619 Indians in Wampanoag country were decimated by foreign diseases; whole villages were destroyed, and the overall rate of mortality is estimated at nearly 90 percent.[8] The Plymouth colonists arrived in that ravaged country in November 1620. The group initially numbered 102; half were dead within six months. How did the pervasive presence of physical remains bear down upon the barely surviving remainder of colonists and natives? What happened to each group's understanding of its place in the colonial arena when the dead began to outnumber the living? How did written records of settlement account for so many dead subjects? Relationships between the living and the dead were multiple: Indians and their dead; colonists and theirs; and the remnants of both populations who looked across the cultural divide at the reduction of the other. I will consider these dead on three intertwined levels: the material level of their physical presence; the interpretive level of their cultural significance; and the representational level of how subsequent histories repeatedly tried to put them to rest. The goal is to read both the events and the strategies that surrounded these catastrophes of colonial settlement without invoking a tragic/triumphalist scene of closure—a closure, as Joseph Roach puts it, that comes of "investing the future with the fatality of the past."[9]

The writing of settlement shows that to read death properly was at once a crucial and a deeply disorderly process. Dead bodies became highly charged sites of cultural crisis, and their treatment ranged from utter abandonment to elaborate, postmortem manipulation. Recovering some of the anxieties produced by these bodies will demonstrate how histories of the living were driven, in part, by the visibility of the dead. The Plymouth colony was rife with conflicts throughout its history, but the problem of mortality was at the center of the problem of settlement during its initial years. It was necessary to place a seal on the meanings of those deaths—experientially, historically, and existentially—not only to dispose of the remains but also to stabilize the remainder. Reading William Bradford's retrospective history in the context of other eyewitness reports, it becomes clear that the means by which Bradford attempted to effect that disposal and stabilization uniquely registers what was so acutely unsettling about these mounting, unburied bodies, particularly in the light of the colony's task of "plantation." Perhaps, then, the most direct way to exhume this historical problem is to begin with the opening of a grave.

The grave was found by a group of scouts sent out to survey the interior from the newly arrived *Mayflower*. They were looking for sources of food, freshwater, arable lands, navigable rivers, and just as important, signs of the native people who called this place home. While a company and crew of over one hundred anxious people waited on the crowded ship anchored in the harbor, the scouts followed a beaten path five or six miles into the coastal woods to arrive at what appeared to be a burial site. After wading through icy water, losing their way in forests, and staggering against winter winds, they were getting sick and increasingly wary of their leaders' intentions to push as far up the river and into the woods as possible. Sixteen discontented men had already quit the trek, and now the eighteen who remained stood in a circle around the opened ground, transfixed and bewildered. They had come upon an especial mystery in the midst of the ubiquitous unknown. It was, as they later described it, "a place like a grave, but it was much bigger and longer than any we had yet seen."[10] They had earlier found what they thought to be a gravesite—heaps of sand purposefully decorated and arranged—but reasoning that the Indians would surely find it odious to discover the grounds disturbed, they ceased their investigation. When the settlers found this site, however, they showed no such restraint. After all, as their report was careful to qualify, this place was only "like" a grave. They lifted the boards that covered the spot and began to dig.

The scouts hauled out the site's treasures one by one. Carefully laid between several layers of woven mat was a fine bow, an intricately carved and decorated plank, an assortment of "Bowls, Trayes, Dishes, and such like Trinkets," and finally "two Bundles, the one bigger, the other lesse." They picked at the knot of the large bundle first and found "a great quantitie of fine and perfect red Powder, and in it the bones and skull of a man." Flesh still clung to the bones of the face. More startling still, the top of the skull was covered with fine blond hair. Packed up with the corpse were a knife, a needle, and some "old iron things," all folded into a sailor's canvas smock. The men then opened the smaller bundle, and the same red powder let out its strong but not unpleasant smell. This bundle contained the skull and bones of a small child, its legs bound up with finely beaded white bracelets, a miniature bow and other child-sized things beside it. The remains of these two corpses held the armed men spellbound for a time as they formed a circle around the unearthed bodies.

What did they make of these mysteriously mismatched things: a sailor's rough canvas and fine Indian beads; bones in red powder and a skull with blond hair; the remains of a child, prettified and bound? As to the material objects, they quickly took "sundry of the prettiest things away" and "covered the Corps up againe."[11] But as to the elaborate ceremonial scene's cultural or spiritual substance—as to its meaning—they were baffled. Ritual burials expressed connections across the chasm of life and death: the relationship between a living person and his final remains; the relationship between the body in the grave and the living hands that committed it there.[12] But the scouts could not fathom how those connections worked at this site; they could not reconstruct a narrative between the living and the dead.[13] Though the evidence was laid bare, the meaning was still buried. Even in its raided state, the grave—its site, its objects, its corpses, and its story—silently resisted interpretation.

The men began to talk: "There was varietie of opinions amongst us about the embalmed person; some thought it was an Indian Lord and King: others sayd, the Indians have all blacke hayre, and never any was seen with browne or yellow hayre; some thought, it was a Christian of some speciall note, which had dyed amongst them, and they thus buried him to honour him; others thought, they had killed him, and did it in triumph over him."[14] Thus far in their forays, the primary concern for the scouts had been careful identification of everything they saw in the New World. As intelligence gatherers, the scouts were meant to report back to the shipboard group the lay of the land, who else was there, and how easily the place might be possessed. In moving from the unknown to the known, these scouts operated by processes of analogy and anomaly, describing things as "like" or "unlike" something they knew until the categories of their own experience approached whatever unfamiliar thing they encountered. Gathered around this mysterious grave and these unearthed corpses, the scouts felt a growing sense of urgency in their inability to read or categorize. Who were these bodies? What was this place? Were these signs of murder and revenge, or of honor and mourning? Their anxiety stemmed in large part from the uncertainty of their own colonial condition, the unfixed meaning of their own potential suffering. Questions about the strange corpses quickly turned into questions about themselves. Will we be honored or triumphed over? How will we die? Whose hands will attend our dead? The unrecognizable "somebodies" removed from the ground, bodies surrounded by elaborate signs of colliding cultures and yet exposed in all their recalcitrant materiality, reflected back upon the intruders what was dangerously unknown about their own colonial condition. Once revealed, these spectacular bodies could not be recontained by any narrative available to them.[15]

The record of these corpses demonstrates that the "ranging and search-ing" of the scouting party was as much about epistemology as it was about geography, and as much about imagination as it was about fact. It also in-dicates that from the start, looking at the dead played an important role in the Englishmen's efforts to "settle" themselves on native ground. If one goal of the early scouting missions was to devise a manner of settling the living, the fulfillment of that goal was soon frustrated by the problem of unsettling remains. How was it that dead bodies came to assert this kind of imperative as English colonists were attempting to establish their settlement at Plymouth? The reasons encompassed both material and abstract realms, ranging from the physical struggle for survival, to the political struggle for control, to the historical struggle for identity in a land undergoing traumatic transformations.

Maurice Blanchot provides a way to connect the special status of the corpse to these particularly colonial anxieties: "What we call mortal remains escapes common categories. Something is there which is not really the living person, nor is it any reality at all. It is neither the same as the person who was alive, nor is it another person, nor is it anything else. What is there, with the absolute calm of something that has found its place, does not, however, succeed in being convincingly here. Death suspends the relation to place, even though the deceased rests heavily in his spot as if upon the only basis that is left to him."[16] The first part of this statement pertains to the corpse's identity. *Who is this body?* It is neither the person who it used to be nor any-one else; this is what Blanchot calls the problem of cadaverous resemblance. The second part of the statement pertains to the corpse's environs. *What is this place?* It is at once an empty space and an emphatic location, a here and a nowhere. Thus while the presence of the corpse transforms undifferenti-ated space, it does so by marking a departure. This is what Blanchot calls the problem of cadaverous presence. Ceremonies for the dead exist precisely to stem both of these problems. At the sanctified site of the grave, the commu-nity gathers, names itself, and reasserts its identity in the face of death's dis-ruption. But if meaningful burial always tries to remedy the disorder of the exposed corpse, the problem of remains at Plymouth Plantation was that in the early years of settlement, cadaverous resemblances and cadaverous pres-ences overpowered the fledgling cultural formation that struggled to con-tain them. The fundamental liminality of mortal remains exacerbated the broader problem of stabilizing a colonial presence, especially since the very nature of that presence broke the bonds between person and place, between "self" and "home." *Who is this body? What is this place?* The presence of the corpse pushed the very questions that already unsettled the emergent colonial condition into a state of crisis.

A Curse in the Wilderness

The mysterious grave and its ambiguous corpses are wholly absent from Bradford's history. In an attempt to rebury those strange bodies for good, Bradford simply omits them from his narrative. His rendition of that early scouting mission concentrates instead on the discovery of buried Indian corn found alongside Indian graves that remain undisturbed. In place of the bones unearthed by Englishmen and the pilfered Indian burial place, then, is a basket of buried corn, which Bradford sees as a sign of divine intervention, "a special providence of God, and a great mercy to this poor people."[17] He reports that the party finds

> a good quantity of clear ground where the Indians had formerly set corn, and some of their graves. And proceeding further they saw new stubble where corn had been set the same year; also they found where lately a house had been, where some planks and a great kettle was remaining, and heaps of sand newly paddled with their hands. Which, they digging up, found in them divers fair Indian baskets filled with corn, and some in ears, fair and good, of divers colours, which seemed to them a very goodly sight (having never seen any such before).[18]

Unlike the corpses, the corn is readily identified. There is no searching for meaning and no variety of opinion: it is seen as a message from a merciful God. However, the surrounding context of the Indian burial site belies this conviction of legibility. Here, Indians are both absent and present. Their footprints, their graves, their cornfields, the remainders of their households, the impressions made by their digging hands—each is another trace, but only a trace, of their absent bodies. Even as Bradford records the details, he cannot situate the place in time, using such terms as "formerly," "new," "the same year," "lately," "remaining." The handprints are "newly made," but the site looks wholly abandoned. This disordered temporality arises from not being able to read signs even when they are entirely visible. For "fear of their safety," the scouts rebury half the corn before returning to the ship, splitting the difference between fulfilling their own present needs and courting the potential anger of an absent people.

Bradford closes out this partially disclosed account by replotting the ambiguous scene in a scriptural context. He uses the biblical type in an attempt to cover over the mysterious traces of Indian life, but his allusion only raises more doubts about the fate of strangers in a foreign land. Narrating the scouting party's return to the *Mayflower* with the cache of Indian corn, Bradford likens them to the biblical men of Eshcol, who "carried with them of the fruits of the land and showed their brethren; of which, and their return, they were marvelously glad and their hearts encouraged."[19] The "men of Eshcol" are the scouting party Moses sends out to Canaan. At the river of Eshcol, these men find a bounty of grapes, figs, and pomegranates, which they carry back to the children of Israel, declaring the wilderness a land of milk and honey. Bradford's analogy concludes with this resonant moment of gratitude and fulfillment. However, the story of Moses's scouts is far from over, for the men of Eshcol also return bearing important intelligence. Charged with taking account of the native inhabitants as well as searching for food, the spies report that "the people be strong that dwell in the land, and the cities are walled, and very great: and moreover we saw the children of Anak there."[20] Bradford's party could make no such declaration about the Indians. There were glimpses and signs of the native inhabitants, but these sightings were confused. Bradford resorts to an awkward construction; for a moment the English scouts do see Indians and try to follow them "by guess," but "they soon lost both them and themselves." Like the elusive native people, and like the colonists who dig up Indian goods, the scouts who trespass in Canaan are both present and absent in Bradford's account of the scouts trespassing in Wampanoag country. We glimpse the biblical interlopers laden with the fruits of the land, but their real significance is withheld in Bradford's text because the story of the Eshcol scouting party actually explains how the first generation of God's chosen people *lost* the Promised Land. As such, and despite Bradford's careful editing, it casts a shadow over the settlement at Plymouth.

A brief synopsis of the biblical story is in order. Upon hearing that the people of Canaan are strong, numerous, and well fortified, many Israelites begin to lose faith in the promise of their deliverance. Convinced that they will die horrible deaths in a foreign land, they weep and clamor, sigh for their abandoned home, and wish that they had died in Egypt. Moses, Aaron, Joshua, and Caleb beg the people to remain faithful. They suspect that the scouts are lying about the threat posed by the Canaanites. After all, the spies' reports include contradictory accounts and at times defame what was promised to be a holy place. To convince the panicked company of the providential gift of God, the leaders remind the Israelites of all the signs of divine favor and protection offered during their journey. However, in the gathering storm of fear and incriminations, God grows angry and throws down a bitter curse upon his people, blocking them from the Promised Land:

> As truly as I live, saith the Lord, as ye have spoken in mine ears, so will I do to you: Your carcases shall fall in this very wilderness. . . . But your little ones, which ye said should be a prey, them will I bring in, and they shall know the land which ye have despised. But as for you, your carcases, they shall fall in this wilderness. And your children shall wander in the wilderness forty years, and bear your whoredoms, until your carcases be wasted in the wilderness. . . . I the Lord have said, I will surely do it unto all this evil congregation, that are gathered together against me: in this wilderness they shall be consumed, and there they shall die.[21]

With this withdrawal of God's favor, all the actions of the Israelites become profane. Their subsequent invasion of Canaan is a futile, abortive war. These God-forsaken pilgrims are attacked, driven back, and finally deserted, their divine history unfulfilled.

There are many parallels between the two scouting stories: the gifted land; the fear of its inhabitants; the murmuring among the larger company; and the pervasive anxiety that the people who embarked upon a divinely sanctioned mission might end up an exiled group on the brink of extinction. The threat of becoming a corpse abandoned in the wilderness was thus not only a material concern for the Plymouth colonists; it was also a typological nightmare. The horror of such an ignominious end is emphasized in the Lord's short but thunderous pronouncement against the first generation of Israelites, during which the curse is repeated five times. This image of dead bodies falling in the wilderness must have struck particular terror in the Pilgrim congregation, especially as it came to pass. As the writer of their history, Bradford would of course want to avoid surveying these fields of death in *Of Plymouth Plantation*, but of course he could not. In planting Plymouth, it was impossible to avoid that landscape, or to fully dismiss the threat of a bad death in the wilderness.

Scores of Wampanoag

Earlier texts documenting exploratory forays into this territory did not have to reckon with the problem of the dead. Their reports were about English encounters with Indian life. If the English settlers on board the *Mayflower* had arrived and sent out a scouting party not many years earlier, they would have encountered a vastly different cultural landscape. In 1603 Martin Pring came to the same place Bradford would later call Plymouth harbor as the master and commander of two ships and nearly fifty men. Pring's expedition was sent out under the authorization of Sir Walter Raleigh to retrace the successful voyage of Bartholomew Gosnold the year before. Coursing the coast, naming islands and inlets, and gathering as much intelligence and sassafras as they could manage, Pring and his men finally came to an anchor. Whereas later surveyors would find abandoned places and eerie silences, Pring's voyage encountered native people fully engaged in the energetic business of life, which included discovering the intentions of these English sojourners. The coastal groups showed no signs that they would be all but eradicated within the course of a single generation. "During our abode on shore," Pring writes, "the people of the Country came to our men sometimes ten, twentie, fortie, or three-score, and at one time one hundred and twentie at once."[22] Pring describes their brass breastplates, their quivers full of "prettie works and compartments," their swift canoes, the arrangement of their homes and fields, the nights of their dances and songs ("twenty [dancers] in a Ring . . . singing lo, la, lo, la, la, lo").

Attending to these details of Wampanoag life, his report continually recognizes the tribe's strength in number. For example, as the English are preparing to leave, a full "seven score" armed Wampanoag men present themselves at the English barricade and ask the four armed English sentinels to step down. The English nervously refuse. What ensues is a series of events, surely mystifying to both parties, involving resounding shots of English ordnance; chaos and furor caused by the two English mastiffs, Foole and Gallant; much Indian laughter, jest, and sport (however genuine or tactical is unknown); and then a mile-wide fire deliberately set by the Indians in their own sassafras-rich woods.[23] For all that was mistaken or misread, the

Pring account shows the two cultures in intimate, repeated (if sometimes chaotic) contact. Pring and his men had been in Wampanoag country for ten weeks, and after this night of disquieting drama, they decided it was time to leave: "[A]nd the very same day that wee weighted Anchor, they came downe to the shoare in greater number, to wit, very neere two hundred by our estimation, and some of them came in their Boates to our ship, and would have had us come in againe: but we sent them backe, and would none of their entertainment."[24] Regardless of what Pring and company made of this solicitation to return, one thing is certain: when they turned their ship away, they did not leave an empty shore behind.

In various guises Indians offered "entertainment" to English voyagers up and down that coast over the next thirteen years. Following Gosnold and Pring, no fewer than thirty French and English expeditions sounded the inlets and explored the "intralls" of what was clearly a fully populated Indian land.[25] In fact, recording the size of the native populations was one of the explorers' most important tasks. Reports from these expeditions also describe the various dispositions of native groups toward the putative visitors. Some offered "kind civility," some "soddainly withdrew them Selves from us into the woods & Lefte us," and some demanded that individual Englishmen visit their villages: "Griffin at his returne reported, that had there assembled together, as he numbered them, two hundred eighty three Salvages, every one his bowe and arrowes." In another case a leader's silent sign pronounced the group's resolve: "seeming as though [the chief] would know why we were there, and . . . pointing with his oare toward the sea, we conjectured he meant we should be gone."[26] Whatever the reception, however, European voyagers found Native American people, not graves.

In a characteristic act of colonial mapping, John Smith lists no fewer than forty separate Indian countries encountered along the coastlines between 1614 and 1615. That just pages later he calls this part of the world "not inhabited" is entirely a matter of colonialist ideology.[27] This ideological emptying of Indian lands would soon make powerful recourse to the rapid, dramatic changes occurring on the New England coastline. In the winter of 1616–17, Sir Ferdinando Gorges sent Richard Vines and a small company out with "provisions for trade and discovery" to spend the winter at the mouth of the Saco River. What Vines found there was a place devastated by war and disease, leaders and warriors felled in battle, and the remaining people so "sore afflicted with the Plague, for that the Country was in a manner left void of Inhabitants."[28] Two years later Thomas Dermer opened a report of his recent

New England voyage with these words: "I passed alongst the Coast where I found some ancient Plantations, not long since populous, now utterly void; in other places a remnant remains, but not free of sicknesse."[29] Between 1616 and 1619 a lethal epidemic swept through coastal New England, following the well-worn routes of Indian trade networks and travel corridors. It decimated native populations, ravaging coastal groups from southern Massachusetts to the central Maine seaboard.[30]

European pathogens were the cause.[31] Although Vines and Dermer refer to the killer as the "Plague," the precise epidemiology of this devastation remains a matter of debate.[32] The evidence is scant but grim. Surviving accounts speak just enough to record the symptoms of a quick and horrid death: headaches and fevers, pustules and lesions; bruising, hemorrhaging, and nasal bleeding; the skin turning yellow, then green, and then cold with death. Although the literature that sought to justify colonial possession erased Indians from a landscape now seen as "void," for colonial writers on the ground, the victims of this epidemic remained dramatically visible for one reason: the living were not able to bury their dead. The rapid spread of sickness and death made it impossible to treat each corpse with the solicitude dictated by tradition. Bodily remains were heaped up in the villages, and bones were left to dry in the sun. Abandoning the dead was, of course, considered abhorrent in Indian cultures. Indeed ceremonial burial was one of the cultural vectors linking Native American groups as far back as the late archaic period (ca. 4000–1500 B.C.). Over time the consolidation of distinctive cultures and regional diversification led to different mortuary customs, but whether bodies were laid out on high platforms, wrapped in leather, filled with copper beads, decorated with jewels, preserved with ochre powder, curled into fetal positions, or covered with mats and planks, the dead were intensely and painstakingly prepared for the afterlife.[33]

The epidemic led to the collapse of both worldly and otherworldly native networks. Foundational spiritual beliefs and cultural means of withstanding hardship failed to mitigate the crisis. Deeply embedded rituals were either constrained or abandoned, which seemed to guarantee the further withdrawal of protections from the spiritual realm. The personal and social structures of kinship were tested to the extreme. Political and economic relationships were reconfigured as groups absorbed survivors or as the remnants of tribes banded together. The balance of power shifted decisively when groups not yet affected by the crisis, in this case the Narragansett, asserted their newfound regional dominance.[34] And ultimately there was the immeasurable human toll, the number of the dead surpassing the number of the living.

The scale and impact of the epidemic are literally incalculable. What happened in New England was part of, as John Murrin writes, "the greatest known demographic catastrophe in the history of the world, a population loss that usually reached or exceeded 90 percent in any given region within a century of contact with the invaders."[35] Mortality in the Plymouth settlement cannot compare to the staggering history of decimation among Native American populations, and on one level the turn to Plymouth at this point can seem problematically reductionist. I risk such a joint consideration, however, in order to analyze the relation between Indian and English mortality during this first season of colonial plantation and to examine the role that mortality—in both its depictions and its occlusions—played in the establishment of Plymouth's colonial settlement and its written history. What follows, then, is a comparison of two kinds of reckoning with catastrophe: the actual disposition of those physical remains left in the wake of death; and the discursive reckoning with those remains in the writing of the colony's history. Beginning in 1620, colonists in Plymouth also died in droves and found their cultural tools insufficient. They also failed to properly bury their dead. Like Indians, they feared that they had brought the disaster on themselves and dreaded the prospect of divine abandonment. For both natives and colonists, the structures of cultural cohesion were crumbling. As places of colonial settlement became inextricably bound up with places of the dead, their afflicted populations bore the burden of the mounting remains and of struggling to define newly shifting identities in a newly contested space. Survivors had to interpret the meaning of dying bodies from within and across cultural boundaries, boundaries that were themselves caught up in the mysteries and violence of encounters in the colonial arena.

A Newfound Golgotha

Ultimately histories such as Bradford's had to succeed in making colonial death meaningful by assigning a vastly different significance to the remains of English bodies scattered in a foreign land. In part, this meaning was established by elaborating a set of desired contrasts between Indian and colonial deaths. The outlines of the contrast promised stability. On the one hand, Indian deaths would depopulate the land and leave it void, littered with the bones of the unremembered dead. They would mark a termination and an absence. Colonial deaths, on the other hand, would populate the "wilderness" with marks and memories of English sacrifice. They would leave the land sacred, hallowed. The memory of the English dead would mark an origin and a presence. Indian deaths would make discrete and local places look like empty space, but colonial deaths properly remembered would turn that empty space into a series of places of English memory and fidelity. The Indian dead would signify the devolution of native communities into anomie: a chaos of civil dissensions and bloody war; great mortality; and abandoned remains. The colonial dead would perform an opposite function. Out of the anomie that everywhere threatened the goals of settlement, they would create nomos: a deeply bound community of faithful and grateful survivors. The Indian corpse had to devolve into pure materiality—carrion—so that the colonial corpse could reach the status of pure figure—seed.

In his *Miraculous Plagues: An Epidemiology of Early New England Narrative*, Cristobal Silva treats this providential interpretation of Indian death in detail, explaining how "a colonial ideology that framed the settlement of New England as a divinely ordained mission, and that understood the epidemics to play a crucial role in that mission," resulted in "the centrality of epidemiological discourse to justification narratives."[36] The providential narrative dovetailed with one of the major civil justifications for the English seizure of Indian lands, which was later articulated by John Locke in his *Two Treatises of Government* (1690). There, Locke elaborates the ancient Roman theory of *vacuum domicillium* as a powerful rationale for English colonialism. Locke's theory of property puts forward two arguments: first, that original inhabitants have no sovereign claim on the land because they live in a state of nature, not as fully developed societies; and second, that property rights require not only habitation but also the addition of human labor, of discernible "improvement" of the land resulting in the development of agricultural, commercial, civil, and political societies. Only this kind of society could maintain rights, hold property, and assert sovereignty. These legal and civil claims made land claims easier to justify for the colonial English, who did not want to be seen as following the Spanish conquest style of colonialism. In New England the debilitation of strong, economically and politically sound Indian cultures due to the devastating spread of disease made it easier still.[37]

The movement from shared, Anglo-Indian specters of death to divergent symbologies—one apocalyptic, one generative—can be traced in the seventeenth-century sources. For example, compare an eyewitness report published in 1622 and a subsequent history published in 1669. Nathaniel Morton's 1669 history, *New-England's Memorial*, presents the story of disease, civil unrest, and the visible remains of bodies among the Indians at Patuxet as a providential clearing of the land: "The Lord also so disposed, as aforesaid, much to waste them by a great mortality, together with which were their own civil dissensions, and bloody wars, so as the twentieth person was scarce left alive when these people arrived, there remaining sad spectacles of that mortality in the place where they seated, by many bones and skulls of the dead lying above ground; whereby it appeared that the living were not able to bury them. . . . Thus God made way for his people, by removing the heathen, and planting them in the land."[38] Yet the source from which Morton lifts his description, while still using the language of a "wasted" people, does not end with the same providential closure. Robert Cushman, reporting on his short residence in Plymouth, writes in 1622, "They were very much wasted of late, by reason of a great mortality that fell amongst them three years since; which, together with their own civil dissensions and bloody wars, hath so wasted them, as I think the twentieth person is scarce left alive; and those that are left, have their courage much abated, and their countenance is dejected, and they seem as a people affrighted."[39] Cushman's account of discouragement, dejection, and fright among Indian survivors populates a landscape of bones and skulls with living, grieving people. In Cushman's estimation, even though the surviving Indians are greater in number and strength than the surviving English, they are too disordered by grief to use their advantage against the colonists: "[They] might in one hour have made a dispatch of us, yet such a fear was upon them, as that they never offered us the least injury in word or deed." And yet that fear was upon the colonists too. As David Stannard writes of the early colonists, "In meeting death, it seems clear, they encountered something their English ancestors never had. What they encountered was themselves and their profound sense of tribal vulnerability."[40] Later histories elaborated the division between the Indian dead on the one side and the healthy English planters on the other, but such absolute demarcations were not felt as sickness and mortality reigned in the settlement.

English colonial ideology may have been based on a theory of *vacuum domicillium*, a world with no one in it, but in the writings of early English colonists, it was also rendered as a place where the loss of life was still visible. In 1625 Thomas Morton, proprietor and "Host" of the raucous settlement at

Merry Mount, arrived at his pleasure dome by stepping over Indian bones.[41] Of the late native inhabitants, he reports,

> they died on heapes, as they lay in their houses, and the living; that were able to shift for themselves would runne away, & let them dy, and let there Carkases ly above ground, without buriall. For in a place where many inhabited, there hath been but one left a live, to tell what became of the rest, the livinge being (as it seemes,) not able to bury the dead, they were left for Crowes, Kites, and vermin to prey upon. And the bones and skulls upon the severall places of their habitations, made such a spectacle after my comming into those partes, that as I travailed in that Forrest nere the Massachusetts, it seemed to mee a new-found Golgotha.[42]

As Morton reads these Indian remains, he also speculates on the relations between the living and the dead. When he sees piles of skulls and bones, he imagines fear and flight but also the possibility of memory and mourning. His parenthetical hesitation at the moment of explanation—"the livinge being (as it seemes,) not able to bury the dead"— reimagines his earlier image of Indians actively abandoning their dead as a situation of unavoidable constraint. In this imaginative reconstruction of the scene, the parenthetical "(as it seemes)" is situated directly between the living and the dead—between the possibility that someone might bear witness to the catastrophe ("but one left a live, to tell what became of the rest") and the impossible silence of the fully dehumanized corpse ("left . . . to prey upon.")

Between these poles of speech and silence, the cadaverous resemblance and the cadaverous presence of the unburied dead stretch out to mark the place as a site of Indian trauma, and not simply as a voided space ready for English possession. Although Morton does present "a place where many inhabited" as now emptied, he ends by memorializing this place as "a new-found Golgotha." Even for an apostate such as Morton, allusions to Christian scripture were never far from reach. In the gospels the evangelists refer to Golgotha as the place of a skull.[43] Golgotha was associated with transgression; it stood outside the city walls and was a place to execute criminals. It was also a place of great holiness: the site of Christ's crucifixion and the legendary burial ground of Adam. Some claimed that the rounded hill of Golgotha physically resembled a skull, the very landscape announcing itself as a place of the dead. When Morton calls this Indian skull-place a "Golgotha," it is a profoundly memorable moment in the text precisely because of the site's mixed connotations. On the one hand, Golgotha evokes banishment and abandonment; on the other, it is a sacred, sacrificial, raised plot of land whose very shape speaks to remembrance. In the same way that Golgotha is a spot marked by death, the cadaverous presence of these Indians remains indelibly mark "that Forrest near the Massachusetts."

When Bradford's history depicts a similar sight, it cannot afford to populate or name the landscape in such a way. With varying degrees of success, Bradford's text tries to control the cadaverous presence of natives by relocating them to a presettlement past and describing their remains in the passive voice.[44] Recounting his first visit to Massasoit's Wampanoag village, he can neither completely excise his encounter with the dead nor meditate on it. He describes it thus: "the people not many, being dead and abundantly wasted in the late great morality, which fell in all these parts about three years before the coming of the English, wherein thousands of them died. They not being able to bury one another, their skulls and bones were found in many places lying still above the ground where their houses and dwellings had been, a very sad spectacle to behold."[45] Native remains are "lying still" above ground, meaning that their insistent presence is at once fixed and belated: they lie still, and still they lie.

For both Morton and Bradford, Indian bones and skulls create a spectacle, a sight both public and unnatural. As such, these remains require notice and narration. The suspended cultural work of burying the dead put a burden on later observers, who needed to enclose the visible remains within a system of meaning.[46] There were various ways to do this. Whereas Morton's "I" walks through the forest near the Massachusetts and actively describes what he encounters, Bradford's account is vague and passive. Bones "were found in many places," but their discovery goes unnarrated. Coming upon the evidence of a mass death, Morton supplements the still bones with an active, if tragic, history: the sick dying in heaps, the survivors fleeing; the corpses rotting; the scavengers picking at the abandoned dead. In contrast, Bradford records the "late great mortality" as a fait accompli, inert and final. The dead belong to a past that he will not reanimate, not even in his imagination. Although he nearly succeeds in circumscribing the spectacle of Indian bones within the already concluded history he devises, the uncanny visibility of the dead breaks through into a present moment in Bradford's last phrase: "a very sad spectacle to behold." That moment of affective recognition hints at the cultural significance of the material remains; it also momentarily problematizes the discursive role of sadness in his historical practice.

For the most part, what allows Bradford to assign a meaning to the crisis of settlement is a discourse of misery endured. His are always a "poor people" whose faith in the midst of suffering sanctifies their mission, whether or not that mission succeeds in earthly terms. Sadness is the Pilgrims' special preserve. They are often in a "sad condition," and letters bring "sad tidings" and send "sad news." Their many losses are "sad and lamentable"; yet they bear "their sad affliction with as much patience and contentedness" as any people can.[47] Sadness is one of the central discursive vehicles through which Bradford attempts to filter the Plymouth colony's complex and fractious relations to colonial, transatlantic, and Indian social and economic orders, and to their own experiences of internal and external disorder. Depicting a settlement that is always on the verge of catastrophe but whose present meaning and future promise are sustained by special providences, Bradford creates for his group a colonial condition that is defined at once by hardship and by grace. A chronicle of afflictions borne in patience allows Bradford to narrate the often-desperate exigencies of colonial experience while still claiming a virtual self-continuity unaffected by rupture, even as it is defined by loss.

As Walter Wenska observes, "The 'cost' of their determination to walk with the Lord, and their eventual deliverance 'from all . . . perils and miseries' (p. 61)—these are, for Bradford, the determinant of the Pilgrim experience and achievement."[48] This requirement that the experience of loss (cost, peril, misery) be linked to achievement is realized by a rhythm of human sorrow and divine glory that contains loss within a larger story of power. Breitwieser discusses this rhythm of "presence/absence/presence/absence/ glorious presence" as a structure for converting the experience of historical loss, failure, and violence into a desire for the futurity of an ideal nation. "There is no loss, really," he writes, "only a reinvestment of riches. In this scheme, the hole in the self turns out to be the space reserved for the coming glory, and the patriot is on the very verge of emerging complete and full."[49] For Bradford, it is not the nation that promises a future perfect form but the surviving plantation that will prove that the costs of becoming colonial were divinely recompensed. The mere survival of the people of sorrows, with their burdens and bitter afflictions, will stand as proof of their promise fulfilled.

Bradford's invocation of sadness relied on making readers participate in the discourse of misery and using their compassion to forge a sense of identification and loyalty. The means of producing this fellow feeling—an ideological commitment to a humble, stalwart, faithful people—was successful in mythologizing Plymouth's first years for future generations. "Descendants" of these "poor people" made a passage through sadness in order to implant the Pilgrim soul as a national imago, and a recitation of settlement hardships became a standard preamble to any stated obligation to secure a triumphal future. Especially in the early and mid-nineteenth century, an oratorical tradition grew up around the 1620 settlement that called for copious tears to be shed at the Pilgrim grave.[50]

For New England culture makers, Bradford's account of sickness and death in the first dreadful seasons of settlement became a poignant and powerful set piece in a developing nationalist imagination. As one schoolbook taught citizens-in-formation, "Their cruel hardships are the spring of our prosperity; their amazing sufferings the seed, from which our happiness has sprung."[51] The sad spectacle of Indian bones that stops Bradford was replaced in the cultural memory by a "melancholy handful of survivors" in the Plymouth colony who had to "conceal the extent of their losses from the jealous Indians."[52] Bradford's moment of compassion at Massasoit's village, an aperture in the text through which other "amazing sufferings" are glimpsed, is finally shuttered by a totalizing English sadness. Because Bradford's sadness comes to occlude the Indian mourners, the spectacle of Indian death is cut off from futurity. Meanwhile elaborate rhetorical performances of melancholy directed toward the Pilgrim survivors guaranteed that the Pilgrim dead would be figuratively committed to the ground again and again as their story passed down through generations and as Indian land was marked by American remembrances. Transfigured into seed, colonial corpses became an ever-renewing source of cultural sustenance. As opposed to their Indian counterparts, they were amply buried—not lying still above the ground, not strewn across it, but sown into it.

"The Rest of Our Friends"

In general, settlers viewed the decimation of native inhabitants as an act of a satisfied God who had cleared the land for his chosen people. However, that interpretation was compromised by watching their own die in droves as well. In terms of the effect on the company's families, only three of eighteen married couples survived intact. All of the colony's principal men—William Bradford, Miles Standish, Isaac Allerton, and Edward Winslow—

were widowed. Only two families did not suffer a loss. Of the children (who had a much better survival rate than the adults), eleven among the twenty-five to survive were orphaned of one or both parents. Half of the free single men died, as did eight of the eleven servants.[53] Such mortality must have produced deep anxiety in the covenanted people, for whom it could not but signal a dangerous disorder. The stark fact was that within six months of the Pilgrim landing at Plymouth, half of the English company was dead. Of this calamity William Bradford famously writes, "[I]t pleased God to visit us then with death daily, and with so general a disease that the living were scarce able to bury the dead, and the well not in any measure sufficient to tend the sick."[54] At times the number of "the well" dwindled to seven, six, or even fewer. Over fifty were dead, the surviving majority was gravely ill, and only half a dozen functioning adults remained among them.

Even if some settlers were able to keep faith in the midst of this extremity, the deaths presented a grim imperative. While several colonial reports document the sight of Indian carcasses and bones strewn about depopulated sights, the corresponding question remains unanswered: what did the settlers at Plymouth do with their dead? On the issue of burial, the record is almost silent. The oldest gravestone on Burial Hill is dated 1681, although it is thought that burials here began shortly after the hill served as a strategic high ground for an armed fort from 1622 to 1676.[55] In the absence of any earlier markers, traditional memory holds that the first year's dead were buried on a hill just below the fort, that graves were dug hastily at night and leveled to conceal the number of the dead, and that corn was planted over these shallow graves to further disguise the settlement's losses.[56]

In addition to this physical concealment, these deaths were largely untallied and unnamed in the earliest reports sent back to England. For example, although the writers of *Mourt's Relation* spend pages describing how they broke the seal on the elaborate Indian grave to unearth its baffling corpses, they do not mention that Bradford returned from that expedition to find that his wife, Dorothy May Bradford, had drowned. While the scouting party could not fathom how that blond-haired body had come to rest in an Indian grave, they also could not speak of what may have driven Dorothy Bradford over the side of the *Mayflower* and into the icy water.[57] Hers was one of four English bodies consigned to the harbor's bottom before the group ever left the ship. This first relation from Plymouth chronicles neither those four deaths nor those that followed, not even as a record of labor; the digging of graves must have accounted for a prominent physical activity during the first months of settlement.[58] The dead were neither counted nor accounted for.

The silence surrounding these bodies—half of the original group—is broken by one contemporary source: a text dictated by a passenger who arrived at Plymouth in the aftermath of that first horrid season. In May 1622 a small boat from a fishing vessel called the *Sparrow* came into Plymouth harbor bringing irritable letters from London and extra mouths to feed. These papers and people were utterly unwelcome; both bore the marks of Thomas Weston, the dodgy English ironmonger and colonial promoter already well known and distrusted by the Plymouth settlers.[59] Weston was pursuing two different paths of profit. He had hired out the larger ship, the *Sparrow*, to fish the Maine waters; meanwhile he had directed a handful of men to take the shallop and head inland to set up a trading settlement near Plymouth.

While the colonists at Plymouth regarded the new arrivals with skepticism, the new men contemplated their would-be hosts in utter confusion. Alarmed to find the company that Weston had told them about so radically diminished, they wondered aloud what had happened to these people. As the passenger Phineas Pratt tells it, the answer was worse than they expected: "We asked them wheare the Rest of our friends weare that came in the first ship. Thay said that God had taken them Away by deth, & that before thayr seckond ship came, thay weare so destresed with sickness that thay, feareing the salvages should know it, had sett up theyr sick men with thayr muscits upon thayr Rests & thayr backs Leaning Against trees."[60] The answer supplied by the Pilgrims as to the whereabouts of the missing has nothing to do with burial. From Pratt's testimony we learn that in the midst of their mortality crisis, the Plymouth colonists set the bodies of their dying men upright in the woods and propped muskets at their sides as a protective ruse. In response to their extreme vulnerability, the Pilgrims established a cadaverous *tableau vivant* of forest sentinels. Sick and dying bodies were employed by those who still had the strength to carry them as symbolic instruments in a traumatic contest for survival.[61]

Plymouth colonists displayed their powerless bodies to neighboring Indians as a fiction of social power, despite the fact that such exposure undermined their own social practices for dealing with the sick and the dead. Back in England, some lessening of solicitude toward the dead and dying was inevitable during times of extreme social breakdown, and yet even during plague and war years, distressed and weakened people clung tightly to their rituals of decency.[62] In Plymouth, with the anxiety over the withdrawal of providential protection mounting alongside the rising death toll, the use of these casualties as armed decoys in the forest must have seemed an appalling breach of taboo, an act of desperation. Regardless of its ostensible necessity, a scheme whereby the dying were put to strategic use to protect the living must surely have seemed a loathsome path to follow.

In 1662 the General Court of Massachusetts legally endorsed Pratt's narrative, which he presented to the court as "A Decliration of the Afaires of the English People that first Inhabited New England." His acts of witness were affirmed as evidence of his "first-comer" status in the colony, and he was given an extensive land grant.[63] As early as 1677, when Increase Mather published a version of Phineas Pratt's story as part of his own *Relation of the Troubles Which Have Hapned in New-England*, the forest guard of sick and dying men was excised from the Plymouth narrative. Mather refers to Pratt as "an old Planter yet living in this Countrey" and writes, "He doth relate, and affirm, that at his first coming into this country, the English were in a very distressed condition, by reasons of famine, and sickness which was amongst them, whereof many were already dead." True, but Mather then continues the sentence with a very different piece of intelligence: "and that they buried them in the night, that the Indians might not perceive how low they were brought."[64] Pratt's declaration does not "relate" or "affirm" anything at all about night burials. Increase Mather inserts the tradition of night burials at the precise moment that Pratt testified to armed bodies leaning up against the trees.

Enough bones have been exhumed from Cole's Hill to show that it was an early colonial burial place.[65] Though night burials and leveled graves may indeed have occurred, what is important here is Mather's act of substitution, which signals a slip in how the dead settlers of Plymouth would be used and remembered. The tradition of night burials admits that there was a strategy surrounding the disposal of the dead, but it was one in which their corpses were hidden and kept from signification rather than one in which their wasting bodies were displayed and intended for signification. While Pratt's account of a ghastly sentinel disappeared, Mather's account of the concealed graves became a cherished story in the Plymouth legend. It served to nullify the disquieting, cadaverous presence while also framing the straitened actions of the survivors into an appropriate discourse of grief. The dead may have been scarce buried, but at least they were in the ground.

In Bradford's writing, Indian bones could be set apart and ambiguous corpses could be omitted, but he still had to face the problem of Plymouth's own "abundantly wasted" bodies. As we have seen, this posed many threats. There was the material threat of being overwhelmed by physical remains: "the living were scarce able to bury the dead." There was the cultural threat of tabooed transgression: they "sett up theyr sick men with thayr muscits upon thayr Rests & thayr backs Leaning Aganst trees." There was the divine threat of being abandoned by God and seeing his prophecy fulfilled: "in this wilderness they shall be consumed, and there they shall die." Given such dangers, Plymouth's historian had to seal the Pilgrim grave if he and his fellow settlers wanted to possess the land.

How strange, then, that in a chronicle that extends to two books and took at least twenty years to write, Bradford's history hardly mentions the dead at all. In rendering his history of that "most sad and lamentable" winter during which half the English population died, Bradford writes, "But that which was most sad and lamentable was, that in two or three months' time half of their company died, especially in January and February, being the depth of winter, and wanting houses and other comforts; being infected with the scurvy and other diseases which this long voyage and their inaccommodate condition had brought upon them. So as there died some times two or three of a day in the foresaid time, that of 100 and odd persons, scarce fifty remained."[66] After describing the period as sad, lamentable, comfortless, and wanting, the text swerves. Immediately following this passage, Bradford devotes lingering attention to the actions of the "six or seven sound persons" who spend their days and nights nursing, feeding, washing, clothing, warming, and attending the sick. That even such a tightly constrained narrative of their Starving Time has since become one of the most celebrated parts of Bradford's text confirms a demand that written histories, and especially a history of origins, somehow account for the dead.

Why does Bradford's history turn so quickly away from the dead? One could argue that perhaps the reason there is no commentary on their burial is because burial did not have a highly symbolic status for the Plymouth community. Changing burial practices in England, and among Puritans especially, downplayed the ritual significance of the body's interment. Separatist populations such as Plymouth's would be especially loath to place emphasis on a ritual act that had no true spiritual basis, adamantly asserting as they did that elaborate burial rites did nothing to change or influence the condition of the soul.[67] Given this, the compassionate toil of the living, who demonstrated their faith by nursing the sick, would be much more important than the material disposition of the dead. However, there is another, rhetorical reason why the English dead are so nearly absent from Bradford's history. In his biblically framed conception of Plymouth history, the dead are carcasses in the wilderness. Bradford turns away from the horrid dying because it is the only way to restore to prominence the faithful actions of the surviving few. He needs to recuperate the faith of Joshua and Caleb amid the murmuring and fearful crowd in order to preserve the promise of possessing the land.

The Word from Wessagusset

Phineas Pratt played an important role in another, little-told story of life and death in these settlement years: that of the failed colony at Wessagusset. Following the traces of the dead in Plymouth leads us to this second settlement, and to another case in which the landscape of death is occluded in Bradford's narrative. Although Bradford gives only a brief account of Wessagusset, Edward Winslow treats it at length in his *Good Newes from New-England* and even discloses that one of the reasons he decided to publish his report was to counteract the "vile and clamorous reports" coming from members of this "disorderly colony" who had returned to England.[68] Despite both Bradford's and Winslow's efforts to put distance between the two settlements, Plymouth was intimately involved in the short and violent history of Wessagusset from beginning to end. Reconstructing this relationship recalls how quickly colonial settlements could fall into extremity and how fatal the consequences could be for both colonists and Indians. It also reveals the willingness of the leaders of the Plymouth colony to put the dead to use in order to define and enforce their political power, for the dramatic end of the Wessagusset settlement resulted in the most spectacular display of an unburied corpse in this colonial arena.

In June 1622, a month after Pratt's arrival, an English ship named the *Charity* and its shallop, the *Swan*, came into Plymouth harbor. On board were the sixty men that Thomas Weston sent to make up the remainder of the company at his planned inland settlement at Wessagusset. The newcomers had little to recommend them to the aggrieved people at Plymouth. A letter that had been sneaked on board the *Charity* warned Bradford that the newcomers were heady and violent young men. Even Weston felt that they were "rude fellows."[69] These "strangers" stayed at Plymouth all summer, recovering from the sicknesses and hardships of their voyage. Plymouth was on rations; each settler was allotted four ounces of bread a day. Witnesses to the ravages of winter, Plymouth settlers knew that it could have been worse and endured the rationing, but Weston's new men were contemptuous of the Pilgrim strictures. They spent the first three months of their colonial lives not only sick and near starvation but also cursing their hosts up and down, fighting among themselves, chronically stealing food, and enduring public whippings for these infractions. When September came, those who were well enough promptly set out northward toward the Massachusetts Bay and the place called Wessagusset, where they planned to live, trade, and prosper. Their leave-taking could not come soon enough for either party.

Before the month was out, Wessagusset settlers came calling to Plymouth again. Their store was already spent, winter was approaching, and the specter of starvation loomed. In search of food, Richard Greene, Thomas Weston's brother-in-law and the leader of the Wessagusset group, proposed a joint trading expedition among the coastal Indian groups. The plan was to use the *Swan* for transport and the Plymouth colonists' scant commodities for trade. This offer was accepted by those at Plymouth, whose harvest, planted by weakened and unskilled hands, had been poor. Greene traveled to Plymouth but sickened, died, and was buried there before the trading course was ever set. It was now October, and the winter of 1622 was looking no better than its predecessor.

Between October and November the *Swan* made three attempts to go in search of food. Only the last of these, commanded by Bradford and piloted part of the way by Tisquantum, could be considered a partial success. Tisquantum, a Patuxet Indian, had been kidnapped in 1614, taken to England, and returned home four years later only to find his entire village dead and gone. Since 1620 he had lived in Plymouth and acted as a go-between, using his position to gain status with both English and native groups.[70] Now he brought the desperate settlers on the *Swan* as far as Chatham harbor. Colonists traded with the people at Nauset, Cummaquid, and Manomet and procured over two dozen hogsheads of corn and beans, but ultimately they lost more than they gained. At Manamoick Bay, into which they were forced by a storm, Tisquantum became feverish and began bleeding profusely through his nose. He died within a few days.[71] The *Swan* was driven by violent gales onto the sands at the inlet of Mattakeeset, where it was beached, fifty miles from Plymouth. Bradford and crew divided as much of their corn as they could physically carry and walked home, leaving the body of the sole native survivor of Patuxet behind them.

By January the colonists at Plymouth were hungry again, but the colonists at Wessagusset were desperate. Without strong leadership or any form of social cohesion, they had completely consumed their scanty provender from November's costly trading journey. Meanwhile a deadly sickness had broken out among the Massachusett Indians, who were their most immediate trading partners. Nevertheless, Weston's men at Wessagusset attempted trade, and then pilferage, and then barefaced theft to keep themselves stocked with corn. The envisioned trading post was becoming an assembly of stragglers, beggars, and bandits. The position of the Massachusett toward the settlement quickly went from provocation, to hostility, to open hatred and contempt. Established social structures among the Massachusett weakened in response to widespread sickness and death, but the Wessagusset community, such as it was, completely collapsed. The new colonists sold whatever they had brought with them from England—their blankets, the clothes off their own backs—for food. They agreed to hard labor and menial work in return for capfuls of corn from the Indians. Dispersing in search of food, some joined the Massachusett, some eked out subsistence, and others starved and died. As Bradford later reports, "One in gathering shellfish was so weak as he stuck fast in the mud and was found dead in the place. At last most of them left their dwellings and scattered up and down in the woods and by the watersides, where they could find ground nuts and clams, here six and there ten."[72]

In February, Wessagusset's second governor, John Sanders, came up with a plan. He and whomever he could gather of the starving Englishmen would conduct one last brazen raid for Massachusett corn, which he was convinced was being withheld from them out of contempt. Then, they would lock themselves up in their palisades until the supply ran out. That was as far as the plan went. Sanders, acknowledging that Plymouth should be aware of such a bold maneuver, sent a letter to Bradford outlining their resolve to commit the violent action and their plot to accomplish it. The news had a dramatic impact, not only at Plymouth but also among the Massachusett, to whom the plan was leaked. Even as the leading men at Plymouth crafted a stern reply to Sanders, the leading men among the Massachusett began to forge a coalition. Receiving a forbidding reply from his erstwhile providers and disciplinarians at Plymouth, Sanders abandoned both his plan and his post. He headed out in an open boat to the fishing waters of Maine in hopes of securing provisions and never returned. In the absence of even a nominal leadership, the situation at Wessagusset went from bad to appalling.

Meanwhile, Miles Standish, the military commander at Plymouth, was also skirting the coast looking for food. His mission was to retrieve the caches of corn and beans that Bradford and the November expedition could not carry home. At Nauset, Cummaquid, and Manomet, Standish's rendezvous with local Indian groups took on an increasingly hostile tone. Standish, who readily displayed arms and threw down ultimatums over trifles, initiated much of the discord. But when calling on Canacum, the sachem at Manomet, Standish was confronted by two Massachusett warriors who assumed an even more aggressive posture than his own. One of them was Witawamut, who made a long, passionate, and pointedly untranslated speech to Canacum, all the while flashing his sword menacingly in the direction of the furious and flummoxed Standish. Standish returned to Plymouth enraged at the insult, and with less than a full burden of corn.

Meanwhile a rumor was spreading, this time about an Indian attack. The word was that the Massachusett Indians were determined to wipe out the trading post at Wessagusset but feared reprisals from Plymouth. Therefore they had put together a coalition that included the coastal people of Nauset, Cummaquid, Manomet, Pamet, and Gayhead to achieve an even more ambitious end. They would take out both the post at Wessagusset and the settlement at Plymouth in a single day. One version of this rumor came from Miles Standish, who took from his encounter with Witawamut that Plymouth was in danger. A second version came from Edward Winslow, who heard it from Hobomok, who in turn was told it by Massasoit, the Wampanoag sachem. Massasoit said that he had been invited to join the coalition but had refused. He now urged Plymouth to make a preemptive strike and cut down the main conspirators, Witawamut chief among them.

A third version of the rumor came from Phineas Pratt. Pratt, a Wessagusset man, escaped from the palisade there and returned to Plymouth as a refugee. Clearly he now thought that even four ounces of bread and the austere lifestyle at Plymouth were better options than imminent starvation or massacre in the Massachusetts Bay. Pratt reported that at Wessagusset, the Massachusett were inching their wigwams closer to the palisade and were awaiting only the completion of some canoes (which two of Weston's men were building in exchange for scraps) to commence their assault. Meanwhile the state of the would-be Wessagusset traders had deteriorated to the point that Indians had taken to throwing dirt in their English faces. Pratt describes himself amid a cohort of corpses in the fort: "I see one man ded before me & Another at my writ hand & An other att my left for want of food."[73] For all Pratt had seen and heard, he could not hide his panic. He knew the Massachusett at Wessagusset had been keeping a close eye on him for days, and even though he tried to escape without notice, armed men trailed his path to Plymouth. Still, even "Faint for want of food, weary with Running, Fearing to make a Fier because of them that pshued [pursued] me," he was not sorry to play the role of messenger. As he reasoned, "if Plimoth men know not of this Treacherous plot, they & we are all ded men."

For Bradford, Allerton, and Standish, the rumors were enough. On March 25, 1623, Standish, Hobomok, and eight armed men went to the Massachusett under the pretense of trade.[74] The pretense was slim, and their arrival was a clear signal to Witawamut and others that a new level of confrontation had begun. Standish gathered as many of Weston's men as he could into the fort and held them there under penalty of death. After a while Indians came to the fort to "trade," but the rules of engagement were an utter mystery to the colonial captain. Witawamut and Pecksnot, the lead warriors, never did attack, but they sharpened their knives in his face, bragged of the European blood their blades had tasted, mocked Standish's small stature, and laughed at the tearful way in which they had seen Englishmen die.[75] This taunting went on for days.

On April 4 Standish realized that he and his men outnumbered Witawamut and his men who had come by for more jeering. The room was closed, a signal given, and Witawamut and Pecksnot were killed with the knives that hung around their own necks. Of the murders, Edward Winslow writes that "it is incredible how many wounds these two Puceses [Pineses] received before they dyed, not making any fearfull noyse, but catching at their weapons and striving to the last."[76] Before the day was out, five more were killed. Of the roughly thirty Massachusett men to survive that disastrous winter's sickness, Standish's men had killed seven. A triumphant Standish carried the decapitated head of Witawamut back to Plymouth, where he was joyfully greeted as a returning hero.[77]

Wessagusset was finished less than a year after its first settlers came ashore. Most of the surviving English refused Standish's offer to return to Plymouth. Instead they boarded the *Swan* and headed north toward the Maine fishing waters to search for food, work, Sanders, Weston, or a passage home. Their dead were left unburied behind them. Of the Indian dead, only Witawamut remained visible, but that visibility was extraordinary. His head was raised on a pike and set on top of the fort at Plymouth, the Pilgrims' central place of worship and defense, where it stood for many years as a spectacle. Over the years many remarked upon it. In a letter written to the London Adventurers in 1623, William Bradford reports on the raid and does not fail to note the ghastly ensign mounted on the settlement's highest ground: "the head of one of them stands still on our forte for a terror unto others."[78] While this intimidating reminder of the killing stood, the death and dispersal of so many native people had ruined trade. "We have been much endamaged in our trade," Bradford continues with some perplexity, "for there where we had most skins the Indainns are rune away from their habitations, and sett not corne, so as we can by no means as yet come to speak with them." Edward Winslow confirmed the connection between intimidation and declining trade, writing later that year that the execution of Witawamut and the others "hath so terrified and amazed them, as in like manner they forsooke their houses, running to and fro like men distracted, living in swamps and other desert places, and so brought manifold diseases amongst themselves, whereof very many are dead. . . . None of them dare come amongst us."[79]

At Leyden the Pilgrims' pastor and spiritual leader John Robinson heard news of the massacre and found the violence outrageous. He admonished them, "Oh how happy a thing had it been, if you had converted some before you had killed any!" Godly people were not supposed to kill potential converts or "be a terrour to poor barbarous people," much less bring a bloody head back to their fort for display.[80] But then again, few things had gone according to plan. Indians were not supposed to throw dirt in the faces of Englishmen, and they were not supposed to mock an English captain, twirling their knives in his face. Trading partners were not supposed to run "like men distracted" into the woods and flee from English people and their goods. The Pilgrim collective body was not supposed to disintegrate so quickly, and the Pilgrim individual body was not supposed to be propped up dying against a tree.

Thomas Morton of Marymount had harsher words for the colonists, assuming the perspective of the Massachusett people to whom the intentions of the English remained opaque or sinister: "The Salvages of Massachusetts, that could not imagine, from whence these men should come, or to what end, seeing them perform such unexpected actions, neither could tell by what name, properly to distinguish them, did from that time afterwards, call the English Planters *Wotawquenange*, which in their language signifieth stabbers, or Cutthroates."[81] Morton coined many sobriquets for the Plymouth men, but none more damning than this: "Cutthroates." Bradford had earlier bestowed the name "Pilgrims" upon his group as they headed out to sea, asserting that what the settlers did not know about the New World was ultimately unimportant as long as they knew who they were: "[T]hey knew they were pilgrims, and looked not much on those things, but lift up their eyes to the heavens, their dearest country."[82] They were spiritual voyagers, not colonists, and their spiritual certainty would overcome their material unpreparedness. Instead, the Massachusett judged the Pilgrims solely through the intense interactions they had with them. From this local view expressed by Morton, what is wholly "unexpected" is not what the English found in the wilderness but what they did there. The origin and intentions of these newcomers remained baffling, but the Massachusett had seen enough to name them. They knew that they were cutthroats and that they lifted their eyes to an Indian head impaled on their fort as they filed into their palisades.

Witawamut's Banner

The earliest recorded personal reaction to the head of Witawamut came from an Indian who knew him. Here again Phineas Pratt had a role to play. The Indian who pursued Pratt from Wessagusset soon became the first prisoner to be held in Plymouth fort. Chained and guarded, he was to be kept at least until Standish and company returned from Wessagusset. They would return, as we know, with a grisly trophy. Edward Winslow's *Good Newes from New-England* reports on the prisoner's reaction to the spectacle of Witawamut's impaled head: "Now was the Captaine returned and received with joy, the dead being brought to the fort, and there set up, the Governours and Captaines with divers others went up to the same further, to examine the prisoner, who looked pittiously on the head. Being asked whether he knew it, he answered, Yea."[83] According to Winslow, this unnamed Indian confesses that there was a plot against the English settlers, that Witawamut was among its chief promoters, and that three other principal organizers were still alive. However, the prisoner protests that he himself is innocent and is not even a Massachusett but rather a stranger living among them. He had come to the tribe as a survivor, he claims, when his own people were decimated by disease. Hobomok, himself a "stranger" living among the Pilgrims at Plymouth, vouches for the truth of this confession and appeals for the prisoner's life, although it is later suspected that his testimony was bribed. Eventually the prisoner is released to demonstrate the settlers' benevolence, they claim, but also to carry a message back to the remaining Massachusett: the Massachusett should return the three English prisoners they had taken, leave the palisade and houses at Wessagusset untouched, and above all never forget how quickly and ferociously the English would respond to threats. If any group plotted against the settlement again, they warn, the Plymouth colonists would not rest until they "had utterly consumed them."[84]

Winslow's report of the raid's dramatic aftermath continues, but one moment stands out. The prisoner, writes Winslow, looks at Witawamut's head "pittiously" and upon being asked if he knows him, answers "Yea." That low affirmation resounds as the most precise direct speech in all of the account that follows. This record of an Indian prisoner looking at and claiming connection to the freshly decapitated head of an Indian leader is unique. Although the viewer and the viewed are both held as enemies—one a prisoner in chains and the other impaled on a post—the nature of the piteous gaze gives this moment of recognition the sorrow, mercy, and tenderness that the Pilgrims usually claim for themselves. The piteous gaze communicates both the prisoner's pity toward Witawamut and the power of that pity to move others to compassion.[85] Certainly it was affecting enough for Edward Winslow to record the scene in this way. As we have seen, Bradford uses the connections created by pity to great effect in portraying the sad scenes endured by his poor people. Here, the Indian prisoner's gaze opens up a space in the text where colonial power turns to Indian emotion, where the demand that the prisoner identify the head turns into a display of personal affective bonds between Indians living and dead.

Such recognition also introduces uncanniness into the scene of triumphal return. An object called "[t]he head" is ready to be set up, but the prisoner recognizes Witawamut not as a mutilated trophy but as a cadaverous resemblance (one who is/is not the same person) and as a cadaverous presence (one who is/is not in his place). The liminality of the corpse, somewhere between subject and object, is inherent in the prisoner's gaze. The rest of Winslow's report relocates this uncomfortable ambiguity over Witawamut's head back onto the unnamed prisoner. The prisoner's confession is believed to be true, but Hobomok's "good report" of him must have been bribed. He is released from his chains but is not allowed to leave the fort of his own will. Bradford promises him that there is nothing to fear but then sends him off with an ultimatum and threats of future English aggression. And yet for all the scene's contradictions, it is a singular moment in the early writing from this settlement when a personally intimate relation between the living and the dead is depicted between Indians.

On August 14, 1623, four months after the staking of Witawamut's head, the Plymouth settlers gathered to celebrate the wedding of their governor, William Bradford, to Alice Southworth. Southworth's first husband, Edward, had died that year in Leyden, never having made the crossing. Bradford's first wife, Dorothy, had drowned by tumbling overboard from the anchored *Mayflower*. As the widow and the widower were married "with great cheer," the head of Witawamut still presided over Plymouth fort. Among the guests greeted by this sight was Massasoit, the Wampanoag chief, and his gift-bearing retinue. The Plymouth people, who notoriously shunned decoration, did add one adornment for the happy event. A piece of linen soaked in Witawamut's blood was hung as a flag from the post where the warrior's decaying head perched.[86]

The cultural meanings of the totem are difficult to discipline. Although in one respect, the ideological function and political implications of Witawamut's head could not be clearer, the mutilated corpse also reveals internal colonial tensions that are impossible to excise fully from its display.[87] The display of traitors' heads was not uncommon in early modern London, but when the head of Witawamut held such symbolic primacy in the first years of Plymouth, it placed the visibility of human remains at the apex of the settlement's representational order. *Who is this body? What is this place?* For a weakened community in exile, and often in doubt and crisis, that cadaverous fixture was problematic at best. Though meant to convey strength both to settlers inside the fort and to enemies outside, the totem actually spoke to the very disorder it was meant to combat.

Given the broader significance of the dead in settlement history, Witawamut's silent corpse must have created disquieting reverberations at the wedding feast. Scattered bones were one thing; an impaled head was another. The sight made it clear that the authority of the Plymouth settlement rested in its military power. It also recalled the crisis of widespread Indian mortality and the Indians' inability to control the disposition of their own dead. Moreover the head proved that the colonists would use the threat of terror even against a people socially disordered by grief and loss. The wedding feast made reference to the Plymouth dead too—it was, after all, a marriage of widow and widower—even as it celebrated the colony's potential for recovery and repopulation. In a perverse sense, the power represented by the presiding spectacle of Witawamut's head and the bloody banner supplanted the vulnerability represented by the scarce buried remains of the twenty-four husbands and wives who had died since their landing. At the same time, the decaying head recalled those ambiguous remains disinterred from the first mysterious grave, the ones that haunted the scouts precisely because they were unable to read them. Thus even as the corpse was purposefully erected as a sign with a clear and menacing meaning, its very presence created an atmosphere in which significance could not be fully disciplined.

In Plymouth, the visibility of the dead was brought about by acute conditions, but it also offered an opportunity for powerful representational practices. However, some forms of representation that were meant for those on the ground became problematic when the events of settlement were shaped into a history of origins. In the case of the propped-up forest guard, the display of dying bodies was considered so transgressive that those written histories had to radically disavow any evidence of it. In the case of Witawamut, the corpse that was forced into a position of high visibility also cast a shadow on the communal ideals of the colonists whose power the display enforced. In both instances, the use of these bodies signaled the aggressive posture of a precarious new regime contending for authority in the area, of a group that would use the dead and dying strategically to fortify its survivors and to display a capacity for violence through which it sought to secure power. The problem was that this narrative was completely at odds with the narrative of suffering and election that William Bradford later used to sanctify the project of plantation. Therefore these spectacular bodies, so crucial to the political landscape of Plymouth, were added to the roster of corpses that disappeared from his history of settlement.

Bradford's treatment of the debacle at Wessagusset is similarly occluded. He states that a messenger (who we know was Phineas Pratt) arrives in Plymouth and confirms existing rumors of an Indian conspiracy. He continues, "This made them make the more haste, and dispatched a boat away with Captain Standish and some men, who found them in a miserable condition, out of which he rescued them and helped them to some relief, cut off some few of the chief conspirators, and according to his order, offered to bring them all hither if they thought good, and they should fare no worse than themselves, till Mr. Weston or some supply came to them."[88] Remarkably, that is the whole of Bradford's report on the raid at Wessagusset. In the rest of the long paragraph that follows, Bradford provides details about Weston's men taking leave of Wessagusset, focusing particularly on

Standish's beneficent and stabilizing oversight of their departure. As with his account of the first winter at Plymouth, Bradford quickly dispatches the specter of death and instead erects a display of moral fortitude in the face of mortal danger. He ends the Wessagusset saga in a meditation on pride, humility, and comparative suffering: "This was the end of these, that some time boasted of their strength (being all able, lusty men) and what they would do and bring to pass in comparison of the people here, who had many women and children and weak ones amongst them. And said at their first arrival, when they saw the wants here, that they would take another course and not to fall into such a condition as this simple people were come to. But a man's way is not in his own power, God can make the weak to stand. Let him also that standeth take heed lest he fall."[89]

What was important, then, to Bradford's historical enterprise? Not the armed confrontation that quashed an Indian coalition's potential attack on English settlements, nor the economic aftermath of the dispersal of both Indians and colonists from Wessagusset, nor the political potency of that first banner to be raised at Plymouth—Witawamut's impaled head trailed by a piece of linen soaked in his blood. As we have seen, descriptions of all of these elements were prominent in colonists' writing immediately following the raid (including Bradford's own correspondence), but they are nowhere to be found in Bradford's *Of Plymouth Plantation*. What was important to Bradford's history was to schematize the story of Weston's men and the Indian conspiracy in such a way that the Plymouth settlers, in their long-suffering piety, remained distinct from both the profane English and the duplicitous Indians. Only forty miles north of Plymouth, there had been a disastrous winter of disease, starvation, conspiracy, and social collapse. This crisis involved several groups of people who were intricately connected, and it changed the social and economic landscape for all of them. Nonetheless the story of Wessagusset had to be written as a thing apart. Bradford had to disavow Plymouth's participation in this disaster as much as possible, obscuring both the events and their cultural reverberation, in order to control the disruptive meaning of the unnatural deaths in the pages of his history.

Surely, Bradford's near elision of Wessagusset was in part a response to suspicions aroused by Plymouth's role in executing the raid. Bradford's contemporaries and modern historians alike have noted that Plymouth's leaders had a vested interest in seeing the Wessagusset venture disband and fail so that they could consolidate power in their own settlement and secure its political and economic prominence. They readily took advantage of their neighbors' vulnerability by pushing an already unstable situation into violent crisis and then framing the story in a way that made them seem like faultless bystanders.[90] True perhaps, but there is a specific textual anxiety around the Wessagusset raid that has to do not only with politics but also with the problem of remains. Bradford's terse description of the murders at Wessagusset—that Standish and his men had "cut off some few of the chief conspirators"—is embedded in a story framed as a rescue mission. This articulation not only exonerates the Plymouth leaders but also, more generally, minimizes the alarm, extremity, and violence of the winter and early spring of 1623. Even if the image of Witawamut's head mounted on Plymouth fort was seared into the memories of all who witnessed it, Bradford the historian cannot allow that dismembered corpse into his narrative. But neither can he fully deny it. Like so many other uncanny remains, the head is both present and absent. He writes that they "cut off" the chief conspirator, not that they cut off his head.

Bradford's text then pushes his wary treatment of this violence and its totem even further away by immediately returning to a portrait of the Plymouth colonists as a suffering people. The presence of Witawamut's head is obscured by the historian's invocation of the "women and children and weak ones" of Plymouth, these nonpolitical, "simple people," silent and powerless before the boastful mockery of lusty men. By narratively conjuring the distinctiveness of an explicitly feminized, infantilized, enervated people, humbled but not humiliated in the poignancy of their desperation, Bradford's history conceals colonial scenes of calculated violence. Even more broadly, the righteous quality of suffering thus imagined also removes his people from the temporal exigencies arising from their connections to coastal Indians and neighboring settlers. It first identifies suffering as the only available response to "such a condition as this simple people were come to" and then negates the possibility of different kinds of suffering experienced by Massachusett and Wessagusset people. Many bodies disappear into the rhetorical shadows in *Of Plymouth Plantation*: the piled up dead; the pantomime of English sentinels; the decapitated fierce opponent; the emaciated figures of would-be traders. None is visible in Bradford's account. However, histories can also "make the weak to stand" and thus offer a different form of protection and control. In Plymouth's history, it is the afflicted bodies of women and children and enfeebled men that are made a spectacle in Bradford's discourse of sadness and misery.

A Dead Reckoning

During the final years of his history's composition, Bradford was still concerned with setting colonial deaths in Plymouth to rights. The vexing question would not rest: how could he preserve the memory of the colonial dead without confronting the agitating problem of remains? Bradford's encomium for William Brewster, perhaps the longest and most elaborate portrait in this history, can be read as an attempt to resolve this problem. Central to the story of Elder Brewster's life is the story of his death, which Bradford tells in detail, literally breath by breath: "He had this blessing added by the Lord to all the rest; to die in his bed, in peace, amongst the midst of his friends, who mourned and wept over him and ministered what help and comfort they could unto him, and he again recomforted them whilst he could. . . . [H]e died without any pangs at all. A few hours before, he drew his breath short, and some few minutes before his last, he drew his breath long as a man fallen into a sound sleep without any pangs or gaspings, and so sweetly departed this life unto a better."[91] In bed, at peace, surrounded by friends; hearing whispered prayers and words of comfort; breathing into death as into a deep, sweet sleep—this was a scene that Bradford could narrate as an emblem of a good death in the wilderness.

Brewster represented the last link to the leadership of the Leyden congregation. It was especially crucial that his death be narrated as ordered and exemplary and in contrast to the morally compromised Pilgrim settlement, which had deviated from its founding idealism. Yet even as Bradford composed this peaceful death scene, the first years of settlement were stubbornly fixed in his mind, for in the very next sentence, the historian moves from the honored deathbed to his ever-present memory of the early settlement's terrible struggle for survival. "I would now demand of any," he challenges, "what he was the worse for any former sufferings? What do I say, worse? Nay, sure he was the better, and they now added to his honour." This internal defense is laid at the threshold of what Bradford calls a "memorial to the just," a textual monument that, unlike the dead, will neither fall nor rot. To see how important this kind of monument was to Bradford's history, compare his treatment of Brewster's death to his treatment of the death of the Pilgrims' first governor, John Carver. On a hot day in April 1621, Carver stumbled feebly out of a planting field, fell unconscious, died, and was, in Bradford's cryptic phrase, "buried in the best manner they could."[92] Unlike Carver's tersely narrated death, Brewster's death occasions page upon page of chronology, description, and honorific memory, ultimately leading to an awed mediation on the marvelous longevity of the Pilgrim Fathers. Surely the horror of such a staggering number of early deaths, which Bradford's narrative so anxiously circumvents, was providentially resolved by the long lives of those survivors. Surely the Promised Land was not lost, despite the carcasses wasted in the wilderness. Even though Brewster's eulogy forces Bradford to refer to the litany of perils that befell so many, he devotes himself to the task because it allows him to claim decisively that Plymouth's dead should be held up to view only because they were everywhere upheld, and not abandoned, by God.

Eventually, *Of Plymouth Plantation* trails off into silence; the last entry reads, "Anno 1647. And Anno 1648," followed by blank pages. However, Bradford continues the struggle to find a proper place for the dead in his history. Having reached an impasse, Bradford takes up another method of accounting: a double entry register of life and death at Plymouth. First, he composes a list that names and enumerates the immigrants of 1620. Then he composes another list covering "the decreasings and increasings of these persons and such changes as hath passed over them and theirs in this thirty years."[93] In two columns, with an entry for each family group, Bradford first identifies those who came over, those who died, and what progeny they left behind. He then does the math and records the number of their ultimate "increase." For example, the entry for Miles Standish reads, "Captain Standish his wife died in the first sickness and he married again and hath four sons living and some are dead," with the number "4" written in the second column. The entry is tidy; what survives is the new remainder of "four sons living." Standish's first wife and their dead children sink into one column, while the four living sons remain visible in the other. The entry below this reads, "Mr. Martin, he and all his died in the first infection, not long after the arrival," and for this family the number column is left blank. The deaths are recorded, but the "zero" does not appear in the ledger. With no living to count, the dead simply disappear. Whatever use such a reckoning would prove to anyone in the future, Bradford believed that he would "rest in my own benefit" after composing it. He initiates this new task of recounting with the words, "I will therefore take them in order as they lie." Naming and numbering the dead as he never could in his narrative account, Bradford steadily combats the problem of remains by calculating the natural increase of the remainder. Unlike a discursive reckoning, this kind of double entry accounting lets him represent a Pilgrim progeny "sprung up" like seed, despite a past of rampant death and a present of continuing departure. Released from the requirements of narrative, Bradford can finally approach the dead rationally, methodically, and "take them in order as they lie."

In the end, this history cannot allow for corpses to overwhelm the living. It cannot have bodies falling indiscriminately, or strewn promiscuously, or propped up in the woods, or erected on stakes. Even as he exhausts his own historical practice, Bradford still works to get the names and dates and memories of those bodies all lined up in order. Finally, it is a way to bury the dead. In a history of origins, the corpse has to be forced underground to become seed for the perpetuation of a hallowed narrative. In the end, perhaps, the dead were the most important crop the people at Plymouth planted. But if Bradford's history makes a great effort to control the problem of remains, it also cannot help but leave behind an enigmatic trace. The settlers were "scarce able to bury the dead," he writes, and historical memory has enshrined the phrase. "Scarce": the sense of frustration and inadequacy embedded in that word has garnered appreciable pity for the Pilgrims' plight, but it also leaves a small space open through which the grim disquiet of settlement history can be glimpsed.

CHAPTER 4

Barbados: Wild Extravagance

[T]he place being extreme beautiful and lovely, could not but secretly harbor in it the Spirit of Love, a passion not to be governed. And therefore I hope, you will pardon my wild extravagancy.
—Richard Ligon, *A True & Exact History of the Island of Barbados*

For English people in the seventeenth century, the West Indies existed as a place of astonishing but intractable extremes. The strange climate that produced a fruit as wondrous as the pineapple also brought hurricanes that could wipe out a settlement in a day. Sugar was the source of unimaginable wealth, but planters drank themselves to death with the rum thrown off by its manufacture. Barbados was the jewel of the English empire; it was also "the dunghill whereon England doth cast forth its rubbish."[1] It was, to use a phrase from the colonial literature, a place of serious "Commodities and Incommodities."[2] The tropics were places of strange beauty and gratification, if only one could figure out how to survive them. When Richard Ligon arrived in Barbados in 1647, he learned that "few or none of them that first set foot there" only twenty years before "were now living" (23).[3] The more recent white transplants he encountered "were so grievously visited with the plague, (or as killing a disease), that before a month was expired after our Arrival, the living were hardly able to bury the dead" (66). Although the scarce-buried dead in Barbados did not incite the kind of typological crisis that they did in Plymouth, it was impossible to ignore the fact that colonial life in the West Indies often meant miserable conditions, rampant sickness, and early death. And yet the torrid zone was also represented as a place of undreamed-of splendor and consummate pleasures. In his first introduction to the tropics, the sixty-two-year-old Ligon saw two young African sisters coming down to fill their calabash vessels at a well and was instantly transported into such raptures that he felt compelled to ask his readers to excuse his "wild extravagancy." Ungovernable passion, he confessed, was the very nature of the place. It was difficult for English settlers to reconcile the presence of these simultaneous dangers and desires, and almost from the moment English people began to set themselves up in the West Indies, they represented their experiences there through a language of excess and inordinate extremes.

Tropes of the prodigious and the volatile, of the luxurious and the dangerous created what I call a "colonial tropic," a discursive framework of extremity and extravagance through which West Indian colonials described lives that could not be imagined in England. The colonial tropic embedded excess in the nature of the place by using a language of intensifiers: such unaccountable pleasures; such insurmountable perils; such extraordinary differences. The rhetoric bound danger to desire and then defined that fusion as the essential condition of West Indian coloniality. As in other colonial places, this discourse was built around the seemingly inescapable intensities of settlement life that suspended the norms of Englishness. Writing settlement in this way displaced the violence and avarice of colonial plantation by creating a situation in which the environment itself seemed to enact a force—foreign, irreconcilable, ungovernable—upon settlers, who succumbed what they could not resist. In Barbados violence and avarice later returned undisguised and in full force on the sugar plantations, but by that time a model of excess had already been fully associated with the space of the tropics, an inescapable condition to which nature was seen to admit no alternative.

I use the term "colonial tropic" to refer at once to tropical places and to linguistic tropes—that is, both to the English colonies of the equatorial zone and to the figural and discursive structures through which that colonial space was constructed. My use of the term borrows from Srinivas Aravamudan's study of the "tropicalization" of colonial discourse in the eighteenth century but applies it differently to the settlement period.[4] I agree with Aravamudan that the discourses that sought to define colonized places and people instead generated a rhetorical surplus, destabilizing the representational system they were meant to secure. It is also clear that these texts' investment in creating an exotic other instead created patterns of ambiguity and ambivalence, and that the political aim to normalize colonization was continually frustrated by this ungovernable textual malleability.

However, as much as the earliest constructions of this colonial tropic seem to lay the groundwork for "tropicalization" of colonial others in the eighteenth-century English literary forms that Aravamudan studies, settlement-era writing was shaped by different contexts, genres, and motivations. In this earlier period, the colonial tropic sought to define English settlers themselves in the still precarious sites where their colonial condition was first emerging.

In the early Caribbean, as in other sites of early settlement, permanent plantation was not a foregone conclusion. English colonies were destroyed, driven off, resisted by native inhabitants, and threatened by other European colonial powers. In this rough experimental phase, even when English claims over the islands held, the settlements were often internally in utter disarray. From these disorderly outposts, colonial writers from this period struggled to employ what Barbara Shapiro calls "a discourse of fact" by writing first-hand reports that put "particular emphasis on 'particular' things, practices, or events . . . both human and natural."[5] With the authority of the eyewitness, those who lived "beyond the line" described the dramatically different natural world of the tropics, but they also could not help but emphasize how Englishmen were being transformed by their experiences in these unfamiliar environments. Although the intention was to inform, the colonial tropic introduced a turbulent rhetoric in these texts, one in which sudden reversals between extreme states ended up affirming the radical unfamiliarity of their colonial condition. In the early seventeenth century, then, becoming colonial in the tropics also meant becoming an other to England, as settlers became identified with the space of the tropical otherness their writing described.

In addition to referring to a place and to a way of constructing that place, the colonial tropic refers to a movement beyond limits that was seen to define the behavior of Englishmen who ventured there. To European eyes, the West Indies was a place "beyond the line." During this era this piratical arena was demarcated by a policy of "no peace beyond the line," regardless of European international treaties. Because no nation could afford to retaliate against, recompense, or defend the activities of rogue agents, the forceful will of individual actors replaced the rule of law.[6] To move "beyond the line," then, was to move into a space beyond boundaries, one that did not accord with established relations between states. Movement into the tropics also seemed to bring on a state of moral turpitude—indolent, profligate, violent behavior that likewise trespassed boundaries. The inherent dynamisms of the West Indies were thought to make it impossible for men to remain upright there. An early visitor's conviction that men could not "lie long quiett in these parts" was widespread.[7] It was as if Englishmen in the tropics were pulled off their moral axis by some force embedded in the very nature of these places, resulting in the disordered societies they invariably produced. As Karen Kupperman has demonstrated, English fears of what "hot places" would do to their temperate bodies were everywhere articulated, but these torrid dangers were not limited to the physical body alone.[8] To move to the West Indies was also to move inexorably toward debauchery, corruption, and avarice. Although the image of the profligate Barbadian colonist would persist throughout the eighteenth century, in the earliest literature it was soon established that Englishmen could no more tame their own natures in the tropics than they could tame the wild nature that surrounded them.

This early literature demonstrates that we can analyze early Caribbean settlement using a similar framework as we did with Roanoke, Plymouth, and Jamestown: the first forms of coloniality emerged from the crises of settlement, and becoming colonial was often represented through accounts of what catastrophes befell settlers at these outposts. Here too places where Englishmen were becoming colonial were represented as sites of exception, where difference and violence were often proximate terms. Although West Indian settlements were different from settlements in North America, they were not entirely so. To be sure, the distinctions are readily apparent: location; climate; geography; demography; archipelagic relations; native populations; a longer and more complex history of European colonization; and eventually, of course, the plantation. As Antonio Benítez-Rojo writes, "[O]ne of the most reasonable ways to explain the regular difference that we notice in the area is to begin with the plantation; still more, I think that its multiplied presence may be used in establishing the differences not just within the Caribbean itself but also in its relation to Europe, Africa, Asia, North and South America."[9] However, when we use the entrenchment of the plantation complex in the second half of the seventeenth century as a starting point, we position the first waves of settlement as a historical "not-yet"—a vague or floating precursor to a fully articulated slave society.

Alternatively, working up to the plantation rather than back from it exposes a colonial discourse that described settlement through representations of ungovernable conditions, a discourse that was operative from the very beginning of English writings from the West Indies. Beginning *before* the plantation, then, better shows the connections between the West Indian and North American colonies, as well as their differences. Therefore this chapter begins with two early texts from the English West Indian archive that demonstrate how English identities and behaviors deteriorated in the places of tropical settlement as they too, like the North American colonies, were located beyond the bounds of Englishness. The central text discussed, Richard Ligon's *A True and Exact History of the Island of Barbados*, depicts the natural, social, and economic orders in Barbados as the colony stood at the threshold of the sugar revolution and the plantation complex. In it, a discourse of deliberate systemization contends with the intensities that still defined life in the colony twenty years after its founding. In Ligon's account of the beginning of the sugar economy, the excess that characterized the colonial tropic from the start of settlement becomes deeply embedded in the plantation system, as it revolves around the extravagant surplus and intensifying violence of an emerging slave society. "Wild extravagancy" was a quickly changeable state, and whether it was located in the context of natural beauty, sudden wealth, dissolute behavior, or brazen cruelty, its profuse qualities remain linked to the unstable excesses that characterized coloniality in England's West Indies.

A West Indian Hourglass

The first English-sponsored settlement on the "Wild Coast" of Guiana was set up in 1604 with forty-six men and boys. Their plan of action was not exactly clear. Although such a tiny group of English colonists could not compete with the Spanish on the Orinoco River or the Portuguese on the Amazon, they thought they could occupy a little land on the Wiapoco River and survive. They were wrong. Like so many of England's tenuous attempts to secure a foothold in the Americas, the Guiana settlement was on the brink of collapse within a year of its founding. In 1605 a ship carrying reinforcements—needed supplies and new settlers—to the colony was diverted from its purpose by storms, mutinies, and dwindling provisions. For the captain and crew, supplying a puny outpost in Guiana was not a priority. After seventeen weeks at sea, with patience and resources growing shorter daily, the seamen turned on their passengers and left sixty-seven of them to fend for themselves on the island of Saint Lucia. The Guiana colony was wiped out while awaiting supplies, and the marooned men fared little better; only four of them ever made it back to England. No account from the failed Wiapoco colony exists, but John Nicholl, one of the men stranded by the supply ship, wrote a "true and tragicall discourse" upon his return from Saint Lucia, relating all that happened on that "Island of Caniballs, or Men-eaters in the

West-Indyes."[10] Its title invited English readers to peer into *An Houre Glasse of Indian Newes*, where would be revealed "the most lamentable miseries, and distressed Calamaties indured by 67 Englishmen."

Nicholl delivers the wondrous and woeful tale his title promises, beginning with the men's perilous sea passage, their arrival at Saint Lucia, and their attempt to settle on the island. The small English party bought "houses" from "an Indian Captaine called Anthonie" and lived there for several months in sometimes friendly, sometimes tense relation with the native population, who, as "Captaine Anthonie's" name indicates, were already familiar with European colonizers and seafarers.[11] Eventually the stranded Englishmen proved to be like other colonists: eager to mine the island's resources while depending on the locals for food. At that point the Indians decided to oust them. While some members of the English company were on a mountain looking for gold and the rest were happily following their Indian hosts in hopes of a meal, the first ambush began. In his report Nicholl pulls back from the scene for a moment to list for his reader, and himself, a litany of disasters:

> In all these extreme dangers and imminent Calamites which all this while we endured, let the Christian Reader judge in what a perplexed state we were plunged, seeing still one misery to follow another, and each misery farre exceeding the former: As first, our danger at Sea to be famished: then a comfortless remedy against famishment, to be left in a farre remote and unknowne place, amongst a cruel, barbarous and inhumane people, without hope of ever having any meanes to recover the sign of our native and deare country and friends: Then the losse of our Captaine (and others) which before (in all extremity) was still some comfort unto us: And now (lastly) these lamentable stratagems of the massacre of our fellowes and friends, therein seeing as in a Glasse, the utter ruine and Butcherly murthering of our owne selves.[12]

In this passage it is not just the Christian reader who peers into the *Houre Glasse of Indian Newes*. The men who watch the massacre peer "in a Glasse" as well, one in which their ruin is both foretold and reflected in the deaths of their friends and fellows. As in an hourglass, their time is measured and running out, but as in a mirror, they see their "owne selves" being killed. To both writer and reader, these deaths seemed inevitable from the moment the

English were stranded on the "Island of Caniballs," but the hourglass could be turned over again and again to watch the sand spiral down to its inescapable fate. The extreme dangers, imminent calamities, and exceeding misery were part of a colonial drama both predictable and spectacular. The combination of wonder and peril, of irresistible intrigue and the certainty of terror in the wild tropics of America kept Nicholl's readers turning the pages.

Peter Hulme and Neil Whitehead identify Nicholl's narrative as "the most detailed and valuable account of Carib-European contact before the full-scale attempts at settlement on the islands of the Lesser Antilles in the 1620s."[13] As a hinge between exploration and colonization, *An Houre Glasse of Indian Newes* has both historical and literary significance for early West Indian settlement. Nicholl's is the earliest English report in which the West Indies figures as something other than a stopover or a site of plunder. Sir Francis Drake famously raided the area by land and sea, and ships would often stop there to refresh and re-provision, but the Wiapoco settlement, which was Nicholl's original destination, represented the first English attempt at living in the torrid zones. It was also on this 1605 journey to Guiana that the English made their first claim on Barbados. Stopping there for much-needed provisions, the ship's crew erected a cross and carved these words into a nearby tree: "James K. of E. and of this island." Although no settlement was established, this act was unambiguously a ceremony of possession.[14] The marooned company did not set out to settle Saint Lucia—and they hardly could have, given the native population's ability to defend the island—but within the first days of their island sojourn, Nicholl began to refer to Saint Lucia as "home." Sent out as English planters bound for Guiana and abandoned en route, the company found themselves in the strange position of being colonists without a colony.

In addition to its historical primacy, Nicholl's text is important in its modes of representing the West Indies. At this initiating moment, we can see in the *Houre Glasse* important elements that would continue to characterize the English colonial tropic. Chief among these is the depiction of wild extravagance as a primal and primary condition that expressed the essence of the islands. To the English, nothing native to the tropics—its people, vegetation, weather—could ever be moderate. The "Carribees" were seductive, inscrutable, lush, and lurid places where Englishmen would be exposed to outrageous fortune (good or ill) beyond imagining. This early text also demonstrates that well before sugar production transformed the colonial Caribbean, those islands were depicted as places of misery. Left comfortless in a remote land, enduring misery upon misery, and vulnerable to treacherous savages, the English in Nicholl's story face the same perils as English settlers face in other catastrophic colonial narratives. Across these accounts, there is first and foremost the devastating realization of how far the outpost is from the home culture, and how easily forgotten. If any illusion of a sustaining connection existed when Nicholl and his fellows were deposited on Saint Lucia, it was surely severed by the parting actions of the sailors. After telling "Anthonie" that the marooned men planned to cut his throat, the sailors quickly boarded the ship and fired on the stranded settlers before sailing away.

Second, there is in these accounts an emphasis on the settlers' suffering as unprecedented. "[M]y selfe with my associates have had a wofull experience," Nicholl claims, "as ever (in my judgement) had any creatures living under the Canopie of Heaven."[15] Like the first settlers in Roanoke, Jamestown, and Plymouth, Nicholl asserts that to be an Englishman in the New World is to live in a "tragicall" state. Third, one finds the claim that the misery of settlement remains unspeakable. "To speak of the misery we indured there," Nicholl writes, "it is impossible; for I cannot express it."[16] All he can do is relate the catastrophe endured in the Americas, "each misery farre exceeding the former," and ask an ideal and sympathetic reader to imagine that which defies description.[17]

Finally, as in descriptions of the first North American settlements, native people who resist colonization play a central role. Saint Lucia is not only populated; it also exists within a dense network of Amerindian groups able to mount counterstrategies to colonial invasion. As Hilary McD. Beckles writes, during the early settlement period, "[t]he English and the French . . . were aware that most of their settlements would have to come to terms with Kalinago [Carib] resistance."[18] When Barbados became the center of England's colonial efforts in the Caribbean, however, representation of native resistance disappeared from accounts of its settlement because the island no longer had a permanent Amerindian presence. This was in part because of the reorganization and consolidation of native communities onto other islands in response to colonial threats. Early writing about Barbados thus occludes a larger history of violent confrontations between colonizers and native peoples, focusing instead on political wranglings between English factions on the island or on depictions of nature that sought to demonstrate empirical mastery of the tropics. Because these texts do not depict Amerindians who retain control of their territory, the "uninhabited" island of Barbados becomes an arena in which the prospects and dangers of colonizing the West Indies can be discussed exclusively in terms of English politics or tropical nature. Nicholl's 1607 text from Saint Lucia provides a background against which this rhetorical disappearance of original inhabitants is made visible.

From the first moment to the last, Nicholl's narrative depicts both the nature of the place and its people as wild, overwhelming, and beyond reckoning. He describes the Caribs who first approach the English boat as the strangest, ugliest, most demonic men he has ever seen: "all naked, with long blacke hair hanging downe their shoulders, their bodies all painted with red, and from their eares to their eyes, they do make these strokes with red, which makes them looke like Divels."[19] Here are the fabled, "most cruell Caniballs, and man-eaters" of the New World in the flesh. However, instead of attacking the passengers and crew, the "Anticke" natives surprise them by bringing a bounty aboard: "Tobacco, Plantains, Potatoes, Pines, Sugar Canes, and diverse other fruits, with Hens, Chicken, Turtles & Guavas."[20] These exotic pleasures arouse in the starving shipmen new appetites and satisfy them as promptly. Repeatedly and increasingly Nicholl's story turns like this from fear to pleasure, from fascination to panic. Sudden reversal is the text's dramatic mode.

For example, when the first tropical storm hits the island, Nicholl describes a "most horrible" scene: "it began to raine, thunder, and lighten so extreamly . . . and so it continued all night, with the most horrible thunder claps that ever I heard, with lighting and raine as light as day."[21] The men wait it out by sitting all night before fires, smoking, drinking, singing "with extraordinary mirth, little forseeing the danger that befell to us the next day." The next morning they invite the Indians into their houses "and were very merrye and pleasant with them, and gave them Aqua Vitae which they delighted much in." Spirits high and steadily imbibed, the men "fell to a singing of Catches with the Carrebys." Looking back on it through the hourglass/mirror of his tale, Nicholl ruefully notes that the English could have killed the natives all there and then: "We had a hundreth and above of them within our houses without either bowe or arrows."[22] But they drank and sang together instead. The uncanny proximity of fear and mirth, danger and camaraderie, ominous thunder and merry music creates an atmosphere of unsettling paradox. The necessary conditions for ordering knowledge and determining action are destabilized by the turbulence, unpredictability, and extreme difference of the tropics. Inherent in that difference is the combination of danger and extravagance that, even at this early juncture, characterized English writing from the West Indies.

When the massacre of the English begins, it does so in an atmosphere of friendship. Indians and Englishmen walk together in good company into an Indian village, where they "had beene often times well used." Nicholl describes their state as "careless and secure," forgetful that if their companions were truly the notorious cannibals of America and not just last night's drinking partners, to be simultaneously careless *and* secure would not have been an option.[23] Soon the heat grows so oppressive that the English need to disrobe and disarm in order to keep up with the Indians' pace. One Englishman, "lighte and coole" after removing his gun, is "playing arme and arme with two Carrabye" out ahead of the group when the Indian leader, making "as though he would imbrace him," slashes his body straight through with a long sword instead. Suddenly arrows fly from everywhere and Indians fall flat to the ground, "shouting and crying in a most hellish noyse, naming us by our names when they hit us." Nicholl calls it a "butcherly Murthering" but describes it as a display of extraordinary precision. He recounts how, in addition to calling out the name of each man they target, the Indians "purposed to make choyse in which place to hit us, of some they shot in the faces, others through the Shoulders, and of others they would naile their feete and the ground together."[24] Nicholl receives two arrows in the back as he flees the scene. The fighting continues for six or seven days, until the English "hold out a flag of Truce," which is promptly accepted upon condition that they leave the island.

Thunder and singing, frolic and ambush, playful intimacy and hellish screams—these strange and sudden reversals structure Nicholl's colonial tropic. Peter Hulme suggests that because the English were unable to reconcile their image of "the cannibal" with the experience of native hospitality, and because they were unable to see that their own incursionary actions led to violent conflict, the only narrative that they could construct was "a narrative of treachery in which the initial kindness was a ruse to establish trust before the natives' 'natural' violence emerged from behind the mask."[25] While Europeans regularly attributed this kind of treachery to Indians, Nicholl's discourse does not limit the reversals to natives alone. The miseries upon miseries that the marooned settlers suffer on this island reverse their own situation from Englishmen embarked for the New World to colonials whose traumatic experience has made them as "wofull . . . [as] any creatures living under the Canopie of Heaven." Nicholl records their catastrophe in stunning detail—even to numbering the twenty arrows he extracted from one fellow's dying body—in his effort simultaneously to give a close account of these events and also to communicate their chaos. The method through which he pursues that task is to shuttle from one extreme to the other—from the giant turtles who give up seven hundred eggs at a time, to the arrows that come quickly on every side; from the men who walk boldly into the Indians' village, to the men who are lost in a "wildernesse of woe."[26]

Although Henry Colt's 1631 journal neither asks for nor shows compassion for West Indian colonial settlers, it stands as another expression of an English colonial tropic in which torrid places, extravagant rhetoric, and unruly behavior combine. Colt was a member of the Essex gentry who set out to establish a plantation on the island of Saint Christopher, which the English and the French had split between them after having massacred all the native inhabitants. At that point Barbados was so far from being a major point of entry to the English West Indies that Colt's ship tacked back and forth for five days looking for it, leading him to conclude that it would be easier to find a sixpence thrown into the heath than to find Barbados. Finally arriving, he was appalled. The whole place was "desolate and disorderly," reeking of "slowth & negligence."[27] Although his journal was written for his son, Colt could not help but address the planters directly, the better to direct his tirade against their dissolution.

After complaining of the gnats, ants, and unpleasant heat, he berates the planters—all young, unbridled men—for drinking, fighting, and otherwise indulging their "younge and hott bloods" and "fiery spirits." Then he turns to their abuse of the land: "Your grownde & plantations shewe whatt you are, they lye like the ruins of some village lately burned,—heer a great timber tree half burned, in an other place a rafter singed all black. There stands a stubb of a tree above two yards high, all the earth covered black with cenders. [N]othinge is cleer."[28] The disorder was not only pervasive; it was also contagious. While Colt is spared the sickness he calls "the danger of the Tropick," he soon grows distempered in other ways and begins an extraordinary drinking binge, increasing his habitual intake of "2 dramms of hott water" at a meal to a full 30. There seems to have been no limit to the excess. Colt admits that despite his age and wisdom, if he had stayed only a few days more, "I doe believe I should have binn brought to the encrease of 60." He lays his rapid degeneration squarely at the feet of the locals: "In a few dayes you corrupted me."[29] The servants are idle, hanging around the ship all day, shirking their duties and looking for handouts. The free settlers are no better; in fact, Colt reports, "I never saw any man at work."[30]

Considering the hot weather, hot water, hot blood, and hot tempers, Colt concludes that the "Devill" must govern the island: "Sureley the Devill the spirit of discord has great power in America, & loosed he is as well amongst Christians as Infidells; & wonder nott why the naturalls warr soe much the one with the other. Who is he that can lie long in quiett in these parts? For all men are heer made subject to the power of this Infernall Spiritt. And fight they must, although it be with their owne friends. Ther be poysonous trees whose gumm hurteth the eyes of such as hewes them downe, & divers sorts of fruit & trees not yet known."[31] This passage begins with the certainty that America is the devil's dominion and ends with a seeming non sequitur about an unknown diversity of flora as yet undiscovered. Tropes of the New World as both forbidding and beckoning had been intertwined from the first accounts of European exploration; the difference here is that the figure of the distempered settler intervenes. Although settlement seeks to master and possess the land, in Barbados the process works in reverse, the land mastering and possessing the settlers. In these parts, the conditions for settlement could not hold. Work, knowledge, cohesion, and cooperation all dissolved into torpor. Even the land seemed to resist an English-style "improvement." A poisonous tree may well spit in the face of the man who tries to fell it, and blind him. However, as in later reports from the colonial West Indies, Colt in his journal toggles between being disgusted by tropical excess and fascinated by its potentialities. Regardless of the impossible conditions he describes, Colt is also convinced that opportunity is everywhere.

Because of the climate, the air, and the soil, things on Barbados grew "with a marvelous swiftness." There were good fishing, good harbors (once you found them), and a natural abundance of food. In addition to the native fruit, fish, and fowl, the island was full of wild hogs, which were originally left by the Portuguese so that their ships could reprovision there, but whose population had swelled to such an extent that the English settlers were killing fifteen hundred a week. Colt was shocked by this rate of slaughter, writing that the settlers sometimes caught hogs, tied them up, and then were too lazy to go back and collect them, leaving the animals to starve. On the one hand, it was an outrageous waste to kill so many, but on the other hand, the hogs were unbelievably delicious. Colt confesses, "I eat one of them baked in a pye at ther governours & it liked me soe well, as I durst sware ther fathers & predecessors that lived & dyed in England weer never fed dayly with so good meat."[32] These hogs were a symbol for the extravagant and often wasteful excesses that were embraced in colonial tropics. It was clear to Colt that the settlers' English ancestors who had never tasted such good meat were better men by far, and yet here were corrupt young planters throwing a finer flesh to their dogs without thinking twice.

Despite its alarming corruptions, Barbados stirred Colt's imagination and desire. The Barbadian settlers led his body and mind to shameful debauchery, but Barbados itself was intoxicating. It excited in him the desire to possess: "[T]o confesse truly all the Ilands that I have passed by & seen unto this day, not any pleaseth me soe well. . . . Would it weer my owne & thus seated in any part of Europe. I will nott say whatt I could be in short time, if the princes of Europe by force of covetousnesse would not take it from me."[33] This fantasy neatly encapsulates one problem of colonizing the tropics. Holding possession of the island could make a man great in ways he could scarcely imagine, but only if the island were somehow portable, "seated in any part of Europe." However, if such a thrilling place were safely transported into familiar waters, it would immediately be vulnerable to the rapacious grasp of princes and kings. The problem was that one had to be in the tropics in order to possess the islands, but to be in the tropics was to enter a state of dispossession. Fifty years later, large-scale sugar production made a version of Colt's fantasy possible. In place by the 1670s was a vast social and economic machinery that allowed absentee plantation owners and slave-trade profiteers to transport incredible wealth from the West Indies to Europe while shielding themselves from the horrors of the sugar islands. They were thus princes and arrivistes at once. But in 1631 sugar was not yet the vehicle that at once bound England tightly to the West Indies but simultaneously allowed, through its material and cultural refinement, for English people to disavow the depths of that connection.[34]

Colt could look with disdain at uncultivated land, uncouth planters, and undisciplined servants. He could surmise that even with its natural beauty, the tropical world was probably an outlying precinct of hell. He could drink too much at every meal and smack his lips over hog pie at the governor's table, but he could not quite pin down what the English might do in the West Indies that would be "worthy of ourselves."[35] The contradictions of life in the tropical zone were ever present but resisted summation. Many times in his journal, Colt stops to catalog the natural products of the island—their shape, form, taste, and use. He describes something strange and new, but he can never be sure whether it will delight or disgust, harm or heal. Sometimes the answer is both. "The prickle Apple," he reports, is "a good moyst fruit. But the prickle pear within [is] as red as blood, keep but your fingers from the pricking & itt may be placed amongeth the best fruits of all."[36] To some extent Richard Ligon's *True & Exact History of the Island of Barbados* is about this problem: how a man could consume the best of the fruits of the West Indies but keep his fingers from the pricking.

Obtaining High Perfection

Ligon's extensive account of life on Barbados from the late 1640s to the early 1650s is the central text of the early West Indian archive. During this period the sugar revolution that would fundamentally change the course of England's Atlantic world was under way. Ligon was in Barbados only from 1647 to 1650 before his own "grievous and tedious sickness" forced him to return to England (198). All the same, he measured his stay not in terms of years but in terms of sugar: "from my first arrival on the Island, when planting there, was but in its infancy, and but faintly understood, to the time I left the place, when it was grown to a high perfection" (147). To appreciate the explosive growth achieved by reaching this "high perfection," consider that in 1637 there was no sugar production at all in Barbados; in 1645, 40 percent of the island was planted with sugar; and by the 1670s, this island of 166 square miles produced 65 percent of all the sugar consumed in England. Barbados had become, as Philip Curtin writes, "the most specialized economy in the world."[37] The population of the island changed radically in response. In the first part of the 1650s, both European and African populations stood at about twenty thousand. By the 1680s the white population still numbered around twenty thousand, but the black population had grown to about fifty thousand, a growth rate of 150 percent. By the decade's end, Barbados was "four times as densely settled as England," and three-quarters of its people were enslaved.[38] This dizzying transformation is often depicted through numbers, percentages, and growth rates and concomitant denotations of economic, demographic, and ecological upheaval. However, literary analysis too is a method for understanding historical change, and a close reading of Richard Ligon's careful record of Barbados allows us to move more slowly and deliberately through the tensions of these turbulent years.

Ligon's history is the first of its kind, a wide-ranging account of colonial life in the Caribbean in the mid-seventeenth century. It is hybrid in form, taking on the natural history of the island, the social history of its inhabitants, and the personal history of Ligon's experiences and copious observations during his sojourn there; but its final function is unique. His *History of the Island of Barbados* is the first detailed how-to manual for curing sugar and procuring enormous wealth from its manufacture. For readers curious about the English West Indies at this time, there was no topic of greater interest. Sugar is both the frame and the engine of the text. The title page prominently advertises that in addition to giving a history and map of Barbados, the book provides copper engravings of "the Ingenio that makes the Sugar," as well as detailed information about the buildings, tools, and arrangements necessary to set up a plantation. Four fold-out engravings are devoted to the construction and running of sugar works: detailed plans of the *ingenio*, or sugar mill—heavily indexed and shown from different perspectives—and blueprints for the first and ground floors of the curing house, also drawn to scale with all parts labeled and indexed. Ligon also offers two itemized accounting tables calculating annual profits and "An Estimate of the expense . . . yearly to keep this Plantation in good order."[39] These illustrations are the center around which his *History of the Island of Barbados* turns.

However, this key industrial information functions in tandem with another order of knowledge. Five equally elaborate engravings are devoted not to the specialized commerce of the island but rather to Barbados's unique natural history. These engravings are finely cut figures of botanical wonders: the prickled pear; the pomegranate in blossom; the banana tree in full fruit; the astonishing Palmetto Royal in both her "Younge" and Olde" states; and finally that paragon of exotic pleasures, the pineapple, which Ligon calls the "Queene Pine." Although the extravagant nature of the island and the industrial technology of its manufactures might seem to exist at opposite ends of the colonial enterprise, early Barbados can be read through these deeply connected modes of imagining consumption in the West Indies: aestheticized rarities alongside rationalized commodities. Ligon's history invites its reader to contemplate the figures and forms of nature in her most prodigal, unabashed display and the figures and forms of capital in its most regulated fashion. These two orders of contemplation, in turn, give rise to both the production of desire and the desire for production. When Richard Ligon offers in his *History* "the sum of all I know of the Island of Barbadoes," that sum is meant to represent both orders of colonial knowledge and desire—the true nature of the island and an exact calculation of its economic benefits—that were coming into being at the end of the 1640s (177).

Ligon's *History of the Island of Barbados* does more than record Barbados's transformation into a sugar island. It also marks a transition in the colonial tropic, one in which the language of uncontrollable excess, which was the primary mode of early writings, begins to inspire a second mode of discourse: an attempt to manage the tropical world through exhaustive catalog and description. This attempt is elaborate but remains incomplete. When John Nicholl describes running through the deep woods with two Indian arrows stuck in his back, he informs his readers that in those woods "did growe aboundance of Guiano trees, whose fruit is as big as an Apple, and verie pleasant to eate: the greene ones are wholesome for the bloodie flux."[40] The incongruity between describing the curious flora and describing the arrow "directly against my hart" characterizes the disjunctions in the earliest West Indian colonial literature.[41] Ligon explores Barbados from a more secure position by far. His list of the "Several Trees growing upon the Island" stretches over almost fifteen pages, but even at the end of his catalog he finds that he has not exhausted them all: "which way soever I have travelled . . . I have still found trees, such as I had never seen before, and not one of those I have named" (137).

The man running for his life and the naturalist's promenade could not seem more different, but both register an obligation to identify and describe exotic nature in a context that defies mastery. In 1631 Henry Colt indulged in a wistful flight of fancy, musing that something about Barbados could put him on par with princes, "Would it weer my owne." Colt's wish emerges in Ligon's text as a proposed method actually to make the island's riches one's own: a rationalized program for plantation, extraction, and profit. However, reading Ligon's text we also learn that those plantations are constantly vulnerable to catastrophes of fire, disease, and weather, as well as to the destabilizing effects, and potential consequences, of endemic violence toward servants and slaves. These forms of violence, observes Susan Scott Parrish, seemed even more "inchoate and in process because the ultimate social organization of the colonial plantation order predicated on a slave society had yet, in the 1640s, to take on the solidity of a foreordained fact."[42] Despite Ligon's overriding commitment to truth and exactitude, then, his history still cannot restrain the movement toward ungovernability. The structures that attempt to organize and delimit the difference of the tropics continually fail to contain that world, especially in terms of the violent extremes and social upheavals erupting from the emerging plantation complex.

Appetite beyond Measure

In 1647 the island of Barbados was no longer as difficult to find as a six-pence thrown upon the heath. By then ships were following familiar sea lanes through the Atlantic, and it was acknowledged that, in one way or another, the best course to Barbados was by way of Africa. Indeed this was Ligon's path. Not long into Ligon's journey, his ship, the *Achilles*, met up with another ship "coming from Guinny, but bound for London." The gentlemen passengers on the *Achilles* received gifts from the gentleman captain of the London-bound ship: gold; elephant teeth; and other "such rarities as he brought from Guinny, and Binny." That the first colonial exchange represented in Ligon's Atlantic journey is African already marks his text as belonging to a different era than Nicholl's or Colt's. The *Achilles* was bound for Saint Jago, one of the Cape Verde islands off the coast of Africa, to trade English cloths and Spanish hats for "Negros, Horses, and Cattle; which we were to sell at the Barbados" (42). As Keith Sandiford has noted, by 1647 the Cape Verde islands had become "strategic crossroads in the trade, travel, and colonizing activities of four continents . . . a vital nexus between Africa, Europe, and the New World."[43] For Ligon, the tropics, and the movement through it, existed in this broader field of exchange. The figures in this field of action in the late 1640s are not marooned men hoping for rescue or servants too lazy to cultivate a crop of tobacco. Rather they are English traders who travel between London, Africa, and the Caribbean; enslaved Africans who are purchased on the Cape Verdes and then transported to Barbados; and sugar planters who are only years away from bringing their "great work" to a state of high perfection.

Geographically and tropologically, Ligon approaches Barbados through Saint Jago, beginning his history of the English colony by first considering somebody else's tropical island. This mode of approach allows him to "try" the tropics and accrue primary experiences there without incurring potentially damning identification. Ligon begins his own discourse in an Iberian tropical scene; the text's acclimatization occurs through the observation of another's extravagance and degeneracy. Saint Jago may be just a stop along the way to the West Indies, but it sets a template for how Ligon's text will employ the colonial tropic by establishing excess as inherent to the torrid zone. Once in Barbados, the nature of the desire incited by that excess changes from the sensual to the accumulative. As the text approaches nearer to "the sweet Negotiation of Sugar," the increasingly sexualized desire for consummation that Ligon describes at Saint Jago is displaced by a description of the rationalized pursuit of profit in Barbados. Nevertheless the passage through Saint Jago initiates a discourse of volatility that will underlie even Ligon's most methodical explications of sugar making and his most precise records of its economies, for even in those sections most intently focused on commodification, the dangerous forces of violence and avarice that fuel the sugar system are never far from view. Despite Ligon's attempt to discipline his text when passing from the Iberian scene to the English one, the intensities that are established as the "nature" of the place on Saint Jago become on Barbados a colonial condition in which extravagant riches and deadly ruin are equally at hand.

Saint Jago is both ravishing and unbearable. It refuses human control. Repeated recourse to the intensifying "so" registers its excessive and relentless qualities. According to Ligon, the flowers are "so fresh, so full of various greens . . . so full of variety, of the most beautiful colors, as if nature had made choice of that place to show her Master piece" (50). Negative experiences too are intensified. The air is "so torridly hot," "painfully and piping hot," a heat "so great, so insufferable" that Ligon feels scalded inside and out. While on his trip Ligon dines at the house of local governor Padre Vagado. Ascending the precipice on top of which the padre's house sits, he and his companions feel like they are going to die. Their legs almost collapse because of the "so painful and violent . . . motion" of the climb. By the time they arrive, it seems to them that they are "in fitter condition to be fricasseed for the Padres dinner, then to eat any dinner our selves" (51). From the very start, then, the tropical order sets up an exchange in which beauty and pain are brokered through a language of excess. What is striking about the Saint Jago episode is not only the sharp difference between a nature that blooms and one that scalds but also their similarity in rendering Ligon powerless to resist.

Dinner at the padre's house offers a primary site of tropical profligacy that expresses itself through both decay and desire. The padre himself is a specimen of colonial degeneration. He is fat and sweaty, his eyes so sunken that Ligon imagines he could pluck them from the man's ruined face with a large pin. Of indiscriminate race, the padre is to Ligon's eye "not so black as to be counted a Mulatto, yet I believe full out as black as the Knight of the Sun." The padre rides into the scene in the most unmanly, unseemly way possible, "subject to the will of his horse," who "ran with such violence, as it was a wonder his burthen had not been cast by the way." He has to be taken down from the horse's back and "set on his own legs" by two black servants, relying on their bodies to regain the stability of his own. He cannot catch his breath, heaving and "in such a trance, as for some minutes, he was not in a Condition to speak to us: So sensible an impression had the fear of falling made in him." The padre is in his person, in his government, and in his colonial situation "very much discomposed," unkempt, ineffective, and unsafe (52). Even his horse seems out to kill him. Sandiford reads the carnivalesque elements of Ligon's depiction of Padre Vagado as part of a pattern of inversion, deployed here to dissociate English colonizing prerogatives from the degraded example of the Portuguese.[44] However, the padre's colonial condition also bears continuity with Ligon's descriptions of the dangers into which English colonists may fall, and it exemplifies the kind of excesses that Ligon subsequently strives to govern in his treatment of Barbados.

Padre Vagado's status as governor of the island is practically meaningless, his connection to power having vanished long ago. "[H]e was more like a Hermit, than a Governor," Ligon writes (51). But unlike a hermit, the padre is no ascetic. He is as profligate and indulgent as his near indigence permits. His house bears no markers of social hierarchy. It has only four rooms with unlevel and unswept dirt floors; the walls are hung with cobwebs instead of tapestries, pots instead of paintings. However, signs of physical indulgence are everywhere. His body is bloated, his black mistress is described as seduction itself, and the first person of his household Ligon mentions is "a Mulatto of his own getting" (51). The padre's table offers only four napkins for twelve men, but the feast he sets, which he himself has to serve, is utterly remarkable. Amid the interior decrepitude, the abundance and variety of food are astonishing. Writing ten years later, Ligon can still describe every single dish. "[A]ll Novelties to me," Ligon remembers, "all strange, and all excellent" (53).

Recalling the meal's first course displaying the splendid fruits of the island, Ligon describes the rarities that await Englishmen in Barbados should they be willing to exchange familiar pleasures for tropical ones. Of these pleasures, one in particular is an emblem that represents all the sweet strangeness of the West Indies for English colonials: the pineapple. Ligon enumerates the dishes of the padre's fruit course, "6 in all," but there are actually seven dishes, one too extraordinary to be counted alongside the rest. To "make the feast yet more sumptuous," Ligon writes, "the *Padre* sent his *Mulatto*, into his own chamber, for a dish which he reserved for the Close of all the rest; Three *Pineapples* in a dish, which were the first that ever I had seen" (53). Pineapples incited rapture in European reports of the West Indies. The English were astounded by the fruit, its juice, its growth, but most of all by its total indigenousness. Sensually transportive, it could in no way be transported without rotting. There was simply no way to convey pineapples to those who had not themselves been "beyond the line." Consumable but not commodifiable, they were to be had only on the islands where they grew.

For the English, language could not quite capture the fantastic pleasures to be had from "the Pine." Ligon's is the earliest English text in which the indescribable fruit is obsessively described.[45] In his catalog of Barbadian trees and fruits, Ligon's labor to represent the pineapple exemplifies both the disorientation and the intense desire that animated the tropic colonial imaginary. It is worth quoting in full:

> [A]s the knife goes in, there issues out of the pores of the fruit, a liquor, clear as Rock-water, near about six spoonfuls, which is eaten with a spoon; and as you taste it, you find it in a high degree delicious, but so mild, as you can distinguish no taste at all; but when you bite a piece of the fruit, it is so violently sharp, as you would think it would fetch all the skin off your mouth; but, before your tongue has made a second trial upon your palate, you shall perceive such a sweetness to follow, as perfectly to cure that vigorous sharpness; and between these two extremes, of sharp and sweet, lies the relish and flavor of all fruits that are excellent; and those tastes will change and flow so fast upon your palate, as your fancy can hardly keep way with them, to distinguish the one from the other: and this at least to a tenth examination, for so long the Echo will last. This fruit . . . invites the appetite beyond measure (145).[46]

The pineapple provokes "appetite beyond measure" because of its sharpness as well as its sweetness, and because these "two extremes" follow so fast upon one another as to deny assessment, despite the taster's determination to make "trial" and "examination." Both sense and fancy being confused, all that is left is to want more.

Ligon's long and detailed portrait of the padre's mistress uses the same discourse of desire: exceptional; strange; prodigal; displaying a simultaneity of opposites; exceeding language; and inciting the wish to "try," examine, and possess. Extending the appetite for tropical fruits, which are "the more beautiful, by how much they were the more strange," to an appetite for African women, Ligon elides the enslavement of the African population by associating them with indigenous delicacies.[47] Like the pineapple that marks the "Close" of the fruit course, the padre's mistress appears at the close of the dinner. She is, Ligon writes, "A Negro of the greatest beauty and majesty together: that ever I saw in one woman," just as the pineapple contains "all excellent tastes the world has, comprehended in one single fruit" (54). The padre's mistress can certainly be read in the context of racialized sexual desires and the proprietary rights over slave bodies and labor that European colonials insisted upon. However, analyzing Ligon's description of the mistress more specifically in terms of his extended descriptions of the pineapple suggests an analogous relationship between extravagance and violence in the colonial trope of Caribbean desire. Reading the padre's mistress and the pineapple in terms of each other does more than highlight the similarities between Ligon's description of this woman and that of this native fruit. It also describes the larger continuities among tropical excess, aesthetic ravishment, and the aggressive desire to consume in this first text to make a persuasive case for English settlement in the West Indies.

Throughout his history Ligon, who was also an artist, dedicates himself to the delineation of color and form. Mapping his descriptions of the mistress and the pineapple onto one another reveals striking similarities in these painterly fields. Both spectacles are riots of color. The mistress wears a turban "of green taffeta, striped with white and Philiamort," "a Petticoat of Orange Tawny and Skye Color; not done with Straight stripes, but waved; and upon that a mantle of purple silk, ingrayld with straw Color." Her buskins are "wetched Silk, decked with Silver lace, and Fringe," and her shoes are "white Leather, laced with sky color; and pinked between those laces" (55). The pineapple, which Ligon refers to in the feminine, likewise presents a stunning variety of intermingled colors. "Her" crown, appearing first, shows "frost upon green, intermixed with Carnation, and upon the edges of the leaves, teeth like those upon Saws; and these are pure incarnadine." The blossoms are "Carnation, Crimson and Scarlet, intermixed, some yellow, some blew leaves, and some Peach Color, intermixed with Purple, Sky color, and Orange tawny, Gridaline, and Gingeline, white and Philyamort." The outer markings "vary so in the coloring as if you see an hundred Pines, they are not one like another . . . some of green, some of yellow, some of ash color, some of carnation" (145). Kaleidoscopic, unfixed, and constantly offering new and various patterns to view, the mistress and the pineapple stun

Figure 1. "The Queene Pine," from Richard Ligon, *A Trve & Exact History of the Island of Barbados . . .* , 1657. Courtesy of the Henry E. Huntington Library, San Marino, California.

the eye with elaborate displays of visual pleasure. Nothing is as rare, all is strange, and all is excellent.

In form too the padre's mistress resembles the "Queene Pine" as Ligon describes it in picture and prose. While the pineapple plant grows large into "the perfect shape," the mistress shows "her stature large, and excellently shaped" (145, 54). The pineapple fruit looks like a turban, like the roll of green taffeta with white and burgundy stripes that is the first piece of the mistress's clothing Ligon describes and the one most particular to the islands. As regal as the "Queene Pine," whose crown grows "to perfection," the mistress moves "with far greater majesty, and gracefulness, then I have seen Queen Anne, descend from the Chair of State, to dance the Measures with a Baron of England" (55). The "graceful bow of her neck," which makes the mistress, for Ligon, "the rarest black swan that I had ever seen," echoes the tropic arch depicted in his engraving of the pineapple plant, which bends gracefully to the right, showing its face to the sun but leaning closer to man's grasp, weighted with the promises of her fruit.

The discourse of desire soon turns to devouring. In the case of the mistress, this turn occurs first by a slow and careful scrutiny of her garments, which are given out to the reader one by one. Ligon is careful to note the removal of her veil, how her linen lies close to her skin, how her mantle hangs loosely and carelessly. He remarks upon "her Legs," "her ears," "her neck," "her arms," and last asserts that "her eyes were her richest Jewels: for they were the largest, and most oriental, that I have ever seen" (55). [48] All this probing and disrobing culminates in Ligon's resolution "to make an Essay" to have her "open her lips" so he can see her teeth. Here his mounting passion suddenly turns into an ostensibly objective, if no less voyeuristic, examination. By offering her a gift, a ribbon, to persuade her to open her mouth, he wants "to see whether her teeth were exactly white, and clean, as I hoped they were; for 'tis a general opinion, that all Negroes have white teeth; but that is a Common error, for the black and white, being so near together, they set off one another with the greatest advantage. But look nearer to them, and you shall find those teeth, which at a distance appeared rarely white, are yellow and foul."

To look into "Negroes'" mouths is a practice of the slave trade, a way of assessing the age, health, and fitness of the body before purchase. Ligon's clearly sexual determination to have the padre's mistress open her lips also represents the slaver's forcible and invasive command that the slave display the inside of his or her mouth, the organ of speech and thus subjectivity.

Ligon claims to know that black people's teeth are yellow and foul, but when the mistress opens her mouth, this "knowledge" is instantly disproven and displaced with more talk of royal courts and oriental beauty. When the padre's mistress smiles at the gift he offers, she shows "rows of pearls, so clean, white, Orient, and well shaped, as Neptunes Court was never paved with such as these." The startling juxtaposition between pseudoscientific scrutiny and mythic splendor carries along with it mingled connotations of invasion, desire, and the will to possess. Her smile convinces Ligon that she is offering him sexual favors in exchange for the ribbon. His own desire is expressed less as a product of his will to master her than as a force that tropical beauty is exercising upon him. Although the words are not exactly ascribed to her—she receives Ligon's address through a translator—Ligon reports that she "wished, I would think of somewhat wherein she might pleasure me, and I should find her both ready and willing." After all, he reasons, "she was but the *Padre's* mistress & therefore the more accessible." This consummation is a fantasy and remains so. In the end Ligon, fearing the padre's jealousy, defers to him and to his loosely held proprietary rights over the woman.

In a telling parallel, Ligon wishes that the pineapple could "speak for itself," but this fantasy of animating the object of desire does not preclude the intention to consume it (144). Before one can taste the pineapple, which is so sharp it rips the skin off the roof of your mouth, so sweet it might be a nectar of the gods, and so untamed it invites appetite beyond measure, it must be uncrowned and split open: "[W]hen we come to eat them, we first cut off the crown, and send that out to be planted; and then with a knife, pare off the rind, which is so beautiful, as it grieves us to rob the fruit of such an ornament; nor would we do it; but to enjoy the precious substance it contains; like a Thief, that breaks a beautiful Cabinet, which he would forbear to do, but for the treasure he expects to find within" (145). Here, even if men of conscience would ordinarily resist spoiling the beauty or breaking the case, these native rarities incite such appetite that spoil and theft become necessary. The desire to possess, consume, and consummate is simply irresistible. As with the mistress, when Ligon moves from aesthetic spectacle to the determination to "try," he needs to demote that which he has elevated in order to possess it. The African woman is like a queen, but only the padre's mistress after all; the pineapple is a marvel, but only a fruit in the end. This disenchantment occurs in part through classification, an attempt to stabilize, control, and ultimately possess the tropical "wildness" that incited both fascination and anxiety in English colonials. Although to Ligon the mistress and the pineapple are treasures deserving of elaborate praise, men must also be ready to take them on the spot in order to capture the main chance they offer.

A final pair of scenes in the Portuguese colony on Saint Jago, which lays the groundwork of Ligon's colonial tropic, make the exchanges between desire and violence even more visible. Under the watchful guard of armed soldiers, Ligon's company visits the island's well in order to see "the beauty of the place we had heard so much commended" (57). They are being guarded because the colony's military captain suspects that the English have come to that side of the island on a mission of revenge. Earlier some Englishwomen passengers had been "Ravished" by some "Portugals, and Negroes too" while cleaning their linens, and the captain assumes that the English have come to make the offenders answer for the attack. However, the English colonel assures the Portuguese captain that whatever assault may have taken place, the English "had no intention of revenge." These were easy women, reasons Ligon, prostitutes, and all the men involved agree that they were unworthy of avenging.[49] Violence against these available bodies, regardless of their national affiliation, is practically beneath the dignity of notice. Ligon recalls the episode as a nuisance and does not even want to use the word "Ravished." He writes, "But (it seemed) the Portugals, and Negroes too, found them handsome and fit for their turns, and were a little Rude, I cannot say Ravished them" (56). And yet he records the injury.

His throwaway line about these throwaway women is worthy of note, because in the seventeenth century the verb "to ravish" was rich with meaning. "To ravish" could mean to plunder, seize, or steal, to remove a thing by force. It could also refer broadly to the power to transport, whether that meant to carry someone away violently, to force someone into an emotional condition or state of mind, or to fill someone with rapture. In addition, to ravish a woman could mean to rape her. The word contains within it the excesses of violence, seizure, and transport beyond boundaries that were all elements of the colonial tropic. The disavowed ravishing of these Englishwomen acts as a textual hinge between the scene with the padre's mistress, who is ravishing, seemingly accessible, but ultimately off-limits, and the scene that immediately follows. That scene centers upon twin sisters at the well, creatures who belong to the ravishing splendor of the valley, and who in turn ravish the aging Ligon with their unbearable, youthful beauty. Between these two extravagant examples of colonial desire, the violence of the rapes both exposes and displaces the everyday brutality with which subjects were put to use as objects in this colonial arena.

The rape of the Englishwomen is casually dispatched within a few sentences, but the next scene at the well is an extended paean to the tropical wonder of the young African virgins. Ligon describes these "Nymphs" as natural products of a "valley of pleasure," as "[w]anton, as the soil that bred them, sweet as the fruits they fed on" (59). [50] As with the padre's mistress, Ligon details every piece of clothing and adorning glitter, ending with the irresistible exposure of their "natural beauty": "their backs and necks before, lay open to the view, their breast round, firm, and beautifully shaped." He admits, "I accosted them." Again Ligon's main purpose is to make them speak, and again these girls have an ambivalent reaction to his pursuit. They "appeared a little disturbed; and whispered to one another," he reports, making "gesticulations" while "casting their eyes towards" him. But Ligon assumes that because they accept a trinket from him and smile, they are now his "two Mistresses." Though part of the girls' extravagant beauty is in their doubleness, Ligon fantasizes about the twins merging into a single body, thus offering a single center to penetrate: "had they been conjoined, and so made one, the point of my Love had met there; but, being divided, and my affection not forked, it was impossible to fix, but in one Centre." Like the nature of the island whose excesses not only seduce but also torture, the unfixable center of the twins creates in Ligon ungovernable desire, on the one hand, and frustration, vulnerability, and duress, on the other. Ligon likens himself to a horse that, stuck between two stacks of hay, starves because he does not know which to choose. Ligon describes the girls' beauty as an overwhelming force that attacks him, throws darts at him, forces him to wrestle with his desire. The girls, in his words, "commit rapes upon my affections," ravishing him. After devoting pages to the impossible task of capturing them in prose (it "would ask a more skillful pen, or pencil then mine"), an exhausted Ligon finally asks the reader's indulgence and forgiveness. He has been possessed by a "wild extravagancy," he says, "a passion not to be governed" (61).

Transported by passions that could not be satisfied, Ligon in the very next sentence gathers his wits and turns to the topic of trade. This sharp swerve from extravagant desire to "Trades or Manufactures" reconstitutes a rational exchange between the European and the tropical, but even here a sense of the illicit hovers. The livestock they buy are contraband and must be secreted away. The English pay too high a price for them and charge too high a price for their goods in return. The "traffic" is not regular, and yet by embracing these irregularities, the men are not "great losers by the exchange" (62). The tropical heat and the wondrous pineapple, the discomposed padre and his breathtaking mistress, the ravished Englishwomen and the wanton nymphs at the well—Saint Jago launches Ligon's history into the linked worlds of negative excesses (decay, corruption, violence) and positive excesses (desire, beauty, profit) that the text will continually struggle to govern. Finishing their business, the English company sets off for Barbados. On their way from the coast of Africa to the English West Indies, a little island suddenly appears in view as the sun makes its tropic turn. "[W]e saw it perfectly," Ligon recalls. It was "shaped like the nether half of a Sugar-loaf" (62).

"So Loathsome a Savor"

In this book about sugar, sugar itself makes a very late appearance, not until over two-thirds of the way in. Instead, Ligon insists that he will deal with everything in its proper order. This order includes the situation and site of the island; its sun, air, and water; its food and drink; the commodities imported and exported; "the number and nature" of its inhabitants; its beasts, birds, and insects; and its trees and plants, all before he gets to "the great work of sugar making." Ligon repeatedly introduces the sugar trade but repeatedly forestalls its full explication. While recounting the history of the first settlers, Ligon writes that he "will forbear" a discussion of sugar "till I bring in the Plants," thereby placing the most powerful magnet for capital desire in the seemingly impartial context of natural history rather than the charged context of covetous planters. Thus when sugar does explicitly enter the text, it is only after hearing of the benign "color, shade, and quality of this Plant" that the reader learns about the inciting "worth and value of it, together [with] the whole process of the great work of Sugar-making, which is the thing I mainly aim at" (70).

Why this delay? One explanation is that before delivering his meticulously detailed and much-sought-after knowledge about the production of sugar, Ligon in his *History of the Island of Barbados* first seeks to control other orders of knowledge about Barbados as a way of naturalizing and rationalizing the obvious excesses of the sugar economy: its staggering profits and its systemic violence. By taking things in order, he can create Barbados as a place that can be put in order, a place where one who knows the island can organize that knowledge and usefully impart the information. But there is a problem with this program. However much Ligon's detailed descriptions of island life aim to stabilize the massive turbulence of the sugar revolution, those descriptions are destabilized throughout. The text keeps breaking with Ligon's chosen categorical form as he narrates the immoderate features of both the natural and social worlds, features that the catalog cannot contain. Despite its formal structures, then, the text's pervasive inability to manage excess undermines Ligon's effort to establish systems of knowledge about the island and ultimately marks the colonial site as corrupt and violent.

When Ligon's ship enters Carlisle Bay, he sees twenty-two ships at anchor, auguring an excellent and lively trade. However, the appearance of a healthy, brisk exchange is deceiving: "the Inhabitants of the Islands, and shipping too were so grievously visited with the plague, (or as killing a disease,) that before a month was expired after our Arrival, the living were hardly able to bury the dead" (66). Trying to account for this sickness, Ligon first wonders if it was brought there on ships that carried contagious diseases along with their commodities. He ultimately concludes that the island's people brought it on themselves through their own distemper, bad diet, "drinking strong waters," and general debauchery.[51] Colt's 1631 journal proves that the trope of tropical corruption was not new, and it was in wide circulation in print by the time Ligon's *History* was published, especially in texts that were politically or religiously motivated against the planters.[52] In a metaphorical sense, however, the trading ships and the men whose dissolution is linked to the profits of that trade are joint sources of contagion. Both are involved in the movements and exchanges of the colonial West Indies—the boats "plying to and fro . . . which carried commodities from place to place" and the men of Barbados, who willingly or unwillingly exchanged their former conditions for the "incommodities" of the island. That is to say, a lively harbor, a deadly disease, and a degenerate population are linked phenomena; the disordered society exists in tandem with the trade that supports it. The colonists are wasted not only by disease and debauchery but also by hunger, because they are planting more fields with sugarcane than with food.[53] And because of the trade, Ligon cannot leave Barbados despite this grievous state of affairs. The ship that delivered him is also "infected with this disease," and furthermore it is on its way to Africa "to trade for Negroes" (66).

Although Ligon continually praises the most powerful planters of the island, he cannot help but confess that on Barbados corruption is the air they breathe and the water they drink. Bridgetown is settled haphazardly in a bog below sea level. The air there is of "so loathsome a savor" that the mere act of breathing can make a man sick. Again intensifiers are used liberally: so loathsome a town; so unhealthy a place; so unwholesome; so much sickness reigning so extremely. At the time of Ligon's arrival, the residents of Bridgetown were throwing their dead into the water: "[T]hey threw the dead carcasses into the bog, which infected so the water, as divers that drunk of it were absolutely poisoned, and died in few hours after" (71). Whereas in Plymouth being "scarce able" to bury their dead carried the threat of God's wrath, the Barbadians are unconcerned with divine retribution. Their first impulse is to keep drinking from the water where corpses float. Even outside of this ghastly plague season, water shortage was a continual problem in Barbados. The island's main source of potable water was rainwater collected in ponds, ponds in which slaves also bathed. Ligon finds this practice "loathsome" too. From his standpoint, black bodies taint the water almost as much as corpses, although the planters seem not to care. Ligon, ever ingenious, proposes a solution to the water problem: it would be better, he thinks, to collect rain in a cistern and bring it into the house. Not only would this water be pure, but it would also have the added benefit of preserving the family in the case of a servant or slave rebellion, because planters could boil it and use it "to throw down upon the naked bodies of the Negroes, scalding hot; which is as good a defense against their underminings, as any other weapons" (75). Describing life on the island, then, Ligon cannot even write about drinking water without veering from his orderly aim and into accounts of carcass-filled bogs and the blistering backs of rebel slaves.

Not only are the air and water tainted, but objects also constantly descend into conditions of decrepitude. The moist, unwholesome air makes knives rust before they are even back in their sheaths and renders locks useless and clocks and watches untrue. The "insufferable heat" destroys Ligon's writing tools; his two pieces of wax melt together, and the sealant on his stationery box liquefies, letting all the ink spill out. These knives, locks, clocks, and pens—all instruments for asserting and recording order—are corrupted by the environment, making it useless even to try to maintain them. Ligon complains that you can "take your knife to the grindstone, and grind away all the rust; which done, wipe it dry, and put it up into your sheath, and so into your pocket, and in a very little time, draw it out; and you shall find it beginning to rust all over" (73). Neither can bodies be preserved while diseases "reign" and exercise "power and Tyranny" over all. Ligon is sick the majority of his time in Barbados and describes it as torment. Fevers come first, and then his insides twist with "Bindings, Costiveness, and consequently Gripings, and Tortions in the bowels." Ligon remembers his sickness as a period outside of time. He believes that on three separate occasions, his companions might have thought him dead as his vital signs weakened to the point of disappearance. "[M]y Memory and Intellect suffering the same decays with my body," he writes, "I could hardly give an account of 2/3 of the time I was sick" (194). The air and water, tools, body, and mind are all subject to the natural corruptions that make degeneration a key trope of the text.

Narrating this decay poses a challenge to Ligon's main project. His aim in the *History of the Island of Barbados* is to secure orders of knowledge and control so as to faithfully describe both the nature of the island and the state of the colony for the profit of potential planters. The *History* is not expressly a promotional piece, but its comprehensive survey is intended to propose the best practices for successful plantation. Indeed, Parrish argues that one of the driving purposes of Ligon's work is to propose the outlines for a better commonwealth in the still-experimental field of England's Atlantic colonies, and that Ligon's empirical project is guided by an ethical message of reform.[54] Fulfilling this purpose requires that Ligon find a way to moderate and master the colonial tropics, to harness the profuse natural world, and to temper the society Barbadians have launched. However, in order to render accurately the natural world and the history of the plantation, Ligon is forced to account for the prodigious aspects of each. Even though the rationalized discussion of sugar—its qualities, value, and worth, and the details of how to establish a plantation—is saved for the end, the more volatile human, social, and economic conditions under which sugar is produced pervade almost every aspect of the text. As the technologies of sugar production reach "high perfection," the demands and profits of the sugar trade turn the West Indies into an even greater site of excess. They inspire, as Ligon says of the wondrous pineapple, an "appetite beyond measure," which his text then struggles to govern. Although his text is capacious in both its narrative and descriptive discourses, systemization and excess exist in continual, pronounced tension throughout.

The Torrid Exchange

One example of the contest between measure and excess can be found in the section describing the "tame beasts that are living on the island." This category includes several subsets of animals, which Ligon further orders by their size—for example, camels, horses, oxen, bulls, cows, mules, hogs, sheep, and goats. The structure of the classificatory writing is challenged by its content, however, as narrative interrupts descriptive discourse. We get this story, for example, under the title "Hogs":

> There was a Planter in the Island, that came to his neighbor, and said to him, Neighbor, I hear you have lately bought a good store of servants, out of the last ship that came from *England*, and I hear withal, that you want provisions. I have great want of a woman servant; and would be glad to make the exchange. If you would let me have some of your woman's flesh, you shall have some of my hog's flesh; So the price was set a groat a pound for the hogs flesh and six-pence for the Woman's flesh. The scales were set up, and the Planter had a Maid that was extreme fat, lazy, and good for nothing, her name was *Honor*; the man brought a great fat sow, and put it in one scale, and *Honor* was put in the other, but when he saw how much the Maid outweighed his Sow, he broke off the bargain, and would not go on (112).

In this grotesque drama of weight and measure, we have a spectacle of the complete dehumanization wrought by the labor system demanded by the plantation economy. The labor is needed because of the massive demands of sugar production, while the provisions are needed because planters are using only a small percentage of their land for foodstuffs, dedicating the majority of their plots to the sugarcane and all that was necessary to run the sugar works. The fat woman and the fat hog are both sites of excess in themselves, but being put on the scales together, they constitute an even more immoderate exchange. Weighing Honor, the planters finally fail to honor the bargain they struck. When the human flesh outweighs the sow's, the deal is called off, not because the two objects are essentially incommensurate, but simply because one man's advantage outstrips the other's. Ligon tells the story as almost an amusement, or at least a peculiarity of island life. What is clear, however, is that the story of Honor and the hog have no proper place in a natural history, and yet such is their excess that Ligon cannot resist interrupting his history to include them.

Another example of this kind of narrative interruption occurs when Ligon reports an episode on the plantation of Colonel Walrond, one of the major planters on the island. Several of Walrond's slaves have committed suicide in the belief that they will escape the horrors of plantation slavery

and return to Africa after their deaths. On Walrond's plantation, as it is elsewhere, slave suicide is an act of resistance that will not be tolerated. After
losing "three or four of his best negroes" this way, Walrond cuts the head
off one of the victims and raises it on a pole twelve feet high. Calling all
his slaves to the site, he forces them to march around the pole, a ritual of
extreme order and extreme violence at once. Walrond first asks if the slaves
recognize the head of the suicide victim, which of course they do, and then
asks how the man's body can go to Africa if his head, gruesomely on display,
is still here? "Being convinced by this sad, yet lively spectacle," Ligon writes,
"they changed their opinions, and after that, no one hanged themselves"
(102). The narrative of this "sad, yet lively spectacle" erupts from an ethnographic discourse on the religious beliefs of slaves, once more demonstrat-
ing how the systemic and spectacular bodily violence of the sugar plantation
undermines the organizational categories that Ligon establishes to manage
his *History*. Like the story of weighing Honor, the disquisition on the impaled head is supposed to be a story of rational thinking: one is a deal that
conveniently matches up a person who needs a pig with a person who needs
a woman; the other aims to demonstrate the foolishness of a belief system
by countering it with a physical display of the real. But the hyperbolic and
visceral nature of these scenes belies the rationality they purport to illustrate. Shown in all their grotesquerie, the scenes exemplify the contorted
relationship between systems of management and chaotic experience on the
island of Barbados.

Ligon's most direct attempt to mitigate tropical excess offers another
managing system: a structure of exchange of "temperate" pleasures that
Englishmen might enjoy in their native country for "torrid" ones that can
be had only in the tropics. Toward the end of the *History*, Ligon lays out
the terms of the deal that the prospective planter would make: "[I]f he can
find in himself a willingness, to change the pleasures which he enjoyed in
a Temperate, for such as he shall find in a Torrid Zone, he may light upon
some that will give him an exchange, with some advantage" (177). The project at hand is not a matter of tamping down desire but rather a matter of
managing its relation to disorder. The trick, Ligon proposes, is to figure out
how to make the exchange between temperate and torrid pleasures while
also tending to one's own advantage—to figure out, in Henry Colt's words,
how to get the fruit while keeping one's fingers from the pricking. Ligon
dispenses frankly impossible advice. He urges Englishmen who are willing
to make the torrid exchange to be moderate in all things. Many "may here

find moderate delights, with moderate labor," Ligon writes, "and those taken moderately will conduce much to their health" (183).

Searching for moderate men, Ligon promises to parse "what gainers or losers they will be by the exchange, that makes the adventure," but the text affirms that except for a chance to acquire great wealth, the torrid exchange amounts to almost a complete loss for the English gentleman. Social enticements are few, and nearly all outdoor entertainments prove "too violent" in the heat and ill-suited to the island's physical contours. Hawks have "neither Champion to fly in, Brookes to fly over, nor Game to fly at" (178). Greyhounds have no place to run their courses; they would bruise themselves by bumping into tree stumps and break their necks by falling into gullies. The only hounds the planters keep are bred for the one kind of hunt the island affords: chasing down runaway slaves. In place of the open fields of the English hunt are the caves of Barbados with their deep enclosures, suffocating air, and human quarry: "These Caves are very frequent in the Island, and of several dimensions, some small, others extremely large and Capacious: The runaway Negroes, often shelter themselves in these Coverts, for a long time and in the night range aboard the Country, and steal Pigs, Plantains, Potatoes, and Pullin, and bring it there; and feast all day, upon what they stole the night before; and the nights being dark, and their bodies black, they escape undiscerned" (169). Whereas in England the greyhound is "accounted an excellent breed," in Barbados "[t]here is nothing in that Country, so useful as Lyam Hounds, to find out these thieves." (170). On the island the hunt is no sport. The exchange at hand concerns not only the agreeable things the planters cannot do but also the brutal things they must do.

It is clear that the temperate/torrid exchange suggested in Ligon's *History of the Island of Barbados* sacrifices home pleasures for island profits. To many a planter's ear, the "music of the Spheres" is less enticing than a donkey's bray and "three whip Saws, going all at once in a Frame or Pit." The planters keep their eyes less on the transcendent "beauty of the Heavens" than on their furrowed plots. Vistas, according to Ligon, are broader and more various in England. Flowers smell better in England. Even the sense of touch offers little that is pleasant in Barbados. Ligon divides the feeling sense into "doing" and "suffering," but there is no satisfaction in either. He writes, "[T]he poor Negroes and Christian servants" suffer only a "coercive kind of feeling": the overseer's blows coming down on their heads and shoulders (180–81). Turning from brutality to sensuality, Ligon cannot imagine any pleasure in touching a woman in the tropical heat: "[T]hey are so sweaty and clammy, as the hand cannot pass over, without being glued & cemented in the passage or motion; and by that means, little pleasure is given to, or received by the agent or the patient: and therefore if this sense be neither pleased in doing nor suffering, we may decline it as useless in a Country, where down of Swans, or wool of Beaver is wanting" (181).

Why, then, would you remove yourself from home comforts and travel to such a dangerous, uncomfortable place? Why would you pack up twenty pounds' worth of black ribbon with which to mourn other colonists, who are dying early deaths, and go to Barbados?[55] The pineapple offers "all excellent tastes the world has, comprehended in one fruit," but surely one does not go to Barbados for such transitory pleasures. Rather, one goes for the other plant that invites appetite beyond measure: sugarcane. The moderate man, the man of industry, the man who can make the torrid exchange and use it to his advantage will find in that plant the best sort of excess. He will discover "the ladder to climb to a high degree of Wealth and opulence, in this sweet Negotiation of Sugar" (183). To this man Ligon writes, "I shall let you see that without the help of Magic or Enchantment" how an investment of three thousand pounds could yield nearly nine thousand in the space of a year. The benefit of the torrid exchange is, in Ligon's account, exclusively economic, but that benefit is extravagant. Indeed the book's driving force is the knowledge that "in this sweet Negotiation of Sugar," a planter could triple his initial investment in the first year alone. The temperate life is exactly what should be abandoned as the first condition of entering the colonial tropic. Ligon writes, "And now I have as near as I can, delivered the sum of all I know of the Island of Barbados, both for Pleasures and Profits, Commodities and Incommodities, Sicknesses and Healthfulness. So that it may be expected what I can say, to persuade or dissuade any, that have a desire to go and live there" (177). Ligon's own recital of the island's "Commodities and Incommodities" achieves no balance. Almost every incommodity he mentions is connected to, and yet outweighed by, a single commodity: sugar. It is abundantly clear that the only reason to sail to this distant part of the world is to pursue the profits available to a man who can successfully manage to "bring in the Plants."

When Ligon does "bring in the Plants," he builds a long catalog ranging from the lesser fruits to the wonder of the indigenous pineapple. After an extended proclamation to the glorious queen of tropical fruits, he moves on to the sugarcane, which in contrast was "brought thither as a stranger, from beyond the Line, which has a property beyond them all" (146). The cane's

special property (characteristic) is that it can be made into a property (commodity) so valuable that "a special preeminence [is] due to this Plant, above
all others, that the earth or world can boast of" (146–47). Its single and singular quality of sweetness "has such a benign faculty, as to preserve all the
rest from corruption, which, without it, would taint and become rotten"
(146). In its primitive state, then, sugar's sweetness prevents physical "corruption," even as the plantation complex that developed around the cane's
cultivation, processing, refinement, shipping and sale was corrupt beyond
measure. That plantation complex, like the cane itself, was "brought thither
as a stranger, from beyond the Line" and allowed its architects to possess a
"property beyond them all."

It is important here to note that although in Ligon's prose his descriptions of the pineapple and of the sugarcane follow directly upon one another,
in the printed text the two passages are separated. In the 1657 edition, the
pineapple description ends the catalog of plants "proper and peculiar to the
Island" and is followed by the description of the sugarcane, "a stranger" to
the island. Between these two pages appears the most important series of
engravings offered in *The History of the Island of Barbados*: the map of the
island and the plans for the sugar works. The map unfolds across two pages,
displaying Barbados's topography, the names and estates of every major
planter on the island, and the "ten Thousand Acres of Land which Belong
to the Merchants of London." The map also includes several illustrations of
livestock and labor, most remarkably one of an armed planter on horseback
shooting two barely clad runaway slaves at close range, the smoke from his
gun nearly touching one slave's back. Appearing next are the copper engravings promised on the title page, including the "Plott forme of the Ingenio
that grinds or squeezes the canes which make the sugar"; a full page index
to that diagram that identifies the machine's parts and their uses; a second
view of the sugar mill, again drawn to scale with labeled and indexed parts;
and a two-part engraving of the ground floor and first story of the curing
house, likewise meticulously dimensioned and indexed.

Amid this sequence of industrial blueprints, Ligon curiously places
the botanical illustration of the ripe "Queene Pine," as stately and beautiful as the padre's mistress and magnificently on view. Encrowned, intact,
and still rooted to the ground, the "Queene Pine" stands apart and inclines
away from the cartographical and architectural plots that precede it. Recall
that no profit can be made of the pineapple. The pleasures it offers, much to
the distress of the always enterprising Ligon, are explicitly experiential: "I

have had many thoughts, which way this fruit might be brought into England, but cannot satisfy my self in any; preserved it cannot be, whole; for, the rind is so firm and tough, as no Sugar can enter in; and if you divide it in pieces, (the fruit being full of pores) all the pure taste will boil out" (146). What is the "Queene Pine" doing here among these intensely codified means of production that do to the sugarcane exactly what cannot be done to the pineapple: boil, transform, and preserve the plant precisely so that the "pure taste" of it *can* be "brought into England"? The pineapple's position in this sequence re-naturalizes the colonial tropic of Barbados, partially disavowing its transformation into the relentless engine of England's colonial economy and partially valorizing that ruthless commerce by associating it with a consummate exotic pleasure. The production of desire underwrites the desire for production as the queen of all fruits is, for a moment, the benign stand-in for "King Sugar." Planted by "the great Gardener of the World," the pineapple provides a romanticized, natural frame around plantation manufacture. Although the methods of inscription could not be more different, the *History* flashes this visual reminder of rapturous desire at the very moment it provides "the secrets" of a great commodity to men "covetous of the knowledge." The glance back at the pineapple allows Ligon to introduce his discussion of sugar making by falling back on the rhetoric of the naturalist rather than the manufacturer. He begins with the sugarcane itself and an avowed effort to "fully and amply set her off" just as he has done for the other tropical fruits in his catalog.

But before coming to this description, the reader, if he seriously wishes to become a planter, has presumably spent an exceedingly long time studying those architectural drawings that are the key to Ligon's history. Gone are the corruptions of the air, water, and body; gone are the cisterns of boiling water, the weighed flesh, and the impaled heads. These engravings, with no visual reference to the natural or social world, are pure system and form. Carefully indexed from A to Z, these architectural forms lay out in perfect order what Ligon calls "the soul of Trade in this Island" (156). Reading these large, fold-out engravings, the reader interacts with the text in a new way. The exactitude and efficiency with which the images are rendered invite the eye to pore over them, moving back and forth from index to image, figuring out how the thing works, how the sugar moves through its refinement, and contemplating the process, the outlay, and the outcome. In one 1657 edition, every page of the book is free from marginalia and seemingly untouched except for these, which show signs of heavy use. Clearly the object of intensive

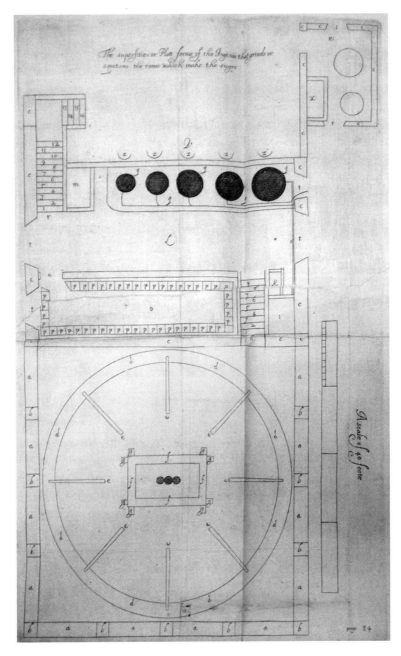

Figure 2. "The superficies or Plott forme of the Ingenio that grinds or squeezes the canes which make the sugar. A scale of 40 foote," from Richard Ligon, *A Trve & Exact History of the Island of Barbados . . .* , 1657. Courtesy of the Henry E. Huntington Library, San Marino, California.

study, these engravings bear the indexical traces of invisible hands: worn edges, scattered blots, the fingerprints of history. Meanwhile the laboring bodies of the slaves who run the works disappear from the plots, and are instead re-enlisted into a table of facts and figures Ligon provides detailing the expenses and profits of running a plantation: the cost for shirts and shoes, victuals and overseers, as well as the compensation for the "decays of our Negroes, Horses, and Cattle, notwithstanding all our recruits by breeding all those kinds" (191). Slaves appear here in ordered columns with numbers affixed, as commodities evaluated in terms of the bottom line. Total sum of expenses: £1,349. Sum of yearly profit: £8,866. Profit cleared: £7,519. "I have as near as I can," writes Ligon, "delivered the sum of all I know of the Island of Barbados both for Pleasures and Profits, Commodities and Incommodities, Sicknesses and Healthfulness." Despite the pervasive disruptions of corruption and violence throughout his text, the torrid exchange represented in these graphs and figures overrides the diverse forms of experiential excess with a singular form of capitalist surplus, one that does not disrupt efforts to systematize but rather, as Ligon has it, becomes the soul of the system itself.

Combustible Matter

The engravings of the sugar works stand apart from the rest of the text because in their meticulous graphical form they present information completely insulated from contingency. Indeed their value is just this freedom from contingency; the precision of the architectural form is meant to guarantee that what is represented in the drawing can be perfectly translated into a material structure. However, in Ligon's textual description of how sugar is actually made, such a perfect translation is marred by pressure, constraint, and accidents—in other words, by the very contingencies the drawings are supposed to eliminate. Sugar making was an elaborate process that required ceaseless labor, especially in its production phase. Because the sugar content of the cane begins to deteriorate as soon as the cane is cut, the crop had to be processed immediately. Therefore during the six months of harvesting, the sugar works ran almost continuously. "And so the work goes on," Ligon writes, "all hours of the day and night, with fresh supplies of Men, Horses, and Cattle" (161).

The process had three major parts: milling, boiling, and curing.[56] The boiling was the most labor-intensive of these steps and required the most skill as well. In the boiling house, five large furnaces heated five copper pots of decreasing size in which the extracted sugar juice gradually cooked down to a syrup. Slaves skimmed and stirred the boiling liquid constantly and, at the right intervals, ladled it from one pot to the next until in the smallest and hottest pot it reached the proper temperature for crystallization. The slave who was the "boiler" would temper the scalding sugar, causing it to crystallize, and then "strike" it by ladling it into a cooling cistern, at which point it would granulate. "The boiler had to be something of an artist," Richard Dunn writes, "for there was no sure way of telling whether the sugar had been tempered enough or too much, or when it was ready to strike."[57] The work was grueling. The heat in the boiling house was hellacious, and as the blistering liquid was stirred and quickly ladled from pot to pot, there was the constant threat of being burned, sometimes fatally. Ligon writes that "being continually drawn up, and keeled by ladles, and skimmed by skimmers, in the Negroes' hands," sugar in this central step of production demanded "much labor" (161).

Great fires fueled the process that transformed cane juice to sugar, but fire also posed one of the most serious dangers on the island. Among the many events that could cause catastrophic loss to the planters, fire could effect such ruin that a planter might "never . . . entertain a hope of rising again" (192). Sugarcane is a highly combustible plant, and fire spreads rapidly in the fields. In the hands of rebellious servants and slaves, fire was the single most powerful weapon available. As the geographer Bonham Richardson reminds us, "All of the slave uprisings in the eastern Caribbean that preceded emancipation in the 1830s involved the use or planned use of fire."[58] Fire erupts several times in Ligon's history, and his treatments of it capture how the threat that catastrophe would strike planters persisted even as the plantation complex became entrenched and the settlement period came to a close.

Combustibility operates as a figure of colonial catastrophe in Barbados, a threat residing at the center of the plantation. In a literal sense, fire was a hazard that demanded careful and constant management, but figuratively, the whole of colonial society in Barbados was a dangerously incendiary world. Thus fire, which produced wealth so systemically but could turn wild and ruinous at any moment, can be seen as a nexus of the most intensive forms of excess on the sugar islands: labor and pain; profit and contingency; the desire for vengeance and the violent regime enforced to prevent it.

The use of fire was central to the process of sugar making, not only in the great furnaces of the boiling houses but also in the creation of the plantations. Since the first years of European settlement in the Caribbean, forest burns were necessary to clear land for planting. Early settlers, to whom the tough tropical vegetation was entirely new, would leave charred stumps, trunks, and limbs of trees to litter the land after these burns and plant haphazardly between them. Recall that to Henry Colt in 1631, the land looked "like the ruins of some village lately burned" with "all the earth covered black with cenders."[59] As sugar cultivation developed, deforestation efforts became more important, and because the slave labor force was also growing, the clearing proceeded at a more rapid pace. Although between 1647 and 1650 Ligon saw such a variety of trees that he feared to describe them all would be "to lose myself in a wood," by 1665 the forests were gone (120).[60] The increasingly large plots of land that the big sugar planters were consolidating required cleared fields for the cane, pastures for horses and cattle, and timber to keep the fires of the boiling houses roaring day and night. Slaves were tasked with the dangerous work of burning the land, the punishing work of clearing it, and the unremitting work of feeding the furnaces and laboring around the clock in the suffocating heat of the boiling houses.

If the dangers of disease, heat, and hurricanes were inextricable from the natural environment of the tropics, then the dangers of fire were inextricable from the human activity of sugar making. Even in the everyday operation of the sugar works, "the violence of the fires" could easily cause "great casualties." The flames threatened to break the brick frame that held the copper pots, to burn the coppers themselves, and to "molder away" the stones at the mouth of the furnace. As slaves fed the fire with heavy, split logs, the weight of the wood might bend or even break the continually "red hot" bars of iron that made up the floor of the furnace. Any of these damages would make "the work stand still," and if work stopped for long enough, the cane would spoil and "not be worth the grinding" (108). In addition to the hazards of the boiling room, accidents happened in the highly flammable environment of the still house where molasses was distilled to rum. Ligon reports that the liquor produced there was so strong that if a flame was brought too close to a cask, "the Spirits will fly to it, and taking hold of it, bring the fire down to the vessel, and set all a fire, which immediately breaks the vessel . . . burning all about it that is combustible matter" (164). In descriptions such as these, fire is a violent and active force that lives, grows, leaps, and consumes the material around it. It is necessary to the functioning of the sugar works and yet continually threatens to destroy them. Ligon tells the story of an "excellent Negro" who was burned to death in a blaze that occurred when he used a candle to illuminate his work of funneling liquor into a cask, losing "the whole vessel of Spirits, and his life to boot" (164). Although Ligon sympathetically refers to the slave as a "poor Negro. . . who was an excellent servant," this final ordering of phrases—"the whole vessel . . . and his life to boot"—identifies each primarily as a lost commodity, valuable but combustible matter ever vulnerable to accidental destruction.[61] Fire was of the utmost necessity to the functioning of the sugar works, and yet it continually threatened to destroy the raw material, the means of production, the laboring bodies, and the products that made up the commodity chain of sugar.

A potentially catastrophic agent at the center of the sugar system, fire was yet more dangerous as a tool of insurrection. As Parrish observes, "the agricultural, industrial and slaving processes were all—literally—highly flammable and explosive; and the captive laborers, either by accident or intent, had ample means to set all on fire."[62] Because fires spread so rapidly, even individual acts of revenge could do extensive damage. Ligon is not sure how to name these acts, first calling them "mischiefs"; then attributing them to "carelessness," "slothfulness," "negligence"; and finally naming them acts of "wilfullness" and "revenge." As he moves through these explanations from the least to most intentional, he narrates how easy it is for a small spark to become a storm of fire that could consume "whole lands of Canes and Houses too . . . to the utter ruin and undoing of their Masters," and how often such blazes happened (95). His discussion of these fires occurs in the section describing a particularly severe labor regime for servants that included poor housing, scant food, insufficient clothing, and brutal beatings in addition to their everyday backbreaking work. "Truly," Ligon writes, "I have seen such cruelty there done to Servants, as I did not think one Christian could have done to another" (94). As he often does in the text, Ligon attempts to mitigate the social ills he identifies by introducing suggestions for or noting indications of improvement, but despite his ameliorative intervention, the vivid depiction of exhausted, hungry, sweating, and often bloodied laborers erupts into a description of fire in the cane fields: "Water there is none to quench it, or if it were, a hundred *Negroes* with buckets were not able to do it; so violent and spreading a fire this is, and such a noise it makes, as if two Armies, with a thousand shot of either side, were continually giving fire, every knot of every Cane, giving as great a report as a Pistol" (95). Here, the canes are not only destroyed but also become weapons in the incendiary scene, every knot exploding like a pistol shot. One of the innovations in sugar planting that Ligon describes is the discovery that if the cane is planted lying horizontally rather than vertically, a new plant will grow from every knot. Now those thousands of sites of prodigious growth detonate in a riotous blast. Ligon figures the fire as a war waged between two great forces in a field of combustible matter, an image that is repeated as he goes on to describe the planning of a major servant rebellion that occurred just before he arrived on the island. This was a different kind of plot indeed, one in which the "high perfection" of rationalized production was subject to the dangerous destructive forces of human activity.

If Ligon could not be sure of the origin of some fires, the intentionality of this "long plotted conspiracy" is clear to him: the servants would "join together to revenge themselves" upon the masters. Ligon pays careful attention to how the servants' words were "spread throughout the Island," from complaints of the "sufferings" and "intolerable burdens" of their "slavery," to the resolution to take action, to the extensive planning designed "to draw as many of the discontented party into this plot, as possibly they could." The result of such a spread, according to Ligon, was that the majority of servants on the island were involved and ready to "fall upon their Masters, and cut all their throats, and by that means, to make themselves [not] only freemen, but Masters of the Island" (96). The plot was discovered the day before it was to be enacted, and eighteen men were hanged. These were identified as the principal designers of the rebellion, men "so haughty in their resolutions, and so incorrigible" that they were thought likely to plan a second revolt. Thus the rebellion, like the fire, is depicted as a violent plan that spreads thick and wide, ignited by men whose desire for revenge is thought to be unquenchable. Ligon's own stated intention for this part of his text is to describe "the number and nature of the inhabitants," but the nature of the Barbadian social world is such that any description of its mixed population of masters, servants, and slaves necessarily gives way to scenes of violence. The fires represent a catastrophe that cuts both ways, bringing misery to the servants at the hands of the masters and exposing the vulnerability of the masters to the vengeance of the servants. Although the rebellion is quashed, the inflammatory atmosphere persists, "the materials there being all combustible, and apt to take fire" (95).

At this juncture, Ligon introduces slaves into the roster of inhabitants by asking why they, as a majority population, do not rise up against their masters and "commit some horrid massacre upon the Christians, thereby to enfranchise themselves, and become masters of the island" (96). He offers three reasons why: first, slaves are given no weapons; second, they are "held in such awe and slavery, [and] their spirits are subjugated to so low a condition, as they dare not to look up to any bold attempt"; and third, they "are fetched from several parts of Africa, who speak several languages, and by that means, one of them understands not the others" (96–97). Ligon's parsing of systematic subjugation, along with his ensuing description of the market for slaves on Barbados, is a stark reminder that by this time, Atlantic slavery was becoming the most profound catastrophe in the colonial world. Slavery institutionalized catastrophe and permanently changed its nature. Ligon gives us Barbados in the midst of that institutional transition, when the planter class was coming to power, the slave society was taking shape, and the miseries of settlement were being passed on from displaced Englishmen to enslaved Africans. Excess and contingency continued to be fundamental to West Indian coloniality, but they now existed in relation to the enormity of the violence that defined the slave system.

Although he believes that Africans are meant to be enslaved, Ligon protests against some aspects of slavery on Barbados—especially the fact that masters would not let their slaves become Christians—and often depicts individual slaves in positive terms. In his final analysis, slaves are entered into a table of costs and profits, but Ligon's interest in slave society leads to some detailed descriptions of their lifeways beyond their labor. Michael Craton suggests that Ligon's curiosity about slaves as both individuals and social groups rests on the certainty of control over them. Ligon, he writes, gives "a far more benign and optimistic account than could have been written fifty years later, when the local plantocracy had survived five major slave plots within thirty years."[63] But rebellion was a threat even in the transition period that Ligon chronicles (witness the cisterns of boiling water). Just as Ligon opens his formal account of slaves with the specter of their revolt, he closes it with the story of one "bold attempt," a plotted slave rebellion in 1649.

The plot took shape in a time of scarcity, when slaves were no longer given even their scant rations: "So that some of the high spirited and turbulent amongst them, began to mutiny, and had a plot, secretly to be revenged on the Master; and one or two of these were Firemen that made the fires in the furnaces, who were never without store of dry wood by them. These villains, were resolved to make fire to such part of the boiling-house, as they were sure would fire the rest, and so burn all, and yet seem ignorant of the fact, as a thing done by accident" (105). The weapons of rebellion, dry wood and fire, were always close at hand. That the very means of production could so easily be used as agents of destruction caused tremendous anxiety to planters, no less so because the act of setting fire could always be denied and ascribed to accident. Fire's inherent instability and volatility put the potential for both productive and destructive excess in the hands of the enslaved, who were held in "such awe and slavery" specifically to prevent rebellion but who, the planters well knew, had the "high spirited and turbulent amongst them."

In the technical drawing of what Ligon calls the "Plott forme of the Ingenio that grinds or squeezes the canes which make the sugar," such destructive potential is absent. Unlike his narrative discourse, the graphical exists outside of human time and its unmanageable events. The fires are here, but not the potentially plotting firemen. And yet even in this depiction of the *ingenio*, whose value lies precisely in its exactitude, the furnaces are the only things that are out of place. Visually they have to be moved out from under the copper boiling pots to be seen in the diagram. Ligon writes, "they cannot be expressed here, by reason they are under the Coppers; yet, I have made small semi-circles, to let you see where they are" (151). Thus the "Plott" of the *ingenio* doubly displaces what fuels the work, not only because it does not picture the slaves whose ceaseless labors run the whole operation, but also because its birds-eye view cannot properly place the fires in the line of sight. The plot of the conspiracy to set fire to the boiling room and let the conflagration blaze until it "burn[s] all" is likewise hidden from sight, secret, and occluded from surveillance of the masters and overseers until it is displaced by some other slaves who report it. The failure of oversight in both of these cases represents a view from the top that both is and is not able to picture the incendiary elements at the heart of the sugar system.

Ligon concentrates such attention on the actions of the slaves who betray the conspirators and expose the plot because he knows that the management of the plantation relies on the slaves' allegiance to the master. Dramatizing this allegiance is meant to combat the major disruption caused by the threat of rebellion by assuring readers that most slaves will put their masters' interests before their own. Therefore he discusses the aftermath of the discovery at much greater length than the plot itself. According to Ligon, so many slaves are willing to offer witness against the plotters that the grateful master offers them all "a day of liberty" and "a double proportion of victual for three days." The slaves refuse the boon. This causes great consternation on the part of the master, who cannot figure out why, in a time of scarcity and a life of hard labor, the slaves will not accept the reward and who therefore suspects that there is still "some discontent amongst them." It is clear that the fears provoked by the planned rebellion have not dissipated. Even if this plot was isolated to one plantation and discovered before it took place, it must have provoked the kind of alarm Michael Craton refers to when he writes, "Almost invariably the whites were deluded by the quiescence, or apparent acquiescence, of their slaves, so that when rebellions occurred, the shock at the suddenness gave way to horrified amazement at subsequent revelations of widespread plotting and secret planning."[64] When the master summons "three or four of the best of them" to ask why the slaves have refused the reward, he learns that it is "not sullenness, or slighting the gratuity" that prompted the refusal, but rather a conviction that they should not be recompensed for doing what they believe is their duty. It is, according to Ligon's report, "an act of Justice, which they thought themselves bound in duty to do, and they thought themselves sufficiently rewarded in the Act" (105–6). They do suggest, however, that if the master should at any other time "bestow a voluntary boon upon them," they would accept it.

Here, the economy of obedience and reward that is meant to offset the threat of rebellion and return power to the master does not run smoothly. The slaves do more than deny the master's recompense; they posit a future exchange in terms that they themselves define: free gift, free acceptance. In refusing the reward, the slaves refuse a strict reciprocity in which their loyalty would be paid for, and thus owed. Their duty may be "bound," but justice is theirs to decide. In the desperately constrained context of their slavery, their sacrifice of a day's freedom and three days' food because the offer is not strictly "voluntary" is a striking example of allegiance not to the master, as Ligon suggests, but rather to their own collective dignity. Ligon praises the actions, but sees them only as submissive. He asserts that the noble qualities of honesty, conscience, humility, and faithfulness reside in many slaves but proposes that one reason for their loyalty is that "they set no great value upon their lives" (106). The reasoning is jarring; the cheapness of life stands in stark contrast to the moral values Ligon has just been describing. However, Ligon's proposal recognizes that for a slave to value his or her own life would put him or her in direct opposition to both the master and the social death imposed by chattel slavery. Putting no personal value on their lives is thus seen as both a condition and a demonstration of loyalty to the master.

Nowhere is this clearer than in Ligon's haunting image of slaves trying to extinguish fires in the cane field by throwing their bodies onto the flames.

In the section where he links the servants' ill-treatment to the setting of fires, Ligon writes, "And I have seen some *Negroes* so earnest to stop this fire, as with their naked feet to tread, and with their naked bodies to tumble, and roll upon it; so little they regard their own smart or safety, in respect to their Master's benefit" (95). The scene is horrid and difficult to imagine. Yet, Ligon claims to have seen it and considers it an inspiring demonstration of the slaves' earnestness, loyalty, and complete dedication to protecting the master's profit, even to the point of sacrificing their lives. If servant labor, which was on the decline, was still associated with unmanageability, the text asserts here that slave labor was so effectively managed that the priorities of protecting the main commodity, sugar, would usurp the priority of protecting one's own life. The image of naked slave bodies tumbling into the cane fire is a concentrated figure for a system in which those bodies were valued only insofar as they could be given to the demands of sugar production. What is barely spoken here is that these lives are already sacrificed, consumed in and by the cane field before it starts to burn. Part of what gives this image such power is the slaves' purported spontaneous participation in their own destruction, the claim that they are determined to inflict injury on themselves in order to save the cane. Ligon's placement of the scene in the context of the servant revolt emphasizes the importance of this ascription of motive. It is an adamant fantasy, in which slavery's voracious consumption of human life is sacrificially cleansed by the slaves' supposedly eager affirmation of the fact that the master's profit is always paramount. The maintenance of this fantasy was crucial to the planter class, even as the fires onto which the slaves threw themselves may have been ignited by the rebellious among them.

Combustible matter was everywhere, and yet the nature of catastrophe had changed. In 1607 the castaway John Nicholl asked his readers to try to imagine "in what a perplexed state we were plunged, seeing still one misery to follow another, and each misery farre exceeding the former."[65] That misery defied expression: "it is impossible; for I cannot express it," he declared.[66] Ligon too points to the daily miseries of life on Barbados, as well as to the "great casualties" that attend the business of plantation, but these miseries and casualties occur in a far different context. The early English settler who was abandoned on the island had been replaced by the planter who successfully made the torrid exchange. The institutionalization of catastrophe in New World slavery brought to a close the seasons of misery that defined early settlement. The colonial tropic was still in operation; life beyond the line was still seen as excessive, precarious, and intense. Being colonial in the West Indies still meant being subject to the volatility of life and death, fabulous wealth and utter ruin, wild extravagance and sudden catastrophe. All these qualities were ascribed to both the nature of the place and the society English people created there.

By the 1650s, however, as sugar production was brought to "high perfection," that society was rapidly turning into a world of masters and slaves. If contingency remained at the center of English coloniality, even that contingency was written into a merciless system of production fueled by the relentless pursuit of wealth, one in which colonists became the architects of catastrophe. Likewise, although the orders of knowledge that Ligon establishes in his text are often interrupted by ungovernable extremes, his discursive modes of catalog and calculation finally represent the privileges of mastery—incomplete to be sure, but functional and above all enforceable. As the miseries of settlement gave way to the atrocities of the plantation complex, violence lost its anarchic character and its connection to settler suffering. Violence was instead a strategy to which the planter had constant recourse. John Nicholl wrote, "[M]y selfe with my associates have had a wofull experience, as ever (in my judgement) had any creatures living under the Canopie of Heaven."[67] No West Indian colonist at midcentury could ever claim the same. Their season of misery ended, a new cataclysmic history had begun.

Standing Half-Amazed

Given the devastating impact that English colonialism had on African and Native American peoples and cultures, we might ask why we should listen to the laments of Englishmen at all. They believed themselves to be the rightful masters of all they encountered, beholden only to a God who set them above others and to a program of empire that would bring them global power. Through their words and through their actions, they insisted on this superiority in countless ways and assumed its prerogatives without question and without apology. Surely what colonists suffered in the early seasons of settlement compares in no way to the disastrous effects that their colonial mission had on others. In light of this, what does their misery matter? If we want to talk about the wages of life and death in the early seventeenth-century New World, why talk about English misery? This is a large question, and a fair one. Throughout the course of pursuing this study, I have asked it myself: why trace the workings of catastrophe through the colonizer? I have arrived at several answers, and each has persuaded me that there is value in incorporating the crisis of early settlement into our understanding of colonial history.

My first reason for concentrating on these difficult seasons emerged from my reading of the literature, from being harrowed by it and feeling compelled to attend, closely and critically, to what I saw as its quality of deep distress. When early English settlers described themselves, they often described themselves in states of misery. We suffer here, they wrote, and in the colonial context, each element of this expression—the subject "we," the verb "suffer," and the place "here"—was made more deeply estranging through its conjunction with the others. Never, they wrote, were there Englishmen left in such misery. If we pass over this fear and suffering as a local, temporary, and ultimately negligible phase, we also pass over how often and how powerfully colonial voices rendered the essential fact of being colonial as a calamity.

Second, if we do not incorporate settlers' suffering into a critical analysis of early colonialism, it remains untouched as a vehicle for national ideology. That ideology is familiarly expressed: settlers suffered for us, so that we might live the blessings of freedom. The past is commemorated as a sacrificial offering to the future, and the colonial gets lost in the dream of the national. In this construction, the complexity of settlement, marked by its many kinds of violence, is narrated instead as a singular story of origins wherein the first "Americans" bravely faced peril to become the progenitors of an exceptional nation. This is a story in which early crises are recoded as heroic endurance and the backward glance is quickly propelled toward a vision of the future. To look closely at crisis during colonial settlement in its own terms, then, is to take suffering out of this orthodox narrative and place it again in a historical context of chaos, violence, and loss.

A third, and related, reason to look at the miseries of settlement is because doing so challenges us to hold suffering and violence in our minds at the same time. This is a difficult task, but it is worth the difficulty because dichotomizing these two states ends by disavowing one or the other. In the end, either one has suffered or one has enacted violence: one state inevitably trumps the other. This move is in keeping with a demand for closure in the historical narrative.[1] Here, much depends on the scale at which the historical narrative of colonialism is told, on where one assigns its beginning, middle, and end. It is hard to resist this demand for closure, especially when on a large scale colonialism was a system of oppression that, through the systematic subjugation of others, consolidated power and benefited from it. However, putting a different frame around the question of suffering and violence, and reading closely within that frame make it possible to create frictions rather than polarities, which in turn challenges us to tolerate tension within the historical narrative. Opening enough narrative space to explore that tension between different forms of brutality gives us a more unsettled, and ultimately more unsettling, view of colonial settlement.

Fourth, paying attention to these seasons of misery begins to locate an area of distinction between the literature of colonization writ large and the more specific features of a literature of colonials. The writing of colonial exploration, justification, promotion, and settlement were integrated and discursively linked elements in an elaborate program of colonial possession.

But we find that at the moment of settlement, a certain difference emerged. The "mixed suffrances of body and mind" that so often defined settlements strained the visions of power and plenty that underwrote the English mission in America.[2] Representing these colonial chaos zones to a non-colonial audience presented a distinctive challenge. Colonial writers needed to find a language that could emphasize the unparalleled nature of their situation while still invoking the connections and continued support that were their lifelines. This language needed to assert difference and connection at once. In trying to negotiate this position, colonial writers called and built on shared rhetorical forms, but their writing took on its most urgent and particular character when it strained the capacity of established discourses to describe the experience of colonial difference. This they registered as a form of crisis particular to their new situation, one that could not be imagined from the other side.

When colonists mapped the land as territory and cataloged nature as commodities, when they looked around them through imperial eyes, when they asserted that God had given them a charge to do his work in a savage land, they participated in a discourse of colonial possession that stretched back to the first European explorers of what was called a "New World." This discourse continued to be elaborated as English settlers attempted to occupy Native land permanently. However, when the eye turned inward, when they depicted themselves and their colonial condition, their writing often turned to a language of fear, uncanniness, bewilderment, entreaty, or grim visions. Writing this way registered a rift between the English ideals that were the basis of colonization and the fractured colonial experiences that were its outcome. It is not that colonial ideology or English rhetorical traditions disappeared because of these experiences; it is that the crises of settlement put such pressure on those inheritances as to open a troubling breach. In this breach, in this space between, colonial identity took shape. That identity was not defined in positive terms; it arose from its own violation. This is why misery became a language of coloniality. It allowed settlers to make recourse to a putative English identity, but it also created their relationship to it as to something that was being irreparably violated. Englishness thus became a virtual, rather than an inhabited, category of being, one that needed to claim its persistence even while describing its deterioration or unrecognizability.[3] That virtual relationship required a kind of splitting, whereby settlers made claims upon and because of their Englishness even as they bore frightful witness to the extraordinary absence of former evidences and guarantees of

that Englishness. In the writing of settlement, the fact that these things happened *to Englishmen* was part of their horror, but the fact that they happened
such a far way off and in such alien and unimaginable circumstances made
them precisely not English, but colonial.

This breach is exemplified in what is perhaps the most anthologized passage of colonial American literature, a close reading of which may construct
a model for how that space between was written. William Bradford looks
out over the land and sees its "weatherbeaten" face looking back at him. In
the tradition of European travel writing, such a moment in which the colonizer casts a sweeping view over the land that he intends to possess has been
described by Mary Louise Pratt as "the monarch-of-all-I-survey" scene. According to Pratt, "The monarch-of-all-I-survey scene" involves an "explicit
interaction between esthetics and ideology, in what one might call a rhetoric
of presence."[4] However, in Bradford's colonial scene, it is not presence but
absence that is first elaborated. Before he portrays the face of the country he
surveys, Bradford discursively opens up a space of distance, absence, and
loss, one that radically separates the colonial moment from the comforts of a
familiar state. He writes, "Being thus passed the vast ocean . . . they had now
no friends to welcome them nor inns to entertain or refresh their weatherbeaten bodies; no houses much less towns to repair to, to seek for succour."[5]
Bradford uses this elaboration of absences to introduce his vision because
before describing what he sees, he needs first to establish what he does not
see. The colonial condition he wants to depict cannot be written until a split
has opened between it and a former condition of Englishness. Even for these
people in exile, Bradford's first claim is that the stabilizing connections that
once existed between identity and the exterior world—connections between
the individual, the social body, and both a natural and built environment—
have undergone a disjunctive transformation. With no friends, inns, houses,
or towns, these "weatherbeaten bodies" are portrayed as being alone, unre-
lieved in their confrontation with the world where they intend to implant
themselves.

The description that follows has been interpreted as a prime example of
the English colonists' projection of prejudice and suspicion onto the land
they were about to subjugate, land that Bradford describes in a vocabulary
of unrelenting hostility and fear: sharp, violent, cruel, fierce, dangerous, hideous, desolate, and wild.[6] It has been called an anticipation of the rhetoric
of the negative sublime, evoking a structure of transcendence to confront
the overpowering qualities of wild nature.[7] It has been read as a discursive

creation of the American wilderness as a place that, while utterly unlike
Europe, must be settled by English people in order to reveal its and their
ultimate meaning and good.[8] All of these readings add to our understanding of the scene in which Bradford imaginatively sets his people apart from,
and yet in confrontation with, what he deeply remembers and discursively
re-creates as a howling wilderness. But in concentrating on the interpretive
consequences of Bradford's description of that wilderness, we often overlook
the way he begins this virtuoso piece about standing at the threshold of the
colonial condition: with a half-amazed pause.

Before his descriptive outpouring, Bradford abruptly stops the time of
his narrative and commands his reader to an astounded halt. He writes, "But
here I cannot but stay and make a pause, and stand half amazed at this poor
people's present condition; and so I think will the reader, too, when he well
considers the same."[9] For a moment, as if compelled by force, writer, reader,
and history itself all stand still and gaze, half-amazed, on the beaten, bewildered, and bereft bodies of the settlers. But why is this astonished pause
necessary? Why can the narrative not go from landfall to a description of the
land? And if we do stop for a dramatic moment, why does Bradford not por-
tray himself as the monarch of all he surveys? The pause is commanded in
order to mark a crucial threshold in his narrative of the rough dealings that
sent the Pilgrim group over the ocean, got them across it, and brought them
to the American shore. It is a space that he "cannot but" open, so that what is
becoming colonial can also come into view. In this opening moment, it is not
the land but his own people's condition before which we stand half-amazed.
Bradford's "poor people" always achieve part of their significance by their
suffering, but his ability to command us into that astounded pause lies more
precisely in their "present condition," the fact that they suffer "such a great
way off," that they have "passed the vast ocean" that "was now as a main bar
and gulf to separate them from all the civil parts of the world," only to cast
themselves into this state of catastrophe.[10] We are called upon to stand half-
amazed because within this moment of shocked time, we are watching the
spectacle of English people watching themselves becoming colonial.

For Bradford, the word "amaze" did not simply mean to be for a moment
astonished; rather it meant to be stunned out of one's wits as by a blow over
the head, to be completely overcome by sudden fear and panic, dread and
alarm. It especially referred to a state of awe inspired by the overwhelming might of God. As a response to miracles, it took the form of trembling
wonder. As a response to holy wrath, it was sheer terror. For example, the

scripture that describes the destruction of Babylon bellows, "And they shall be afraid: pangs and sorrowes shall take hold of them, they shall be in paine as a woman that travelleth: they shall be amazed one at another, their faces shall be as flames."[11] But remember that Bradford the historian stands *half*-amazed. For him to be fully amazed would mean to be hopeless and helpless in the face of divine might, to be struck dumb without any possibility of signification beyond speechless awe. On the other hand, not to be amazed at all would mean that his history had denied the condition that he insistently claims his people to have suffered, that it had not recorded their dread misery. If the colonial subject is split, however—powerfully but only half-amazed—then there is a chance that the fall into terror might be less than total, and that even the language of catastrophe might become a place holder for a former life that is clearly lost. If witness was possible, then the loss of self-recognition might yet admit the potential of a virtual "I" who could view the self rendered through this radical disorientation, and who could present it in a double vision: what that self once was and what it was now becoming. Thus the fantasy of a continuous identity might survive the insistent evidence of a changed one.

Settlers were supposed to establish English presence and English locations in the New World, but absence and dislocation just as often defined the settlement. That these polarities were in such proximity exerted constant pressure on the organization of identity: possession and dispossession; location and dislocation; presence and absence; violence and suffering; conviction and confusion. The first terms in all these sets (possession, location, presence, violence, conviction) are the anchors of a theory of settler colonialism that explains how the colonizing force displaces indigenous populations and consolidates its own claims of sovereignty upon the land.[12] The second terms in these sets (dispossession, dislocation, absence, suffering, confusion) have been co-opted and sanitized by national mythology that enlists the afflictions of the "first settlers" into a narrative of endurance and sacrifice. However, not only were these sets of terms not separated off from one another in the literature written by settlers; they were also portrayed as being in conjunction or in collision with each other. Reading the writing of settlement through the lens of catastrophe offers us a way to read the simultaneity of these opposing categories specifically by not choosing between them but instead by concentrating on the disorder, or crisis, into which these terms themselves fell.

Understanding the workings of catastrophe at the inception of colonial settlement can change some of the ways we think about how the English became colonial. This is, of course, an enormous and much-studied topic. It may indeed be one of the root questions of the field: What did it mean to become colonial? When and where, how and why, and (especially) to whom did it happen? What were its processes and what were its consequences? What were its languages, its claims, and its proofs? Where did patterns overlap, and where did they diverge? In what framework and toward what ends? Models for positing these questions have become more global and comparative, less tied to the contours of a national narrative and more interested in recovering how Native Americans, Africans, Europeans, and Atlantic creoles negotiated a complex network of colonial areas that represented new worlds for all. Clearly the means of devising and elaborating colonial identities were multiple and were specific to time and place and people. Nonetheless, many studies of the colonial world still aim to articulate the emergence, transformation, or development of something that might be called colonial, even while embracing the necessary difficulties and intricacies of that task.

Writing about settler societies in the colonial Atlantic world, J. H. Elliott asks, "What was it that encouraged these transplanted European communities to begin to think of themselves as in some way distinct and separate from the mother country?"[13] In addressing this question, Elliott warns against "assuming that self-definition constitutes a linear process, whereby newborn societies progress by predetermined stages from a condition of total dependence on the mother country to a physical and psychological maturity that ends with full emancipation."[14] He understands that "this process of self-definition [was] sometimes advancing, sometimes retreating, but never static" and that societally, "identities were always uneven, always incomplete, and at times perilously fragile."[15] Elliott is only one of many scholars who emphasize that locating and describing colonial difference does not imply a regular or "preordained" course of development that finds its "denouement" in political independence.[16] But if we now readily acknowledge that colonial identity was not always moving gradually, steadily toward a future sense of independence, I would also stress that it was not always moving gradually, steadily away from a former sense of continuity. The changes were, as Elliott says, uneven, incomplete, fragile. There came critical moments of division when it was abundantly clear that colonial lives could not be—could not even approximate—English lives. In the first period of settlement these critical moments were both acute and widespread. Settlers were the front lines of the colonial mission, but English visions of establishing colonies reflective of the home culture soon gave way to straitened communities living in extreme circumstances. Even when migration was voluntary, these insistently privative transitions were not chosen ends toward which the settler societies directed themselves. Their colonial existence began with the shock of the new, with the brutality and bareness of their experience, and with the distressing breakdown of their supposedly inherent English civility.

This intense confrontation with separateness from the home culture had immediate material and psychological consequences, but the meaning of that separateness still needed to be negotiated. When everything familiar was absent and everything present was strange, settlers' faith in a secure connection to their Englishness became paramount. Instead, it was never more fraught. When colonists stood half-amazed and looked upon themselves, they saw the possibility that the body that had once represented "the civil parts of the world" might not be able to bear the burden of that meaning, much less to manifest its outward forms in a place so deeply defined by difference. This exposed a chaos that writers continually struggled to turn into meaning, a gap they tried, through their writing, to close. However, this search for significance and continuity stood against the precariousness and disorder of colonial life. The upheavals of settlement continued to be pervasive, dramatic, and new. All around whatever disciplines colonial writers were able to impose on their writing, there remained an excess that was caused by the enormous dislocation and disorder, the vulnerability and violence, the instability and insecurity of colonial life. We often talk about identity as a broader "formation" or as something a society "achieves" over time, but settlement-as-catastrophe shows that identity could also take shape through deformation—not as an achievement but as a collapse. When the threat of dispossession was felt so immediately, there was no stable, alternative model ready to take the place of what was lost. Therefore one of the first ways to say "I am colonial" was to speak it not as a formation but rather as a privation: "I am an Englishman who no longer recognizes himself or his actions or his surroundings. I am doing things that seem incredible, but nothing is more real. I am left in the New World in misery."

Over time, becoming colonial was an ongoing project or process of creative adaptation, but it was also a process of recovering from an initial and initiating crisis that forced upon settlers the fact that theirs would not be English lives.[17] Even when day-to-day life within the settlements established some sort of protections, regularity, stability, and coherence, colonists were well aware that their best "improvements" were in a large sense guards against this most immediate history of crisis. Therefore even when the worst of the "seasoning" was over, it continued to register as a gap out of which the colonial had emerged transformed—not better and more resilient, not triumphal, but changed and carrying the memory of having barely survived the ordeal. From the first, colonials had to defend themselves against charges of creole degeneracy: the belief that settlers would necessarily devolve in the New World, where an alien humoral environment would negatively affect their essential constitution, and the proximity to native savagery and barbarism would make the maintenance of any civilized state impossible. "The continuous bombardment of calumny to which settler communities were subjected gave them an early and powerful incentive to develop a more favorable image of themselves, if only in self-defense," Elliott claims.[18] But the question of whether an Englishman could remain English so far from home was not only troubled by metropolitan contempt; it was also troubled by a colonial memory of the deep disorder in which the experiment began and in which it so often persisted. This is part of what Michael Zuckerman calls "the deep disquietude of early American psychic life."[19] If colonists concentrated on building themselves up, eventually focusing on the healthfulness and ease of the place, the improvements they made, and the growth they sustained, they also knew that an environment of total hazard was possible and that in the uncharted space of that hazard, they could both be terrified and become a terror unto others. The "favorable image of themselves" was always in contention with a self-awareness that their short colonial history was inescapably one of suffering and violence.

"But here I cannot but stay and make a pause, and stand half amazed . . . and so I think will the reader, too, when he well considers the same." The archive of settlement is full of moments that can make a reader stand half-amazed. Ralph Lane travels upriver to an imaginary city; his starving men eye the empty, silent shores. Pemisapan jumps up from his death pose and runs. Two bodies are found hanging from the posts of an abandoned fort. Emaciated colonists dig up an Indian corpse and eat it. Paspahegh warriors make the sound of their name fill the air. Men so sick that they cannot stand are propped up against trees with their muskets at their sides. Sugar planters drink water from a bog where dead bodies float. A slave combusts in a distillery. The head of another is impaled and set up at the center of the plantation. English soldiers suddenly shout, "*Oho, Oho,*" and, convinced they are Indians, beat each other with the butts of their guns. All these scenes might bring us to a halt, but there has to be a way of giving a critical account of colonial settlement that does not have to choose between eliding that pause or staying, half-amazed, within it.

The method is neither to exclude these stories nor to treat them as outliers to a more orderly historical narrative. But neither is it to repeat in order to mythologize them. Paul Ricoeur reminds us that "the excesses of certain commemorations" that "attempt to fix the memories in a kind of reverential relationship to the past" are one kind of abuse of historical consciousness.[20] "Let us recall," he writes, "that most events to do with the founding of any community are acts and events of violence."[21] He suggests that one way to remember these events is through narrative, which can serve historical memory in an ethical respect "because it is always possible to tell in another way."[22] My sense in writing this book was that colonial settlement needed to be told in a different way—in part because it is both remembered and forgotten. The nationalist story of settler suffering eclipses settler violence while the broader story of colonialism's violence rarely integrates the crises of settlement. Without reverencing, diminishing, or explaining it away, I felt we did not know what to do with the testimony of suffering in the context of foundational violence. By narratively and analytically constructing the catastrophe as a framework of colonial settlement, I have argued that paying attention to misery's testimony does not detract from seeing violence; indeed it brings violence into high relief. Suffering and violence neither excluded nor annulled each other. Instead, they existed among other acute situations and too-close polarities that initiated the colonial condition.

Misery was not at all the special province of the settlers, but at the start of England's colonial history, they found it crucial to claim that ground. Upon it they stood half-amazed at their changed condition. Representing the initiation of colonial life as a new world of misery allowed settlers to write from within the breach of a ruptured Englishness, to witness the wages of becoming colonial, to express their bewilderment, to justify their violence, and to claim the singularity of their experience all at once. It was, I believe, the framework through which their colonial identities first took form. Reading the records of this critical period of history, we too might stand half-amazed, but only half. The other half must move out of the pause, mindful of its costs, and reckon with the colonial past without losing or getting lost in catastrophe.

NOTES

Introduction

1. Alexander Brown, *The Genesis of the United States* (New York: Russell and Russell, 1964), 487.

2. George Percy, "A Trewe Relaycon of the Proceedings and Occurantes of Momente," in *Captain John Smith: Writings with Other Narratives of Roanoke, Jamestown, and the First English Settlement of America*, ed. James Horn (New York: Literary Classics of the United States, 2007), 1110.

3. Brown, *Genesis of the United States*, 487.

4. William Strachey, *The Historie of Travaile into Virginia Brittania*, ed. R. H. Major (London: Hakluyt Society, 1849), 42.

5. Percy, "Trewe Relaycon," 933.

6. Françoise Davoine and Jean-Max Guadillière, *History beyond Trauma*, trans. Susan Fairfield (New York: Other Press, 2004), xxviii.

7. Ibid., xxii.

8. Thomas Harriot, *A Briefe and True Report of the New Found Land of Virginia* (New York: Dover, 1972), 6.

9. Percy, "Trewe Relaycon," 1099.

10. William Bradford, *Of Plymouth Plantation 1620–1647*, ed. Samuel Eliot Morison (New York: Alfred A. Knopf, 1952), 130.

11. Richard Ligon, *A True and Exact History of the Island of Barbados*, ed. Karen Ordahl Kupperman (Indianapolis: Hackett, 2011), 181, 94.

12. David B. Quinn, ed., *The Roanoke Voyages, 1587–1590* (New York: Dover, 1991), 82.

13. For studies on early modern providentialism, see Alexandra Walsham, *Providence in Early Modern England* (Oxford: Oxford University Press, 1999); and Malcom R. Smuts, *Culture and Power in England, 1583–1685* (New York: St. Martin's, 1999). Walsham argues that while providential thinking was nearly universal, it was never static or monolithic. Smuts identifies providentialism (along with honor, law, and antiquity) as one of the four primary frames of reference for the early modern period. Both argue for a multiple view of providentialism as a fluid belief system producing a variety of discourses, a broadly accepted pattern of thought that could be employed simultaneously by different peoples for different, and conflicting, ends.

On the enormous popularity of providence tales, see J. Paul Hunter, *Before Novels: The Cultural Context of Eighteenth-Century English Fiction* (New York: W. W. Norton, 1990).

14. See Ernest B. Gilman, *Plague Writing in Early Modern England* (Chicago: University of Chicago Press, 2009). Gilman writes, "[T]he English imagination conceived the plague not only as something to be written about, but as itself a form of writing" (73).

15. Lawrence Manley, *Literature and Culture in Early Modern London* (Cambridge: Cambridge University Press, 1995), 74. I thank David Landreth for this reference.

16. Thomas Goad, *The Dolefull Even-song* (London: John Haviland, 1623).

17. Robert Blair St. George, *Conversing by Signs: The Poetics of Implication in New England Culture* (Chapel Hill: University of North Carolina Press, 1998), 8.

18. *Oxford English Dictionary*, 2nd ed., s.v. "seasoning," def. 1e.

19. Joyce Chaplin, *Subject Matter: Technology, the Body, and Science on the Anglo-American Frontier, 1500–1676* (Cambridge, Mass.: Harvard University Press, 2001), 151.

20. Hayden White, "The Historical Event," *differences* 19, no. 2 (2008): 19.

21. Quoted in ibid., 9.

22. Alain Badiou, *Ethics: An Essay on the Understanding of Evil*, trans. Peter Hallward (London and New York: Verso, 2001), 41.

23. White, "The Historical Event," 17, emphasis added.

24. I thank Max Cavitch for this insight and for the vocabulary of "ongoingness."

25. Oscar Handlin, "The Significance of the Seventeenth Century," in *Seventeenth Century America: Essays in Colonial America*, ed. James Morton Smith (Chapel Hill: University of North Carolina Press, 1959), 6, 9.

26. Perry Miller, *Errand into the Wilderness* (Boston: Belknap Press of Harvard University Press, 1957), 6.

27. James H. Merrell, "Indian History during the English Colonial Era," in *A Companion to Colonial America*, ed. Daniel Vickers (Oxford: Blackwell, 2006), 214.

28. Francis Jennings, *The Invasion of America: Indians, Colonialism, and the Cant of Conquest* (New York: W. W. Norton, 1976), 32.

29. Richard Slotkin, *Regeneration through Violence: The Mythology of the American Frontier, 1600–1860* (Norman: University of Oklahoma Press, 1975), 5.

30. This is especially the case in Atlantic histories that compare British and Spanish colonization. See, for example, J. H. Elliott, *Empires of the Atlantic World: Britain and Spain in America, 1492–1830* (New Haven, Conn.: Yale University Press, 2006); and Jorge Cañizares-Esguerra, *Puritan Conquistadors: Iberianizing the Atlantic, 1550–1700* (Stanford, Calif.: Stanford University Press, 2006).

31. T. H. Breen, "Creative Adaptations: Peoples and Cultures," in *Colonial British America: Essays in the New History of the Early Modern Era*, ed. Jack P. Greene and J. R. Pole (Baltimore: Johns Hopkins University Press, 1984), 195.

32. Karen Ordahl Kupperman, *Indians and English: Facing Off in Early America* (Ithaca, N.Y.: Cornell University Press, 2000).

33. See Mary Louise Pratt, *Imperial Eyes: Travel Writing and Transculturation*, 2nd

ed. (London: Routledge, 2008); Richard White, *The Middle Ground: Indians, Empires, and Republics in the Great Lakes Region, 1650–1815* (New York: Cambridge University Press, 2011).

34. See, for example, Jorge Cañizares-Esguerra, *How to Write the History of the New World: Histories, Epistemologies, and Identities in the Eighteenth Century Atlantic World* (Cambridge, Mass.: Harvard University Press, 2001); Walter Mignolo, *Local Histories/Global Designs: Coloniality, Subaltern Knowledge, and Border Thinking* (Princeton, N.J.: Princeton University Press, 2000); Ralph Bauer, *The Cultural Geography of Colonial American Literatures: Empire, Travel, Modernity* (Cambridge: Cambridge University Press, 2009). For "epistemic murk," see Michael Taussig, *Shamanism, Colonialism, and the Wild Man: A Study in Terror and Healing* (Chicago: University of Chicago Press, 1991), 121.

35. See, for example, Elizabeth Manke and Carol Shammas, *The Creation of the British Atlantic World* (Baltimore: Johns Hopkins University Press, 2005); Allison Games, *Migration and the Origin of the English Atlantic World* (Cambridge, Mass.: Harvard University Press, 2001).

36. Andrew Delbanco, *The Puritan Ordeal* (Cambridge, Mass.: Harvard University Press, 1991); Mitchell Breitwieser, *American Puritanism and the Defense of Mourning: Religion, Grief, and Ethnology in Mary White Rowlandson's Captivity Narrative* (Madison: University of Wisconsin Press, 1990).

37. Cathy Caruth, "Introduction," in *Trauma: Explorations in Memory*, ed. Cathy Caruth (Baltimore: Johns Hopkins University Press, 1995), 5.

38. Judith Herman, *Trauma and Recovery* (New York: Basic Books, 1997), 33.

39. Dominick LaCapra, *Writing History, Writing Trauma* (Baltimore: Johns Hopkins University Press, 2001), 41.

40. Moreover, I do not think that the writing of seventeenth-century colonial settlement maps easily onto the testimony from survivors of limit events in the modern age. Trauma theory's concerns with the theory and the practice of recovering the testimony of survivors, providing witness, and working through traumatic history have also centrally been a concern with the continuing repercussions of the catastrophes of our contemporary age, especially the Holocaust. In their introduction to *Testimony: Crises of Witnessing in Literature, Psychoanalysis, and History* (New York: Routledge, 1991), Shoshana Felman and Dori Laub write, "[T]he historical trauma of the Second World War, a trauma we consider as the watershed of our times . . . [is] a history which is essentially *not over*, a history whose repercussions are not simply omnipresent (whether consciously or not) in all our cultural activities, but whose traumatic consequences are still *evolving*" (xiv, emphasis in original). Reading the literature of seventeenth-century colonial settlers is a different endeavor, not only because of the distance between their historical conditions and our own, but also because colonialism itself can be marked as a catastrophe whose continuing repercussions we still feel today.

41. Catherine Gallagher and Stephen Greenblatt, *Practicing New Historicism* (Chicago: University of Chicago Press, 2001), 20.

42. Ibid., 56.

43. Lawrence Stone, "The Revival of Narrative: Reflections on a New Old History," *Past and Present* 85 (November 1979): 23.

44. Myra Jehlen, "History before the Fact; or, Captain John Smith's Unfinished Symphony," *Critical Inquiry* 19, no. 4 (Summer 1993): 690.

45. Two exceptions are E. Thomas Shields and Michael G. Moran. Both read Lane's report as a model of colonial apologia, a reading I complicate through analyzing the epistemological uncertainty of the text itself. See E. Thomas Shields, "The Literature of Exploration," in *The Oxford Handbook of Early American History*, ed. Kevin J. Hayes (Oxford: Oxford University Press, 2008), 33–35; Michael G. Moran, "Ralph Lane's 1586 Discourse of the First Colony: The Renaissance Commercial Report as Apologia," *Technical Communications Quarterly* 12, no. 2 (2003): 125–54.

46. Russell Menard argues that the "sugar revolution" that is commonly held to have happened in Barbados in the mid-seventeenth century should really be seen as a "sugar boom," given the context of the island's history of agricultural diversity, the use of slave labor, and the export of tropical commodities in the 1630s. See Russell Menard, *Sweet Negotiations: Sugar, Slavery, and Plantation Agriculture in Early Barbados* (Charlottesville: University Press of Virginia, 2006).

47. Hayden White, *Metahistory: The Historical Imagination in Nineteenth-Century Europe* (Baltimore: Johns Hopkins University Press, 1973), ix.

48. Ibid., 11.

49. Ibid., 2.

50. Ibid., xiii.

Chapter 1

1. Richard Hakluyt et al., *The Principall Navigations, Voiages, Traffiques And Discoveries Of the English Nation*, 2nd ed. (London: George Bishop, Ralph Newberie and Robert Barker, 1598/9–1600), 292–93. All additional references to White's narrative will be cited in the text from David B. Quinn, *The Roanoke Voyages, 1584–1590: Documents to Illustrate the English Voyages to North America under the Patent Granted to Walter Raleigh in 1584*, vol 1. (New York: Dover, 1991).

2. Richard Slotkin, *Regeneration through Violence: The Mythology of the American Frontier 1600–1860* (Norman: University of Oklahoma Press, 1973); Toni Morrison, *Playing in the Dark: Whiteness and the Literary Imagination* (New York: Vintage Books, 1993).

3. This consensus can be found in the full-length histories of Roanoke as well as more telescoped treatments. See Karen Ordahl Kupperman, *Roanoke, the Abandoned Colony* (Totowa, N.J.: Rowman & Allanheld, 1984); David Beers Quinn, *Set Fair for Roanoke: Voyages and Colonies, 1584–1606* (Chapel Hill: Published for America's Four Hundredth Anniversary Committee by the University of North Carolina Press, 1985).

4. Alan Taylor, *American Colonies*, Penguin History of the United States (New York: Viking, 2001), 124, 25.

5. Ibid., 124.

6. Karen Ordahl Kupperman, "Roanoke Lost," *American Heritage* 36, no. 5 (1985): 81–90.

7. The literature on Harriot and White is extensive. A good place to begin is with Mary B. Campbell, "The Illustrated Travel Book and the Birth of Ethnography: Part I of de Bry's America," in *The Work of Dissimilitude*, ed. David G. Allen and Robert A. White (Newark: University of Delaware Press, 1992), 177–95. Stephen Greenblatt's famous treatment of Harriot in his much-discussed article "Invisible Bullets: Renaissance Authority and Its Subversion" will be discussed below.

8. Ed White has persuasively argued that Harriot's systematizing logic of composition was not total and that Algonquian voices are present both in the catalog sections of the text and most notably in Harriot's discourse on Algonquian reactions to disease. In many instances, White stresses, Harriot's writing betrays "textual moments that escape systematicity" and demonstrate instead "an uneven and dynamic" interpretative praxis. See Ed White, "Invisible Tagkanysough," *PMLA* 120, no. 3 (2005): 751–67.

9. Elizabeth's charter to Raleigh was a near copy of the one she granted to Raleigh's half brother, Sir Humphrey Gilbert, in 1578. Gilbert attempted to make England's New World claims in 1583 but got only as far as Newfoundland and died on the voyage back to London.

10. Quinn, *The Roanoke Voyages, 1584–1590*, 82.

11. Ibid., 83.

12. Ibid., 89.

13. Here, I will refer to this region using its Algonquian name, Ossomocomuck. Due to a misunderstanding, the English thought that the area was called "Wingandacoa," which they later found out was a phrase meaning "You wear good clothes." Sometime between December 1584 and March 1585, Raleigh renamed the territory "Virginia" in honor of Elizabeth. See ibid., 99n1 and 116–17. In my later discussion of English texts, I will use the name Virginia, as well as the names of specific villages and tribal seats where the actions took place.

14. Michael Leroy Oberg, *The Head in Edward Nugent's Hand: Roanoke's Forgotten Indians*, Early American Studies (Philadelphia: University of Pennsylvania Press, 2008), 53.

15. Oberg's work is dedicated to foregrounding Algonquian perceptions and intentions throughout the period of English attempts to settle Roanoke. My understanding of English texts has been influenced and enriched by this perspective.

16. First published in Hakluyt *Principall Nauigations, Voiages, Traffiques, and Discoveries of the English Nation* (London: George Bishop and Ralph Newberie, 1589), 728–33. All additional references to Barlowe's narrative will be cited in the text from Quinn, *The Roanoke Voyages, 1584–1590*.

17. Historians regularly charge Barlowe's report with creating entirely unrealistic expectations that contributed in part to later disasters. See, for example, Kupperman, *Roanoke, the Abandoned Colony*, 16–17.

18. For a full explication of the Garden of Eden trope as a rhetorical device prompting group cohesion, see Michael G. Moran, "A Fantasy-Theme Analysis of Arthur Barlowe's 1584 Discourse on Virginia: The First English Commercial Report Written about North America from Direct Experience," *Technical Communication Quarterly* 11, no. 2 (Winter 2002): 31–59.

19. Louis Montrose writes, "An 'inaugural scene' of Elizabethan New World colonialism is textualized in Arthur Barlowe's report to Raleigh"; see Montrose, "The Work of Gender in the Discourse of Discovery," in *New World Encounters*, ed. Stephen Greenblatt (Berkeley: University of California Press, 1993), 183.

20. For a full-length treatment of communications systems and technologies in early New England, see Matt Cohen, *The Networked Wilderness: Communicating in Early New England* (Minneapolis: University of Minnesota Press, 2010).

21. Beginning at this moment and continuing throughout the settlement period, the English regularly marvel at Indians' extraordinary ability to suffer seemingly mortal injuries and survive.

22. Hakluyt, *Principall Navigations,* 731.

23. Lane's "Account" was first published in ibid., 739–48. Lane's time frame begins with Grenville's departure from Roanoke, two months after their landing. All additional references to Lane's narrative will be cited in the text from David B. Quinn, *The Roanoke Voyages, 1584–1590.*

24. Of the report, Quinn writes, "One thing, however, is certain. It was Lane's apologia for returning when he did, and for his actions during his residence on Roanoke Island" (Quinn, *Roanoke Voyages, 1584–1590*, 29). Also see Michael G. Moran, "Ralph Lane's 1586 Discourse on the First Colony: The Renaissance Commercial Report as Apologia," *Technical Communication Quarterly* 12, no. 2 (Spring 2003): 125–54. Most recently E. Thomson Shields Jr. has taken Lane's report as the very type of the colonial apologia, which along with promotional, descriptive, and tragic narrative forms he classifies as the modes of exploration literature (Shields, "The Literature of Exploration," in *The Oxford Handbook of Early American Literature*, ed. Kevin J. Hayes [New York: Oxford University Press, 2008], 33–35). Related to the apologia form is Mary C. Fuller's superb and sustained analysis of how the rhetoric of failure, fantasy, and deferral operated in reports of early English exploration. She writes, "[I]f the history of those early decades is about any one thing, it is about the ways in which the failure of voyages and colonies was recuperated by rhetoric, a rhetoric which in some ways even predicted failure" (Mary C. Fuller, *Voyages in Print: English Travel to America, 1576–1624*, Cambridge Studies in Renaissance Literature and Culture, 7 [Cambridge and New York: Cambridge University Press, 1995], 12). Fuller does not read Lane, and my contention here is that Lane's rhetoric was never really recuperative.

25. One example of how to shrink the story with skill and dispatch can be found in Taylor, *American Colonies*, 124.

26. In a sparse field, for two recent treatments of Lane's text, see the following:

Shields, "Literature of Exploration," 33-35; Moran, "Ralph Lane's 1586 Discourse of the First Colony," 125-54.

27. Theodor de Bry and Thomas Harriot, [America.-Part I.-English.] A Briefe and True Report of the New Found Land of Virginia, of the Commodities and of the Nature and Manners of the Naturall Inhabitants (Frankfurt: T. de Bry, 1590).

28. Thomas Harriot, A Briefe and True Report of the New Found Land of Virginia: The Complete 1590 Edition with the 28 Engravings by Theodor de Bry after the Drawings of John White and Other Illustrations (New York: Dover, 1972), xiii.

29. Ibid., viii.

30. Mary Louise Pratt, "Arts of the Contact Zone," Profession (1991): 34.

31. Ibid, 37.

32. Myra Jehlen, "History Before the Fact: or, Captain John Smith's Unfinished Symphony," Critical Inquiry 19, no. 4 (Summer 1993): 677-92, quote on 690.

33. The first English colony in North America was founded by Sir Humphrey Gilbert in Newfoundland in 1583. Weeks later, his fleet departed due to lack of supplies and Humphrey died on the return journey. For an account of the history of the colony, see David B. Quinn, "Sir Humphrey Gilbert and Newfoundland," in Explorers and Colonies: America, 1500-1625 (London: Ronceverte, 1990), 207-23. For an exhaustive collection of related primary documents, see David B. Quinn, ed., Voyages and Colonising Enterprises of Sir Humphrey Gilbert, 2 vols. (London: Hakluyt Society, 1940).

34. Quinn, Roanoke Voyages, 1584-1590, 245. In their own way, the narratives that open each chapter of Quinn's Roanoke Voyages are as valuable as the primary documents he collects. For Quinn's "Narrative" of the 1585 voyage, see 158-73; for Lane's colony, see 244-55.

35. Oberg, Head in Edward Nugent's Hand, 82.

36. Kupperman, Roanoke, the Abandoned Colony, 83.

37. There was also without doubt a fourth journey into the more desirable Chesapeake Bay. This significant discovery was deliberately repressed in order to keep the location secret—and so textually that journey does not happen.

38. Quinn, Roanoke Voyages, 1584-1590, 893; Oberg, Head in Edward Nugent's Hand.

39. Without knowing the nature of the gathering at Choanoac, Oberg surmises that Pemisapan may have wanted to prompt a confrontation to eliminate threats posed by the Choanoac, the English, or both.

40. James Horn believes that this marks the first time English colonists hear of Wahunsonacock, whom they will come to call Powhatan, but Quinn suggests that the "powerful werowance" is Kecoughtan. See James Horn, ed., Captain John Smith: Writings with Other Narratives of Roanoke, Jamestown, and the First English Settlement of America, Library of America (New York: Literary Classics of the United States, 2007), 31; Quinn, Roanoke Voyages, 1584-1590, 260.

41. For the entire imagined river journey, see Quinn, Roanoke Voyages, 1584-1590, 261-64, quoted here passim.

42. On the role of the counterfactual in later critical military history, see Catherine Gallagher, "The Formalism of Military History," *Representations* 104, no. 1 (Fall 2008): 23–33. Like those military historians engaged in counterfactual analyses, Lane is also concerned with accounting for what he could have done under different conditions. However, Lane cannot make a critical analysis of his actual or possible actions, or of a field of alternate outcomes, because his retrospective view includes no new information about his experience in the field.

43. This passage actually represents a threefold displacement: it is about the gathering at Choanoke, which Lane has already passed chronologically in silence; it is about Pemisapan's warning at the outset of that journey, which Lane believed; and it is about Lane's later conviction that Pemisapan was spreading rumors to both the English and the Choanoke so that they would turn on each other. Quinn describes this passage as "a typical example of Lane's lack of lucidity in composition." He writes, "Having given us a version of his visit to Chawanoac [sic] in March 1586, he now reverts to the background of that expedition, namely to Wingina's [Pemisapan's] stimulation of a great Indian assembly of a hostile character to receive him. He still leaves untold the circumstances in where he braved this assembly, took Menatonon prisoner, ransomed him and, finally, convinced him of his peaceful intentions" (Quinn, *Roanoke Voyages, 1584–1590*, 266 n1). Oberg disagrees about the purpose of the massive gathering, noting that if thousands of warriors had wanted to kill Lane, they would have done so (Oberg, *Head in Edward Nugent's Hand*, 84).

44. Presently the Roanoke River.

45. Whatever communication did happen was likely conducted through the offices of Manteo. Oberg canvasses the likely reactions of all parties in the wake of the Choanoac assembly in order to account for this deep misunderstanding. Offering a few possible scenarios, he admits that it must have been difficult, if not impossible, for anyone to achieve clarity about what was happening. See Oberg, *Head in Edward Nugent's Hand*, 83.

46. In addition to Oberg, see J. Frederick Fausz, "Patterns of Anglo-Indian Aggression and Accommodation along the Mid-Atlantic Coast, 1584–1634," in *Cultures in Contact: The Impact of European Contact on Native American Cultural Institutions, a.d. 1000–1800*, ed. William W. Fitzhugh (Washington, D.C.: Smithsonian Institution Press, 1985), 227–54.

47. Early histories of Roanoke commented on the men's remarkable loyalty to Lane. See, for example, Increase N. Tarbox, *Sir Walter Ralegh and His Colony in America* (Boston: Prince Society, 1884), 155n7: "Whatever may have been said of Lane upon the score of his wisdom and sagacity, it is at least evident that he had the confidence of his men to a remarkable degree."

48. Harriot too refers obliquely to this story in his *Briefe and True Report*, writing that the "wolves or wolvish dogges" of the natives did not, in his opinion, provide good meat. Harriot added that he had no idea how the taste of an Indian dog compared to

the taste of an English one, but perhaps that question could be answered "by some of our company which have been experimented in both." See Quinn, *Roanoke Voyages, 1584–1590*, 357.

49. As Ed White notes, Harriot's report of the invisible-bullets theory and Stephen Greenblatt's critical use of that report have entered the canon of colonial studies together and are rarely separated. See White, "Invisible Tagkanysough." For the first appearance of Greenblatt's much-reprinted essay, see Stephen Greenblatt, "Invisible Bullets: Renaissance Authority and Its Subversion," *Glyph* 8 (1981): 40–61.

50. In addition to White, see, for example, Donald Pease, "Toward a Sociology of Literary Knowledge: Greenblatt, Colonialism, and the New Historicism," in *Consequences of Theory: Selected Papers from the English Institute, 1987–88*, ed. Jonathan Arac and Barbara Johnson (Baltimore: Johns Hopkins University Press, 1991), 108–53.

51. If Lane is mentioned, it is usually only to corroborate Harriot. See, for example, Joyce Chaplin, *Subject Matter: Technology, the Body, and Science on the Anglo-American Frontier, 1500–1676* (Cambridge, Mass.: Harvard University Press, 2001), 172–73.

52. Quinn, *Roanoke Voyages, 1584–1590*, 378, emphasis added.

53. Ibid., 380, emphasis added.

54. Ibid., 378.

55. Ibid., 381.

56. In accounting for this new influence, Lane's report prioritizes the return of the supposedly dead men. He writes that "the King and all touching us" changed "when hee saw the small troupe returned again." Around that time other incidents ("accidents," Lane calls them) contributed to the English gaining the upper hand. Lane's company brought back Skiko, the "most beloved" son of Menatonon, as a prisoner, and soon after Menatonon sent to Lane a great and perfect pearl, perhaps in ransom for his son or perhaps as a reminder of the pearl-rich lands to the north. Finally, a group of Indians representing tribes allied with Menatonon sealed their friendship with the English and, according to Lane, referred to themselves as subjects of the great werowanza Elizabeth. See Quinn, *Roanoke Voyages, 1584–1590*, 278–79 and n2, n3, n4.

57. Lane's own description of the attack is found in Quinn, *Roanoke Voyages, 1584–1590*, 286–88.

58. The title and recurrent leitmotif of Oberg's exhaustive study is *The Head in Edward Nugent's Hand*, but even in Oberg's committed and detailed recovery of an Algonquian Roanoke, he does not interpret this moment of Pemisipan's flight.

59. Harriot, *Briefe and True Report*, 50.

60. Kupperman writes, "We can see how fragile and tenuous the entire colonial enterprise was; everything seems to have hung by a thread, which was easily snapped" (Kupperman, *Roanoke, the Abandoned Colony*, 89).

61. Quinn, *Roanoke Voyages, 1584–1590*, 476.

62. They may have also left a large number of slaves brought by Drake, who arrived with the privateer's fleet but disappeared entirely from the record after July. For some speculations on the fate of "Drake's Africans," see Quinn, *Roanoke Voyages, 1584–1590*, 254–55; Ivor Noël Hume, *The Virginia Adventure: Roanoke to James Towne: An Archaeological and Historical Odyssey* (New York: Knopf, 1994), 53.

63. Quinn, *Roanoke Voyages, 1584–1590*, 497.

64. Ibid., 787–89.

65. Ibid., 480. This captive was probably brought to Grenville's household at Bideford, where "Ralegh, A Wynganditoian" was christened on March 27, 1588, and was buried on April 7, 1589. For the documents, see ibid., 495.

66. Ibid., 790.

67. Ibid., 469.

68. Kupperman, "Roanoke Lost," 94.

69. Quinn, *Roanoke Voyages, 1584–1590*, 503, 15.

70. Some debate exists over whether or not White was with Barlowe, but White writes that the 1587 voyage was his third. See Quinn, *Roanoke Voyages, 1584–1590*, 598. Other indications that White was with Barlowe are found in ibid., 40, 79, 91, 116, 715. Manteo went to England with Barlowe, traveled in both directions with Lane, and now was returning home with White.

71. See Patrick M. Malone, *The Skulking Way of War: Technology and Tactics among the New England Indians* (Baltimore: Johns Hopkins University Press, 1993). For a comparison of English and Indian war tactics, see Fausz, "Patterns of Anglo-Indian Aggression and Accommodation."

72. Harriot, *Briefe and True Report*, 74. For a full reading of this engraving that situates its representational practices between Native American and European modes of inscription, see Michael Gaudio, *Engraving the Savage: The New World and Techniques of Civilization* (Minneapolis: University of Minnesota Press, 2008). The drawing on which this engraving was based is not extant, but we know that several of White's works were destroyed and can safely assume that White had knowledge of these markings.

Chapter 2

1. As Andrew Fitzmaurice has argued, elaborate rhetorical justifications for colonization in these papers also demonstrated English ambivalence over claiming Native American land; see Fitzmaurice, "Moral Uncertainty in the Dispossession of Native Americans," in *The Atlantic World and Virginia, 1550–1624*, ed. Peter C. Mancall (Chapel Hill: University of North Carolina Press for the Omohundro Institute of Early American History and Culture, 2007), 383–409.

2. Philip L. Barbour, *The Jamestown Voyages under the First Charter, 1606–1609: Documents Relating to the Foundation of Jamestown and the History of the Jamestown Colony up to the Departure of Captain John Smith, Last President of the Council in*

Virginia under the First Charter, Early in October 1609, 2 vols. (London: Cambridge University Press for the Hakluyt Society, 1969), 1:53.

3. James Horn, ed., *Captain John Smith: Writings with Other Narratives of Roanoke, Jamestown, and the First English Settlement of America*, Library of America (New York: Literary Classics of the United States, 2007), 933. All further references to this volume will be cited in the text.

4. Karen Ordahl Kupperman, "The Founding Years of Virginia and the United States," *Virginia Magazine of History and Biography* 104, no. 1 (1996): 103. John Kukla, "Order and Chaos in Early America: Political and Social Stability in Pre-Restoration Virginia," *American Historical Review* 90, no. 2 (1985): 277.

5. Edmund Sears Morgan, *American Slavery, American Freedom: The Ordeal of Colonial Virginia* (1975; New York: W. W. Norton, 2003), 48.

6. Bernard Bailyn, *The Ideological Origins of the American Revolution*, enlarged ed. (Cambridge, Mass.: Belknap Press of Harvard University Press, 1992), 162; Stuart Diamond, "From Organization to Society: Virginia in the Seventeenth Century," *American Journal of Sociology* 63 (1957–58): 457–75. For "chaotic factionalism," see also Jack P. Greene, "Changing Interpretations of Early American Politics," in *The Reinterpretation of Early American History: Essays in Honor of John Edwin Pomfret*, ed. Ray Allen Billington (San Marino, Calif.: Huntington Library Press, 1966), 151–84.

7. Kukla, "Order and Chaos in Early America," 276.

8. J. H. Elliott, *Empires of the Atlantic World: Britain and Spain in America, 1492–1830* (New Haven, Conn.: Yale University Press, 2006), 42, 557.

9. See, for example, Edmund S. Morgan and Marie Morgan, "Our Shaky Beginnings," *New York Review of Books*, April 6, 2007, 22–25; James Horn, *A Land as God Made It: Jamestown and the Birth of America* (New York: Basic Books, 2005). These titles are but two examples of these common formulations.

10. Cyril Brett, ed., *Minor Poems of Michael Drayton* (Oxford: Clarendon Press, 1907), 71.

11. Michel de Certeau, *The Practice of Everyday Life* (Berkeley: University of California Press, 1984).

12. Barbour, *Jamestown Voyages under the First Charter, 1606–1609*, 1:25.

13. King of England and Wales James I, *The Order [Banishing Rogues to the New Found Lands]* (London: Robert Baker, 1603).

14. For explication of this metaphor, see Karen Ordahl Kupperman, "The Beehive as a Model for Colonial Design," in *America in European Consciousness, 1493–1750*, ed. Karen Ordahl Kupperman (Chapel Hill: University of North Carolina Press, 1993), 272–92.

15. Robert Johnson, *Nova Britannia: Offering Most Excellent Fruites by Planting in Virginia: Exciting All Such as Be Well Affected to Further the Same* (London: Printed for Samuel Macham, 1609), 19.

16. Robert Gray et al., *A Good Speed to Virginia* (London: Printed by Felix Kyngston for William Welbie . . . , 1609).

17. Barbour, *Jamestown Voyages under the First Charter, 1606–1609*, 1:35, 40, 37.

18. Ibid., 1:50.

19. Ibid., 1:51, 52, 50.

20. Ibid., 1:52.

21. This concentration on commerce is especially the case in treatments comparing the English colonizing adventures to those of the Spanish. See, for example, Elliott, *Empires of the Atlantic World*, 117–19; Barbour, *Jamestown Voyages under the First Charter, 1606–1609*; Alison Games, *The Web of Empire: English Cosmopolitans in an Age of Expansion, 1560–1660* (Oxford and New York: Oxford University Press, 2008).

22. Wesley Frank Craven, *Dissolution of the Virginia Company: The Failure of a Colonial Experience* (New York: Oxford University Press, 1932), 24.

23. Barbour, *Jamestown Voyages under the First Charter, 1606–1609*, 1:53–54.

24. Johnson, *Nova Britannia*.

25. Karen Ordahl Kupperman, *Indians and English: Facing Off in Early America* (Ithaca, N.Y.: Cornell University Press, 2000), 3, notes, "The letters, sermons, pamphlets, and treatises surrounding American colonization all contained the same subtext: 'Do not abandon us.'"

26. Barbour, *Jamestown Voyages under the First Charter, 1606–1609*, 1:78.

27. Ibid., 1:80.

28. The critical scholarship on Smith is vast. For arguments about how slander and failure shaped Smith's writing and its reception, see Jeffrey Knapp, *An Empire Nowhere: England, America, and Literature from Utopia to the Tempest*, ed. Stephen Greenblatt, New Historicism: Studies in Cultural Poetics (Berkeley: University of California Press, 1992); Mary Fuller, *Voyages in Print: English Travel to America, 1576–1624* (Cambridge: Cambridge University Press, 1995). For Smith's texts as the site of a new configuration of experience and authority, see Jim Egan, *Authorizing Experience: Refigurations of the Body Politic in Seventeenth-Century New England Writing* (Princeton, N.J.: Princeton University Press, 1999). For a reading of the importance of incoherency in Smith's texts as a marker of ideological thresholds, see Myra Jehlen, "History before the Fact: Or, John Smith's Unfinished Symphony," *Critical Inquiry* 19:, no. 4 (Summer 1993): 677–92. For an argument about the formal innovations in Smith's framing of encounter, see Ed White, "Captaine Smith, Colonial Novelist," *American Literature* 75, no. 3 (2003): 487–513. For studies of Smith acting in a theater of geopolitical performance and cultural exchange, see William Q. Boelhower, "Mapping the Gift Path: Exhange and Rivalry in John Smith's *A True Relation*," *American Literary History* 15, no. 4 (2003): 655–82; Joseph Fichtelberg, "The Colonial Stage: Risk and Promise in John Smith's Virginia," *Early American Literature* 39, no. 1 (2004): 11–40. For comparative and hemispheric accounts of his encounters and writing, see Bruce R. Smith, "Mouthpieces: Native American Voices in Thomas Harriot's *True and Brief Report of . . . Virginia*, Gaspar Perez De Villagra's *Historia De La Nueva Mexico*, and John Smith's *General History of Virginia*," *New

Literary History: A Journal of Theory and Interpretation 32, no. 3 (2001): 501–17; Astrid M. Fellner, "Performing Cultural Memory: Scenarios of Colonial Encounter in the Writings of John Smith, Cabeza De Vaca, and Jacques Cartier," in *Transnational American Memories*, ed. Udo J. Hebel (Berlin: de Gruyter, 2009), 33–58; Daniel Walden, "America's First Coastal Community: A Cis- and Circumatlantic Reading of John Smith's *The Generall Historie of Virginia*," *Atlantic Studies: Literary, Cultural, and Historical Perspectives* 7, no. 3 (2010): 329–47.

29. Adam Goodheart, "Fear and Love in the Virginia Colony," in *A New Literary History of America*, ed. Marcus Greil and Werner Sollors (Cambridge, Mass.: Harvard University Press, 2009), 21.

30. Steven Olsen-Smith, "Captain John Smith," in *The Oxford Handbook of Early American Literature*, ed. Kevin J. Hayes (Oxford: Oxford University Press, 2008), 60.

31. For example, Frederic W. Gleach claims, "The Indians universally saw themselves as superior to the Europeans at the time of contact and long afterward"; see Gleach, *Powhatan's World and Colonial Virginia: A Conflict of Cultures*, Studies in the Anthropology of North American Indians (Lincoln: University of Nebraska Press, 1997), 55. Helen C. Rountree is among the scholars who explain the Powhatan people's course of action regarding the new arrivals. She writes, "In the early ill-organized and even worse-supplied years of the Jamestown colony, the Powhatans played a waiting game, watching for signs that the English would make useful allies against Indian enemies"; see Rountree, *Pocahontas's People: The Powhatan Indians of Virginia through Four Centuries*, Civilization of the American Indian Series, vol. 196 (Norman: University of Oklahoma Press, 1990), 29.

32. For an argument that fatal apathy was one of a host of physical and behavioral symptoms linked to the colonists' lack of food and nutritive diseases, see Karen Ordahl Kupperman, "Apathy and Death in Early Jamestown," *Journal of American History* 66, no. 1 (1979): 24–40.

33. These oft-repeated numbers are in some dispute. For slightly variant estimates, see Carville E. Earle, "Environment, Disease, and Mortality in Early Virginia," in *The Chesapeake in the Seventeenth Century: Essays on Anglo-American Society*, ed. David L. Ammerman and Thad W. Tate (Chapel Hill: University of North Carolina Press, 1979), 96–125; Virginia Bernhard, "'Men, Women, and Children' at Jamestown: Population and Gender in Early Virginia," *Journal of Southern History* 58, no. 4 (1992): 599–618.

34. Mark Nicholls, "George Percy's 'Trewe Relacyon': A Primary Source for the Jamestown Settlement," *Virginia Magazine of History and Biography* 113, no. 3 (2005): 212–75. In a review, Peter C. Mancall wrote that this reappearance of Percy's text showed colonization "as the conquest that it was"; see Mancall, "Savagery in Jamestown," *Huntington Library Quarterly* 70, no. 4 (2007): 670.

35. Forrest K. Lehman, "Settled Place, Contested Past: Reconciling George Percy's 'A Trewe Relacyon' with John Smith's *Generall Historie*," *Early American Literature* 42, no. 2 (2007): 235–61.

36. Philip L. Barbour, "The Honorable George Percy, Premier Chronicler of the First Virginia Voyage," *Early American Literature* 6, no. 1 (1971): 7–17.

37. John W. Shirley, "George Percy at Jamestown, 1607–1612," *Virginia Magazine of History and Biography* 17, no. 3 (1949): 227–43.

38. Barbour, "Honorable George Percy," 12, 11, 16. For Barbour's far less flattering portrait of Percy, see Philip L. Barbour, *The Three Worlds of Captain John Smith* (Boston: Houghton Mifflin, 1964), 110, 280.

39. Egan, *Authorizing Experience*; Fuller, *Voyages in Print*.

40. Stephen Greenblatt, *Marvelous Possessions: The Wonder of the New World* (Chicago: University of Chicago Press, 1991), 74. The Earl of Northumberland, Percy's brother, held a large collection of travel literature and was deeply interested in colonialism.

41. Kupperman, *Indians and English*, 75–76, discusses how important it was to the English to discover that Indian groups had well-defined structures of social status and deference. In addition to the familiarity that these structures imparted, the existence of a stratified society convinced the English that they could easily insert themselves at its top.

42. That Percy himself was epileptic may contribute a frightening element of identification to this description.

43. Barbour, Nicholls, and Mancall all refer to this catalog as Percy's, in a word, "necrology." See Barbour, *Three Worlds of Captain John Smith*, 280; Nicholls, "George Percy's 'Trewe Relacyon,'" 229; Peter C. Mancall, *Hakluyt's Promise: An Elizabethan's Obsession for an English America* (New Haven, Conn.: Yale University Press, 2007), 280.

44. See especially Egan, *Authorizing Experience*, which argues that the experiential authority claimed by the colonist confronted inherited English notions of authority and the body politic, while still furthering the agenda of colonial power. For treatments of the conjunction of print, authority, and newly emerging structures of identity, see Benedict Anderson, *Imagined Communities: Reflections on the Origins and Spread of Nationalism* (New York: Verso, 1991); Nancy Armstrong and Leonard Tennenhouse, *The Imaginary Puritan: Literature, Intellectual Labor, and the Origins of Personal Life* (Berkeley: University of California Press, 1992); Francis Barker, *The Private Tremulous Body: Essays of Subjection* (Ann Arbor: University of Michigan Press, 1995); Myra Jehlen, "The Literature of Colonization," in *The Cambridge History of American Literature,* vol. 1: *1590–1820,* ed. Sacvan Bercovitch (Cambridge: Cambridge University Press, 1994), 11–168 .

45. For these documents, see Philip L. Barbour, "The Preliminaries," in *Jamestown Voyages under the First Charter, 1606–1609,* ed. Barbour, 13–61.

46. I am employing the model of deterritorialization from Deleuze and Guatarri, for whom deterritorialization represents the breaking up of assemblages into various lines of flight, which allows for change to occur by making formerly fixed relations available for reorganization. This is essential to creative processes but can also lead to what they call "black holes" where a failed line of flight is absorbed into a void:

"[I]nstead of opening up the deterritorialized assemblage onto something else, it may produce an effect of closure, as if the aggregate had fallen into and continues to spin in a kind of black hole. This is what happens under conditions of precocious or extremely sudden deterritorialization"; see Gilles Deleuze and Felix Guatarri, *A Thousand Plateaus: Capitalism and Schizophrenia* (Minneapolis: University of Minnesota Press, 1987), 333–34. I am suggesting that the intense and unexpected conditions under which the initial assemblage of the English Action broke down in Virginia produced, in its sudden deterritorialization, one line of flight that led to a catastrophic black hole.

47. Dominick LaCapra, *Writing History, Writing Trauma* (Baltimore: Johns Hopkins University Press, 2001), has noted a "dynamic interaction between excess and limits" as a "discursive symptom" of registering trauma (xii).

48. Julia Kristeva, *Powers of Horror: An Essay on Abjection*, trans. Leon S. Roudiez (New York: Columbia University Press, 1982), 4.

49. For the concept of habitus and its relation to social practice, see Pierre Bourdieu, *Outline of the Theory of Practice* (Cambridge: Cambridge University Press, 1977), 76–80. For a discussion of using habitus as an analytical approach to colonial history, see Robert Blair St. George, "Introduction," in *Possible Pasts: Becoming Colonial in Early America*, ed. Robert Blair St. George (Ithaca, N.Y.: Cornell University Press, 2000), 7–9.

50. Kristeva, *Powers of Horror*, 2, emphasis added.

51. Ibid., 1.

52. Samuel Purchas, *Purchas His Pilgrims*, 4 vols. (London: William Stansby, 1625), 2:1691. In publishing *Observations Taken out of a Discourse*, Purchas's editorial hand fell most deliberately in cutting Percy off where someone else could take up the story.

53. See, for example, Kupperman, "Apathy and Death in Early Jamestown"; Taylor, *American Colonies*; Horn, *A Land as God Made It*; Nicholls, "George Percy's 'Trewe Relacyon.'"

54. David B. Quinn, Alison M. Quinn, and Susan Hillier, *New American World: A Documentary History of North America to 1612*, vol. 3 (New York: Arno, 1979), 186.

55. For a detailed history and a persuasive defense of this series of conflicts as a war, see J. Frederick Fausz, "An 'Abundance of Blood Shed on Both Sides': England's First Indian War, 1609–1614," *Virginia Magazine of History and Biography* 98, no. 1 (1990): 3–56.

56. For Spelman, see Horn, *Captain John Smith*,, 967–78.

57. The phrases "woes & miseries" (1094) and "Revendge upon the Indyans" (1103) are Percy's, as is the line "A worlde of miseries ensewed" (1099).

58. Nicholls, "George Percy's 'Trewe Relacyon,'" 227.

59. Lehman, "Settled Place, Contested Past," 238, 37.

60. For treatments of the use of the apologia form in colonial reports, see Michael G. Moran, "Ralph Lane's 1586 Discourse of the First Colony: The Renaissance

Commercial Report as Apologia," *Technical Communications Quarterly* 12, no. 2 (2003): 125–54; E. Thomson Shields Jr., "The Literature of Exploration," in *The Oxford Handbook of Early American Literature*, ed. Kevin J. Hayes (New York: Oxford University Press, 2008), 33–35. In my reading, the apologia comprises only one element of Lane's report (see above) and of Percy's *Trewe Relacyon*.

61. Alexander Brown, *The Genesis of the United States: A Narrative of the Movement in England, 1605–1616, Which Resulted in the Plantation of North America by Englishmen, Disclosing the Contest between England and Spain for the Possession of the Soil Now Occupied by the United States of America*, vol. 1 (Boston and New York: Houghton Mifflin, 1890), 348.

62. Ibid., 348, 52.

63. Peter Force, *Tracts and Other Papers, Relating Principally to the Origin, Settlement and Progress of the Colonies in North America, from the Discovery of the Country to the Year 1776*, vol. 4 (Washington:William Q. Force, 1846), 10–11.

64. Brown, *Genesis of the United States*, 348.

65. "Headless residue" is Barbour's phrase; see Barbour, *Jamestown Voyages under the First Charter, 1606–1609*, 1:viii. However, the characterization of headlessness was used as early as 1610. In their *True and Sincere Declaration* (London: George Eld, 1610), the Counsel for the Virginia Company in London writes, "no man would acknowledge a superior nor could from this headless and unbrideled multitude, bee anything expected but disorder and ryott" (15). Robert Johnson, *The New Life of Virginea* (London: Felix Kyngston, 1612) refers to the hundreds of men who arrived in 1609 as "so many members without a head" (unpaginated). The metaphor was another example of distilling a large group into a single body; this one needed but a head to function properly. See also Brown, *Genesis of the United States*, 1:347; Force, *Tracts and Other Papers*, 10.

66. Barbour, *Jamestown Voyages under the First Charter, 1606–1609*, 1:viii.

67. David S. Shields sees "the injury that destroyed Smith's genitals" as "the accident [that] conditioned all of Smith's subsequent career in letters," particularly his "masculine posturing, his preoccupation with the virile body," and his ubiquitous "notion of paternal legacy" (David S. Shields, "The Genius of Ancient Britian," in *The Atlantic World and Virginia, 1550–1624*, ed. Peter C. Mancall [Chapel Hill: University of North Carolina Press for the Omohundro Institute of Early American History and Culture, 2007], 494).

68. Cathy Caruth calls trauma "the story of a wound that cries out, that addresses us in the attempt to tell us of a reality or truth that is not otherwise available" (Cathy Caruth, *Unclaimed Experience: Trauma, Narrative, and History* [Baltimore: Johns Hopkins University Press, 1997], 4). Percy's *Trewe Relacyon*—especially as it is written in the aftermath of another traumatic history, the 1622 Indian uprising that killed 374 Jamestown colonists in a day—can be read as such a speaking from the wound, an attempt to transmit the story of the original injury that continues to resist assimilation.

However, its catastrophic discourse testifies not only to violence the colonists suffered but also to the violence they perpetrated, the destructive force of which also remains unassimilated.

69. In his *America*, part 4 (1594), Theodor de Bry includes an engraving of this famous scene entitled "The Spanish thirst for gold quenched." Knapp, *Empire Nowhere*, 205–6, too notes the similarities between gold hunger and bread hunger in these two scenarios.

70. José Rabasa, *Writing Violence on the Northern Frontier: The Historiography of Sixteenth-Century New Mexico and Florida and the Legacy of Conquest* (Durham, N.C.: Duke University Press, 2000), 3–4, emphasis in original.

71. The bread-stuffed mouths are an excellent example of what Gleach has called an Algonquian "aesthetic of warfare." He writes, "The shrewdness, skill, and wit employed in these actions were the important performative elements in their aesthetics for the victors" (Gleach, *Powhatan's World and Colonial Virginia*, 50).

72. This scandal is much recounted, especially in the antiquarian sources. What passes in silence is the fact that Francis West was the younger brother of Thomas West, Lord De La Warr, who was later sent to rescue Virginia as its governor-for-life.

73. The phrase "charnel house" is from Morgan, *American Slavery, American Freedom*, 101, 110.

74. For "black hole," see n. 46 above.

75. Seth Mallios, *The Deadly Politics of Giving: Exchange and Violence at Ajacan, Roanoke, and Jamestown* (Tuscaloosa: University of Alabama Press, 2006). Mallios writes that the settlers "did not intend to farm or hunt in the Chesapeake. They planned in advance on subsisting off of exchange with the indigenous population for food. And while the Algonquians initially agreed to part with their foodstuffs, the production and consumption of food in indigenous societies had additional symbolic significance that when unrequited had severe consequences" (21).

76. Michael A. LaCombe, "'A Continuall and Dayly Table for Gentlemen of Fashion': Humanism, Food and Authority at Jamestown, 1607–1609," *American Historical Review* 115, no. 3 (2010): 669–87.

77. For a full-length study of plague times in early modern England that treats social, religious, and cultural attitudes and repercussions as well as biological causes, see Paul Slack, *The Impact of Plague in Tudor and Stuart England* (1985; Oxford and New York: Oxford University Press, 2003), especially chap. 1, "Disease and Society." Famine, traditionally related to plague and war, was considered an especially cruel way of death because of the extended suffering it entailed. It was better that the plague take one out in a day than to suffer the slow death of starvation. For medieval precursors, see John Aberth, *From the Brink of the Apocalypse: Confronting Famine, War, Plague, and Death in the Later Middle Ages* (New York and London: Routledge, 2000). For questions about defining "mortality crises" and ascribing deaths to famine as opposed to the general disease atmosphere, see John Walter and Roger Schofield, "Famine,

Disease and Crisis Mortality in Early Modern Society," in *Famine, Disease and the Social Order in Early Modern Society*, ed. John Walter and Roger Schofield, Cambridge Studies in Population, Economy, and Society in Past Time, vol. 10 (Cambridge: Cambridge University Press, 1989), 1–74.

78. For a comparison of narratives written during plague times in England, see Ernest B. Gilman, *Plague Writing in Early Modern England* (Chicago: University of Chicago Press, 2009).

79. Percy and other commanders stole food from the common store as well, as reported in the jointly authored text "The Proceedings of the English Colonie in Virginia": "As for our hogs, hens, goats, sheep, horse, or what lived, our commanders and officers did daily consume them, some small proportions (sometimes) we tasted till all was devoured." See Horn, *Captain John Smith*, 114.

80. Michael Schoenfeldt, "Fables of the Belly in Early Modern England," in *The Body in Parts: Fantasies of Corporeality in Early Modern Europe*, ed. David Hillman and Carla Mazzio (New York: Routledge, 1997), 245. Schoenfeldt later comments that "[t]o chose one's diet is an act of self-fashioning in the most literal sense" (251).

81. Virginia DeJohn Anderson's study of domestic animals in early America, *Creatures of Empire: How Domestic Animals Transformed Early America* (Oxford and New York: Oxford University Press, 2004), identifies "a challenge that no seventeenth-century English farmer had to face" (122): domestic animals escaping into the woods and becoming feral. Within just years the forms of these animals were decidedly altered from Old World types, and their behavior was aggressive and unmanageable. Livestock was supposed to be sheltered, fed, and put to use—culturally they emblematized the civilizing forces of English husbandry. But these feral horses, cattle, and pigs were not English livestock; nor were they native animals. They simply became beasts. I suggest that something similar happened to settlers during the Starving Time.

82. Horn, *Land as God Made It*, 179.

83. For one important study of the cannibal figure in European thought, see Frank Lestringant, *Cannibals: The Discovery and Representation of the Cannibal from Columbus to Jules Verne*, New Historicism, vol. 37 (Berkeley: University of California Press, 1997). Lestringant makes an important distinction between constraint cannibalism and ritual cannibalism: "[W]hen the symbolic intention outweighs the raw horror of the act, as in vengeance cannibalism, the inherent significance of the practice divorces it from brute animality. This makes the cannibal act less 'blameful' and integrates it into a value system—heroism, passionate love, implacable and desperate vengeance—which...brings us back to the human domain of custom" (86). For a comprehensive historiography of anthropological and cultural historical scholarship on cannibalism, see Rachel B. Herrmann, "The 'Tragicall Historie': Cannibalism and Abundance in Colonial Jamestown," *William and Mary Quarterly*, 3rd ser., 68, no. 1 (2011): 73–74.

84. Michel de Montaigne, *Michel de Montaigne: The Complete Essays*, trans. M. A. Screech (London and New York: Penguin Books, 1993), 236.

85. Lestringant, *Cannibals,* 86, has something to say about this kind of punishment: "The taste for human flesh is viewed as an intolerable perversion, and the criminal must be exorcised, or, more radically, consumed in the purifying fire of the stake."

86. For an extensive treatment of this story's circulation and cultural consequences, see Herrmann, "Tragicall Historie."

87. Councell of Virginia, *A True Declaration of the Estate of the Colonie in Virginia, with a Confutation of Such Scandalous Reports as Have Tended to the Disgrace of So Worthy an Enterprise* (London: Printed for William Barret, 1610), 16. Herrmann, "Tragicall Historie," argues that although cannibalism in Jamestown can be neither proven nor disproven, fixation on the story ultimately served to revise the mistaken belief in easy abundance in the New World.

88. Robert Beverley, *The History and Present State of Virginia, in Four Parts* (London: Printed for R. Parker, 1705), 26.

89. René Girard, *Violence and the Sacred* (Baltimore: Johns Hopkins University Press, 1977), 174.

90. Ibid., 170–71.

91. Anti-providential reactions to mass mortality, bordering on the atheistic, was also a severe threat during plague time. See Gilman, *Plague Writing in Early Modern England*. For a meditation on the pervasiveness of the "Great Chain of Being" and the "Circle of Life" in the seventeenth century, see John Demos, *Circles and Lines: The Shape of Life in Early America* (Cambridge, Mass.: Harvard University Press, 2004).

92. As Kristeva writes, "The corpse, seen without God and outside of science, is the utmost of abjection. It is death infecting life" (Kristeva, *Powers of Horror*, 4).

93. Robert Gray, *A Good Speed to Virginia (1609)* (New York: Scholars' Facsimiles & Reprints, 1937), 5.

94. Ibid., 6.

95. Robert Crashaw, "Crawshaw's Sermon," in Brown, *Genesis of the United States,* 360–73.

96. This arc is an example of what Joseph Roach calls "catastrophic closure." Roach writes, "From the heritage of tragic drama in the West, I believe, circum-Atlantic closures especially favor catastrophe . . . redolent of violence and fatality but also of agency and decision. Like catastrophe, with which it often coincides, the illusory scene of closure that Eurocentrists call memory ('what's done is done') incites emotions that turn toward the future, in aspiration no less than in dread ('God's will be done'). The choreography of catastrophic closure—Fortinbras arrives, Aeneas departs, Creon remains—offers a way of imagining what must come next as well as what has already happened." "What comes next" in this case is the permanence of England's first permanent colonial settlement. See Joseph R. Roach, *Cities of the Dead: Circum-Atlantic Performance* (New York: Columbia University Press, 1996), 33.

97. For an extensive treatment of this machination, see Giorgio Agamben, *State of Exception* (Chicago: University of Chicago Press, 2005).

98. William Strachey, *For the Colony in Virginea Britannia: Lawes Divine, Morall and Martiall, &C.* (London: William Stansby, 1612).

99. Ibid.

100. Ibid.

101. Ibid.

102. Fausz, "Abundance of Blood Shed on Both Sides," 33.

103. Despite later episodes of trading and diplomacy, mostly engineered by Wahunsonacock for political reasons, these hostilities continued. Smith distrusted all Paspahegh motives, referring to the group as "churlish and treacherous nations" who were "treacherous villains and ever shall be." In general, English colonists saw only treachery in the actions of the Paspahegh, while the Paspahegh intended those actions as corrective punishments for the Englishmen's intrusion onto their land and breaches of behavior. According to Gleach, *Powhatan's World and Colonial Virginia*, 52, "This concept of the corrective, moral nature of war is crucial to an understanding of the events in colonial Virginia."

104. William Strachey, *The Historie of Travell into Virginia Britania (1612)* (Nendeln, Liechtenstein: Kraus Reprint, 1967), 109–10.

105. Fausz, "Abundance of Blood Shed on Both Sides," 53; Rountree, *Pocahontas's People*, 55.

106. Smith's *Generall Historie* only briefly records that Percy was sent "to correct some injuries of the Paspaheghs" and that he "tooke the Queene and her children prisoner whome not long after they slewe" See Barbour, *Jamestown Voyages under the First Charter, 1606–1609*, 2:236. Contemporary reports from Strachey, De La Warr, Gabriel Archer, and Henry Spelman do not record the event at all.

107. Strachey, *Historie of Travell into Virginia Britania (1612)*, 66–67.

108. A force this large would obviously represent an organized alliance of native groups attempting to lay siege on the fort while it was under Percy's charge. For estimates of the Paspahegh population during this period, see Bruce G. Trigger, ed., *The Handbook of North American Indians*, vol. 15: *Northeast* (Washington, D.C.: Smithsonian Institution, 1978), 257.

109. Bruce Smith, "Mouthpieces," 504, makes an excellent point about visual vs. aural fields: "The field of vision is linear, while the field of hearing is spherical. As a result, visualized objects appear at a fixed distance from the viewer, while sound invades the listener's person, penetrating the listener's body, setting off reverberations in the listener's very bones. Even an object moving towards me remains 'out there,' in a space apart from where I stand and see, but a sound physically overwhelms me. It compromises my separateness." In this light, not only the air and woods but also the surviving settlers' bodies rang with the sound of "Paspahegh."

Chapter 3

1. Samuel Eliot Morison, ed., *Of Plymouth Plantation, 1620–1647 by William Bradford, Sometime Governor Thereof* (New York: Alfred A. Knopf, 2002), 95.

2. Mitchell Breitwieser, *National Melancholy: Mourning and Opportunity in Classic American Literature* (Stanford, Calif.: Stanford University Press, 2007), 8.

3. For two different interpretations of how the annals of Bradford's second book depart from the providential design of the first book, see Robert Daly, "William Bradford's Vision of History," *American Literature* 44, no. 4 (January 1973): 557–69; Walter P. Wenska, "Bradford's Two Histories: Pattern and Paradigm in *Of Plymouth Plantation*," *Early American Literature* 13, no. 2 (Fall 1978): 151–64.

4. Morison, *Of Plymouth Plantation*, 46.

5. Michelle Burnham, "Merchants, Money, and the Economics of 'Plain Style' in William Bradford's *Of Plymouth Plantation*," *American Literature* 72, no. 4 (December 2000): 695–720; Michelle Burnham, *Folded Selves: Colonial New England Writing and the World System* (Hanover, N.H.: Dartmouth University Press, 2007), 46–67; Douglas Anderson, *William Bradford's Books: Of Plimmoth Plantation and the Printed Word* (Baltimore: Johns Hopkins University Press, 2003).

6. Morison, *Of Plymouth Plantation*, 62.

7. Ibid., 95.

8. John M. Murrin, "Beneficiaries of Catastrophe: The English Colonies in America," in *The New American History*, ed. Eric Foner (Philadelphia: Temple University Press, 1990), 3–4.

9. Joseph Roach, *Cities of the Dead: Circum-Atlantic Performance* (New York: Columbia University Press, 1996), 35.

10. Dwight B. Heath, ed., *Mourt's Relation: A Journal of the Pilgrims at Plymouth* (Bedford, Mass.: Applewood Books, 1963), 27. The jointly authored book that, since 1736, has come to be known as *Mourt's Relation* was originally published in London by John Bellamie in 1622 under the title *A Relation or Journall of the Beginning and Proceedings of the English Plantation Settled at Plimouth in New England, by Certain English Adventurers both Merchants and Others*. Regarding its authorship, the editor Heath states, "It is almost certain that the principal author was Edward Winslow, although it is generally believed that William Bradford also had a hand in the effort" (xiii). The grave scene is found in the modern edition on 27–28, from which I quote passim.

11. Heath, *Mourt's Relation*, 28.

12. For an extensive study of both colonial and native burial practices and the dynamics of their mutual interpretations, see Erik R. Seeman, *Death in the New World: Cross-Cultural Encounters, 1492–1800* (Philadelphia: University of Pennsylvania Press, 2010).

13. The arrangement of planks that the *Mayflower* scouts found would indicate

an honored burial. For the incorporation of European objects into Native American burials, see Daniel Richter, *The Ordeal of the Long-House: The Peoples of the Iroquois League in the Era of European Colonization* (Chapel Hill: University of North Carolina Press, 1992), 52. The scouts' ability to interpret the grave's contents was, of course, dependent on their knowledge of Indian funerary rites. Here anxiety over the inability to interpret the grave stems not only from the Plymouth men's lack of contextual knowledge but also from the ambiguity of the particular corpse with the shock of blond hair.

14. Heath, *Mourt's Relation*, 28.

15. For a theory of corpses as "spectacular bodies," see Lorna Clymer, "Cromwell's Head and Milton's Hair: Corpse Theory in Spectacular Bodies of the Interregnum," *The Eighteenth Century: Theory and Interpretation* 40, no. 2 (1999): 91–112. I am much indebted to Clymer's essay's opening formulations and to our conversations on the topic of the dead.

16. Maurice Blanchot, "Two Versions of the Imaginary," trans. Ann Smock, *The Space of Literature* (Lincoln: University of Nebraska Press, 1982), 256.

17. Morison, *Of Plymouth Plantation*, 66.

18. Ibid., 65. His account of the scouting mission is on 64–66.

19. Ibid., 66.

20. Num. 13:28, King James Bible.

21. Num. 14:28–35 passim, King James Bible. This curse applied to the first generation only, as Moses had pleaded for God's mercy upon their progeny. In begging forgiveness, Moses imagined that if all were struck down by a pestilence and killed (and such was God's original intention) their enemies would say that the Lord could not deliver his chosen people. God relents, but only after imposing this curse that forbids the unfaithful from ever seeing the Promised Land. This story is also told in Deut. 1:19–46, where the emphasis is on Moses's instructions and warnings to the second generation, that they might gain the salvation their parents forfeited.

22. Charles H. Levermore, ed., *Forerunners and Competitors of the Pilgrims and Puritans*, vol. 1 (Brooklyn, N.Y.: New England Society of Brooklyn, 1912), 63. Further quotations will be taken from this reissue. It is not clear whether Pring himself wrote the report, had it written for him, or availed himself of a convenient combination of these means. The report was first published in 1625 in Samuel Purchas's collection *Purchas His Pilgrimes* under the title "A Voyage Set Out from the Citie of Bristoll at the Charge of the Chiefest Merchants and Inhabitants of the Said Citie with a Small Ship and a Barke for the Discoverie of the North Part of Virginia, in the Yeere 1610 under the Command of ME Martin Pring." Here, I will use the name "Pring" as a conceit of authorship, a name for those unrecorded seventeenth-century practices that brought this report into the historical record.

23. For the native practice of controlled forest burns, see William Cronon, *Changes in the Land: Indians, Colonists, and the Ecology of New England* (New York: Hill and Wang, 1983), 47–51. In this particular case, however, the intentions motivating the burn may have gone beyond the ecological.

24. Levermore, *Forerunners and Competitors of the Pilgrims and Puritans*, 67.

25. The principal explorers of the period from 1602 to 1616 were Bartholomew Gosnold, Martin Pring, Samuel Champlain, George Weymouth, John Smith, Thomas Dermer, Nicholas Hobson, Raleigh Gilbert, and George Popham. Several Jesuit missionaries were also active in New France during this time.

26. Levermore, *Forerunners and Competitors of the Pilgrims and Puritans*, 325 ("kind civility"), 368 ("soddainly withdrew"), 334 ("Griffin at his returne"), 323 ("pointing with his oare").

27. From John Smith's 1616 report, *A Description of New England*. See James Horn, ed., *Captain John Smith: Writings with Other Narratives of Roanoke, Jamestown, and the First English Settlement of America*, Library of America (New York: Literary Classics of the United States, 2007), 137, 139.

28. James Phinney Baxter, ed., *Sir Ferdinando Gorges and His Province of Maine*, vol. 2 (Boston: Prince Society, 1890), 19. The section of Gorges's report chronicling Vines's winter journey, which Gorges hoped would reinvigorate his endeavors in this colonial arena, is provocatively titled "A resolution to put new life into that scattered and lacerated Body." Despite the scenes of Indian death, Gorges notes that "Vines and the rest with him that lay in the Cabbins with those People that dyed some more, some lesse, mightily (blessed be GOD for it) not one of them every felt their heads to ake while they stayed there."

29. Levermore, *Forerunners and Competitors of the Pilgrims and Puritans*, 579.

30. See John W. Verano and Douglas H. Ubelaker, eds., *Disease and Demography in the Americas* (Washington, D.C.: Smithsonian Institution Press, 1992); Dean R. Snow and Kim M. Lanphear, "European Contact and Indian Depopulation in the Northeast: The Timing of the First Epidemics," *Ethnohistory* 35, no. 1 (Winter 1988): 15–33. Also see Arthur E. Spiess and Bruce D. Spiess, "New England Pandemic of 1616–1622: Cause and Archaeological Implication," *Man in the Northeast* 34 (1987): 71–83.

31. The historiography on these epidemics is large. In addition to those sources cited above, see, for example, Noble David Cook, *Born to Die: Disease and New World Conquests, 1492–1650* (Cambridge: Cambridge University Press, 1998); Cronon, *Changes in the Land*; Alfred Crosby, *The Columbian Exchange: Biological and Cultural Consequences of 1492*, 30th anniversary ed. (Westport, Conn.: Praeger, 2003); Henry F. Dobyns, *Their Numbers Became Thinned* (Knoxville: University of Tennessee Press, 1983), Francis Jennings, *The Invasion of America: Indians, Colonialism, and the Cant of Conquest* (New York: W. W. Norton, 1975); David S. Jones, *Rationalizing Epidemics: Meanings and Uses of American Indian Mortality since 1600* (Cambridge, Mass.: Harvard University Press, 2004).

32. Environmentally, tree ring evidence points to extreme weather patterns in the years preceding the great mortality. The detrimental impact on food supply probably left local populations even more vulnerable to the effects of disease. Historical epidemiologists have tried to identify the disease. Some have ruled out smallpox and

yellow fever, while others have made a case for sudden, severe hepatic failure. Most agree that the killer was born of a virus spread through contact between European and Indian traders. The conformity between the epidemic's boundaries and those of native trade routes argues for a disease spread through human contact. See Spiess and Spiess, "New England Pandemic of 1616–1622," especially 72, 77; Neal Salisbury, *Manitou and Providence: Indians, Europeans, and the Making of New England 1500–1642* (New York: Oxford University Press, 1982).

33. Seeman, *Death in the New World*, 170. See also Salisbury, *Manitou and Providence*, 17–19; Karen Ordahl Kupperman, *Indians and English: Facing Off in Early America* (Ithaca, N.Y.: Cornell University Press, 2000), 135–38.

34. See, for example, Salisbury, *Manitou and Providence*, 103ff; Kupperman, *Indians and English*, 34ff.

35. Murrin, "Beneficiaries of Catastrophe," 7.

36. Cristobal Silva, *Miraculous Plagues: An Epidemiology of Early New England Narrative* (Oxford: Oxford University Press, 2011), 26–27. See especially chap. 1, "New England Epidemiology," 24–61.

37. For an extended account of Locke's *Treatises* as a defense of English colonial policy in America, see Barbara Arneil, *John Locke and America: The Defense of English Colonialism* (Oxford: Clarendon, 1996).

38. Nathaniel Morton, *New-England's Memorial: Or, a Brief Relation of the Most Memorable and Remarkable Passages of the Providence of God, Manifested to the Planters of New-England, in America; with Special Reference to the First Colony Thereof, Called New-Plymouth*, Applewood's American Philosophy and Religion Series (1669; Bedford, Mass.: Applewood Books, 2009), 37. Silva, *Miraculous Plagues*, 29–32, explores the link between epidemiological discourse and agricultural tropes, arguing that colonial justification narratives essentially established "a metonymy between land and body" and used the language of a landscape left "void" by epidemics in order to justify English possession of the land.

39. Cushman was in Plymouth from November 9 to December 13, 1621. This quotation is from the "Epistle Dedicatory," which prefaced the published version of Cushman's sermon "The Dangers of Self-Love," preached at Plymouth on December 9, the first anniversary of the first landing. It originally appeared in print in London in 1622. For a reprint, see Robert Cushman, "Cushman's Discourse," in *Chronicles of the Pilgrim Fathers of the Colony of Plymouth, from 1602 to 1625*, ed. Alexander Young (Boston: Little and Brown, 1841), 253–68; the quotations in this paragraph appear on 258.

40. David Stannard, *The Puritan Way of Death: A Study in Religion, Culture, and Social Change* (New York: Oxford University Press, 1977), 117.

41. Thomas Morton first visited New England in 1622 and returned in 1625 with Captain Wollaston, who founded a settlement at Mount Wollaston (present-day Quincy, Massachusetts). When Wollaston left the new settlement for Virginia, Morton assumed leadership, renaming the settlement Mare Mount and maddening the Plymouth settlers as much by his rival fur trade as by his sybaritic lifestyle.

42. Thomas Morton, *New English Canaan, or New Canaan Containing an Abstract of New England, Composed in Three Bookes* (London: Printed for Charles Greene and sold in Pauls Church-yard, 1637), 23.

43. See Matt. 27:33, Mark 15:22, and John 19:17.

44. The important exception is Bradford's extended description of Indians dying of smallpox (Morison, *Of Plymouth Plantation*, 270–71).

45. Morison, *Of Plymouth Plantation*, 87.

46. Again I refer the reader to the articulation of "corpse theory" in Clymer, "Cromwell's Head and Milton's Hair." Clymer proposes that because of the corpse's ambivalent status as an object, it must be encased by narrative meaning.

47. Morison, *Of Plymouth Plantation*, 62, 263, 35, 77, 84.

48. Wenska, "Bradford's Two Histories," 154.

49. Breitwieser, *National Melancholy*, 9.

50. For a history of how schoolbook orations consolidated New England as the site of American literature and national origins, see Nina Baym, "Early Histories of American Literature: A Chapter in the Institution of New England," *American Literary History* 1 no. 3 (Autumn 1989): 459–88.

51. John Pierpont, *The National Reader: A Selection of Exercises in Reading and Speaking, Designed to Fill the Same Place in the Schools of the United States*, 28th ed. (Boston: C. Bowen, 1836), 201. Examples of the sacred claim can be found in orations throughout this volume. The first edition of Pierpont's *National Reader* was introduced into the public grammar schools of Boston in 1829. It contains countless images of weary Pilgrims traversing bleak shores.

52. W. H. Bartlett, *The Pilgrim Fathers; or, the Founders of New England in the Reign of James the First* (London: A. Hall, Virtue & Co., 1853), 131.

53. In nineteenth-century American histories, invocation of these winter deaths at Plymouth is practically compulsory. See, for example, John Abbot Goodwin and Making of America Project, *The Pilgrim Republic: An Historical Review of the Colony of New Plymouth, with Sketches of the Rise of Other New England Settlements, the History of Congregationalism, and the Creeds of the Period* (Boston: Ticknor and Company, 1888), 184, 186.

54. Morison, *Of Plymouth Plantation*, 95.

55. James Deetz suggests that graves on Burial Hill prior to 1681 were marked with wooden "grave rails," which did not survive. See James Deetz and Patricia Scott Deetz, *The Times of Their Lives: Life, Love, and Death in Plymouth Colony* (New York: W. H. Freeman, 2000), 311.

56. This oral history comes through Thomas Faunce, an elder in the first church of Plymouth, to Plymouth resident Deacon Ephraim Spooner, to Plymouth historian Abiel Holmes, who recorded it in print in 1805. See Abiel Holmes, *American Annals; or, a Chronological History of America, from Its Discovery in 1492 to 1806*, 2 vols. (1805; Cambridge, Mass. and London: Reprinted for Sherwood, Neely, and Jones, Paternoster-Row, by J. F. Dove, St. John's Square, 1813).

57. There has been some historical controversy over whether or not Dorothy Bradford's death was a suicide prompted by her despair at the prospect of colonial life. For a vociferous refutation of this interpretation, see George Ernest Bowman, "Governor William Bradford's First Wife Dorothy (May) Bradford Did Not Commit Suicide," *Mayflower Descendant* 29, no. 3 (July 1931): 97–102.

58. Assuming, that is, that all the dead were buried. Following this assumption, one historian claims, "That year, that first winter, they had to dig seven times as many graves for the dead, as they were building houses for the living"; see George B. Cheever, *The Journal of the Pilgrims at Plymouth, in New England, in 1620* (New York: John Wiley, 1848), 225.

59. Weston's support had been instrumental in financing the settlement at Plymouth, but as an adventurer, he was equally ready to manipulate and mislead settlers in his pursuit of his own profit, which he soon did.

60. Pratt's narrative was first recorded as a deposition before the General Court of Massachusetts in 1662 and first printed in *Collections of the Massachusetts Historical Society*, 4th ser., vol. 4 (Boston: Little, Brown, 1858), 474–87; this quotation is from 478.

61. I thank Ann Fabian for reminding me that if the sick had actually offered themselves for this duty, it would be a powerful example of *communitas* and no little act of courage. Even so, the intention of the group—to signify strength by using weak bodies—remains the same.

62. Clare Gittings writes, "Given the speed and ferocity of the disease, it is surprising how tenaciously the rituals of decent burial were maintained during plague time"; see Gittings, "Sacred and Secular: 1558–1660," in *Death in England: An Illustrated History*, ed. Peter C. Jupp and Clare Gittings (New Brunswick, N.J.: Rutgers University Press, 1999), 150.

63. *Collections of the Massachusetts Historical Society*, 474–87.

64. Increase Mather, *A Relation of the Troubles Which Have Hapned in New-England, by Reason of the Indians There: From the Year 1614 to the Year 1675 . . . Together with an Historical Discourse Concerning the Prevalency of Prayer, Etc* (Boston: John Foster, 1677), 17.

65. Cole's Hill is widely remembered as the Pilgrim burial ground, but James Cole did not arrive in Plymouth until 1630. The first mention of Cole's Hill in the Plymouth Records is on March 6, 1669, when "Coles Hill soe Caled" was deeded to Nathaniel Warren. See *Records of the Town of Plymouth, Published by Order of the Town*, vol. 1: *1636–1705* (Plymouth: Avery & Doten, Book and Job Printers, 1889), 266.

66. Morison, *Of Plymouth Plantation*, 77.

67. Stannard, *Puritan Way of Death*, 101.

68. Edward Winslow, *Good Newes from New-England, or, a True Relation of Things Very Remarkable at the Plantation of Plimoth in New-England (1624)* (Bedford, Mass.: Applewood Books, 1996), 6.

69. Ibid., 105–6.

70. For more details, see Neal Salisbury, "Squanto: Last of the Patuxets," in *Struggle*

and Survival in Colonial America, ed. Gary B. Nash and David G. Sweet (Berkeley: University of California Press,1981), 228–46.

71. Morison, *Of Plymouth Plantation,* 114.

72. Ibid.

73. *Collections of the Massachusetts Historical Society,* 483.

74. Winslow, *Good Newes from New-England.* Winslow's is the most extensive contemporary account of the raid on Wessagusset; it was published in London the year after these events took place. For his report, from Pratt's news-bearing arrival at Plymouth to Standish's conquering return, see 38–44.

75. Indians regularly mocked Englishmen who cried in front of their enemies. Here Winslow reports that Witawamut "had oft boasted of his own valour, and derided their weakness, especially because, as he said, they died crying, making sour faces, more like children than men" (Winslow, *Good Newes from New-England,* 23).

76. Ibid., 42–43.

77. A later, extended treatment of the history of Wessagusset is found in Charles Francis Adams, *Three Episodes of Massachusetts History* (Boston: Houghton, Mifflin, 1869), 59–104. Adams ends his narrative with the demise of the Massachusett Indians, concluding, "Massacre thus completed the work of pestilence." The story of Wessagusset is also preserved in verse by Longfellow in his much-reprinted *The Courtship of Miles Standish* from 1858. In his popular ballad, Longfellow depicts the totem of the raid: "And as a trophy of war the head of the brave Wattawamat / Scowled from the roof of the fort, which at once was a church and a fortress, / All who beheld it rejoiced, and praised the Lord, and took courage. / Only Priscilla averted her face from this spectre of terror, / Thanking God in her heart that she had not married Miles Standish" (Henry Wadsworth Longfellow, *The Courtship of Miles Standish, with Illustrations by Howard Chandler Christy* [Indianapolis: Bobbs-Merrill, 1903], 124).

78. See "A Letter of William Bradford and Isaac Allerton, 1623," *American Historical Review* 8, no. 2 (1903): 294–301.

79. Winslow, *Good Newes from New-England,* 46–47.

80. In Morison, *Of Plymouth Plantation,* 375, Robinson's letter is reprinted as an appendix. For an extended argument on reintegrating the letters into the text of the history, see Anderson, *William Bradford's Books.*

81. Morton, *New English Canaan,* 112.

82. Morison, *Of Plymouth Plantation,* 47.

83. Winslow, *Good Newes from New-England,* 50.

84. Ibid., 51.

85. Both senses of the word "piteous"—full of pity, and exciting pity in others— were in active use throughout the seventeenth century.

86. See the letter of Emmanuel Altham to his brother, written from Plymouth in September 1623: "And [the head of Witawamut] is set on the top of our fort, and instead of an ancient, we have a piece of linen cloth dyed in the same Indian's blood, which was hung out upon the fort when Massasoit was here" (Sydney V. James, ed.,

Three Visitors to Early Plymouth: Letters about the Pilgrim Settlement in New England during Its First Seven Years by John Pory, Emmanuel Altham and Isaack De Rasieres [Plymouth: Plimoth Plantation, 1963], 31). If Massasoit also looked on Witawamut's remains piteously, Altham does not mention it. The colonists did not intend to intimidate Massasoit but presumably to celebrate the alliance between the Wampanoag and the Plymouth people. Remember that according to Winslow, Massasoit warned the settlers of a regional Indian conspiracy through Hobomok and urged the English to make a preemptive strike. Since then three other sachems involved in the coalition had died of disease, and Massasoit consolidated power among those groups. In the context of this diplomacy, Plymouth leaders likely assumed that the head would remind Massasoit of their strong alliance and the costs of challenging it.

87. For "the spectacle of the scaffold," see Michel Foucault, *Discipline and Punish: The Birth of the Prison,* trans. Allan Sheridan, 2nd Vintage ed. (New York: Vintage, 1995), 32–72.

88. Morison, *Of Plymouth Plantation*, 118.

89. Ibid., 118–19.

90. This interpretation is put forward by George F. Willison, *Saints and Strangers: Lives of the Pilgrim Fathers and their Families* (Cornwall, N.Y.: Cornwall Press, 1945), 214.

91. Morison, *Of Plymouth Plantation*, 324.

92. Ibid., 86.

93. Ibid., 443.

Chapter 4

1. The comment is by Henry Whistler, a visitor to Barbados in 1655, quoted in Richard Dunn, *Sugar and Slaves: The Rise of the Planter Class in the English West Indies, 1624–1713* (Chapel Hill: University of North Carolina Press, 1972), 77.

2. Richard Ligon, *A True and Exact History of the Island of Barbados*, ed. Karen Ordahl Kupperman (Indianapolis: Hackett, 2011), 177. All further quotations from Ligon will be taken from this volume and cited in the text. The 2011 work is a much-needed recent edition of Richard Ligon, *A Trve & Exact History of the Island of Barbados: Illustrated with a Mapp of the Island, as Also the Principall Trees and Plants There, Set Forth in Their Due Proportions and Shapes, Drawne out by Their Severall and Respective Scales; Together with the Ingenio That Makes the Sugar, with the Plots of the Severall Houses, Roomes, and Other Places, That Are Used in the Whole Process of Sugar-Making* (London: Printed for H. Mosely, 1657).

3. Richard Dunn devotes a chapter to the analysis of death rates on all the sugar islands throughout the seventeenth century; see Dunn, "Death in the Tropics," chap. 9 in Dunn, *Sugar and Slaves*, 300–335. For a wide-ranging study of the history and culture of mortality in Jamaica, see Vincent Brown, *The Reaper's Garden: Death and Power in the World of Atlantic Slavery* (Cambridge, Mass.: Harvard University Press, 2008).

4. Srinivas Aravamudan, *Tropicopolitans: Colonialism and Agency, 1688–1804* (Durham, N.C.: Duke University Press, 1999).

5. Barbara J. Shapiro, *A Culture of Fact: England, 1550–1720* (Ithaca, N.Y.: Cornell University Press, 2000), 84.

6. For an attempt to locate the line beyond which there was not peace, see Garrett Mattingly, "No Peace beyond What Line?," *Transactions of the Royal Historical Society*, 5th ser., 13 (1963): 145–62.

7. Vincent T. Harlow, *Colonising Expeditions to the West Indies and Guiana, 1623–1667*, Works Issued by the Hakluyt Society, 2nd ser., no. 56 (London: Printed for the Hakluyt Society, 1925), 73.

8. Karen Ordahl Kupperman, "Fear of Hot Climates in the Anglo-American Colonial Experience," *William and Mary Quarterly*, 3rd ser., 41, no. 2 (April 1984): 213–40.

9. Antonio Benítez-Rojo, *The Repeating Island: The Caribbean and the Postmodern Perspective*, trans. James E. Maraniss, 2nd ed. (Durham, N.C. and London: Duke University Press, 1996), 39.

10. John Nicholl, *An Houre Glasse of Indian Newes: Or a True and Tragicall Discourse, Shewing the Most Lamentable Miseries, and Distressed Calamities Indured by 67 Englishmen, Which Were Sent for a Supply to the Planting in Guiana in the Yeare. 1605. Who Not Finding the Saide Place, Were for Want of Victuall, Left a Shore in Saint Lucia, an Island of Caniballs, or Men-Eaters in the West-Indyes, under the Conduct of Captain Sen-Johns, of All Which Said Number, Onely a 11. Are Supposed to Be Still Living, Whereof 4. Are Lately Returnd into England; Written by John Nicholl, One of the Aforesaid Company* (London: Edward Allde, 1607), unpag. Nicholl's narrative is reproduced in Peter Hulme and Neil L. Whitehead, eds., *Wild Majesty: Encounters with Caribs from Columbus to the Present Day, an Anthology* (Oxford: Clarendon, 1992), 64–79.

11. As Doris Garraway reminds scholars of the colonial Caribbean, the term "Carib" was always political and ideological, not ethnographic. The ascription "Carib," she writes, "became a generic label for Indians deemed hostile to Christians. Allegedly identifiable by a conflation of undesirable traits, including anthropophagy and aggressiveness toward the Spanish, they were subject to legal enslavement." See Doris Lorraine Garraway, *The Libertine Colony: Creolization in the Early French Caribbean* (Durham, N.C.: Duke University Press, 2005), 40.

12. Hulme and Whitehead, *Wild Majesty*, 77–78.

13. Ibid., 62.

14. For the planting of the cross, see Sir Robert Hermann Schomburgk, *The History of Barbados: Comprising a Geographical and Statistical Description of the Island; a Sketch of the Historical Events since the Settlement; and an Account of Its Geology and Natural Productions* (London: Longman, Brown, Green and Longmans, 1848), 258. For a comparison of English, French, Spanish, and Portuguese ceremonies of colonial possession, see Patricia Seed, *Ceremonies of Possession in Europe's Conquest of the New World, 1492–1640* (Cambridge and New York: Cambridge University Press, 1995).

15. Hulme and Whitehead, *Wild Majesty*, 66.

16. Nicholl, *An Houre Glasse of Indian Newes*, from Nicholl's "Dedicatory" letter to Sir Thomas Smith, organizer and governor of the East India Company and a central figure in the Virginia Company; this letter is not reprinted in Hulme and Whitehead, *Wild Majesty*.

17. Ibid.

18. Hilary McD. Beckles, "Kalinago (Carib) Resistance to European Colonisation of the Caribbean," *Caribbean Quarterly* 38, no. 2/3 (June–September 1992): 3.

19. Hulme and Whitehead, *Wild Majesty*, 68.

20. Ibid.

21. Ibid., 72.

22. Ibid., 73.

23. Ibid.

24. Ibid., 75.

25. Peter Hulme, *Colonial Encounters: Europe and the Native Caribbean 1492–1797*, 2nd ed. (London: Routledge, 1992), 131. For a more expansive treatment of colonial attributions of treachery to Native Americans, see Karen Ordahl Kupperman, "English Perceptions of Treachery: The Case of the American 'Savages,'" *Historical Journal* 20, no. 2 (June 1977): 263–87.

26. Hulme and Whitehead, *Wild Majesty*, 67.

27. Harlow, *Colonising Expeditions to the West Indies and Guiana, 1623–1667*, 65–66.

28. Ibid., 66.

29. Ibid.

30. Ibid.

31. Ibid., 73.

32. Ibid., 93.

33. Ibid., 69.

34. For a wide-ranging study of the connections between the refinement of visual culture relating to the West Indies and the manufacture of refined sugar, see Kay Dian Kriz, *Slavery, Sugar, and the Culture of Refinement: Picturing the British West Indies, 1700–1840* (New Haven, Conn.: Yale University Press, Published for the Paul Mellon Centre for Studies in British Art, 2008).

35. Harlow, *Colonising Expeditions to the West Indies and Guiana*, 91.

36. Ibid., 94.

37. Philip D. Curtin, *The Rise and Fall of the Plantation Complex: Essays in Atlantic History* (Cambridge: Cambridge University Press, 1990), 84.

38. These figures are from ibid., 82–84.

39. These tables are found in Ligon, *True and Exact History of the Island of Barbados*, 190–91.

40. Hulme and Whitehead, *Wild Majesty*, 71.

41. Ibid., 76.

42. Susan Scott Parrish, "Richard Ligon and the Atlantic Science of Commonwealths," *William and Mary Quarterly* 67, no. 2 (April 2010): 210–11.

43. Keith Sandiford, *Theorizing a Colonial Caribbean-Atlantic Imaginary: Sugar and Obeah* (New York: Routledge, 2011), 60.

44. Sandiford, *Theorizing a Colonial Caribbean-Atlantic Imaginary*, 59, 64–67.

45. For a French iteration of Ligon's description, see Charles-César, Comte de Rochefort, *The History of the Caribby-Islands*, trans. John Davies (London: J. M. for Thomas Dring and John Starkey, 1666), 58–59. For a study of the pineapple's role in the development of the Enlightenment concept of "taste," see Sean R. Silver, "Locke's Pineapple and the History of Taste," *The Eighteenth Century: Theory and Interpretation* 49, no. 1 (Spring 2008): 43–65.

46. That Ligon devotes three pages to describing the pineapple attests to its significance.

47. The tradition of "naturalizing" African bodies in order to justify their enslavement is a long one. For an example of how this practice applies particularly to women's bodies, see Jennifer L. Morgan, *Laboring Women: Reproduction and Gender in New World Slavery* (Philadelphia: University of Pennsylvania Press, 2004).

48. The padre's mistress is extravagantly described on 54–56, from where the quotations in this and the next paragraph are taken.

49. Ligon mentions that they were "taken from Bridewell, Turnboule Street, and such like places of education" (56).

50. This scene is lavishly narrated over several pages, 58–61, from where these quotations are taken.

51. Susan Scott Parrish reads Ligon's assessment of the plague in the political context of the interregnum. Parrish argues that by placing the etiology of the wasting sickness next to his praise for the beauty of the trees, Ligon is struggling with a humanist quest to find a potentially harmonious commonwealth. She writes, "Ligon lays out this abrupt juxtaposition of health and death, of social balance and social ills, to introduce Barbados as a puzzle. The vegetatives indicate a potential harmony in the island that the humans, by their debauched behavior, have put in discord" (Parrish, "Richard Ligon and the Atlantic Science of Commonwealths," 225). I believe this initial juxtaposition can also be read as one of the many torrid exchanges Ligon describes in his depiction of the colonial tropic.

52. When Barbados's mostly royalist colonists refused to be enlisted in Cromwell's Western Design, a pamphleteer declared, "[C]ertainly these islanders must be the very scum of scums, and meer dregs of corruption"; see I. S., *A Brief and Perfect Journal of the Late Proceedings and Success of the English Army in the West-Indies* (London, 1655), 11. For a screed against the moral and religious life on the island, see John Rous, *A Warning to the Inhabitants of Barbadoes* (London, 1656). Rous, a Quaker, opens his text with the following: "O Barbadoes, Barbadoes! who

excels in wickedness, pride and covetousness, oppressing, cheating and cozening . . . the wrath of God shall be revealed in flames of fire against you, ye Earth-worms" (Rouse, *A Warning*, 1).

53. On Colonel Modiford's plantation, where Ligon lived, only 14 percent of the acres were planted with food for his household and more than 130 slaves and servants.

54. Parrish, "Richard Ligon and the Atlantic Science of Commonwealths."

55. Twenty pounds' worth of "Black Ribbon for mourning" is among the purchases Ligon suggests for would-be planters (184).

56. See Dunn, *Sugar and Slaves*, 190–97, for a detailed explanation of the sugar-making process.

57. Ibid., 194.

58. Bonham C. Richardson, *Igniting the Caribbean's Past: Fire in British West Indian History* (Chapel Hill: University of North Carolina Press, 2004), 31.

59. Harlow, *Colonising Expeditions to the West Indies and Guiana*, 66.

60. See also J. R. McNeill, *Mosquito Empires: Ecology and War in the Greater Caribbean, 1620–1914* (Cambridge: Cambridge University Press, 2010), 27; Karen Ordahl Kupperman, "Introduction," in *History of the Island of Barbados,* 19; Richardson, *Igniting the Caribbean's Past,* 27.

61. Myra Jehlen explores how Ligon's worldview allows him to be simultaneously sympathetic to slaves and unbothered by their status as commodities; see "History Besides the Fact: What We Learn from *A True and Exact History of Barbados,*" in Myra Jehlen, *Readings at the Edge of Literature* (Chicago: University of Chicago Press, 2002), 179–91.

62. Parrish, "Richard Ligon and the Atlantic Science of Commonwealths," 227.

63. Michael Craton, *Testing the Chains: Resistance to Slavery in the British West Indies* (Ithaca, N.Y.: Cornell University Press, 1982), 107–8.

64. Craton, *Testing the Chains*, 100.

65. Hulme and Whitehead, *Wild Majesty,* 77–78.

66. Nicholl, *An Houre Glasse of Indian Newes*, from Nicholl's "Dedicatory" letter to Sir Thomas Smith, not reprinted in Hulme and Whitehead, *Wild Majesty.*

67. Hulme and Whitehead, *Wild Majesty,* 66.

Afterword

1. Hayden White writes, "The demand for closure in the historical story is a demand, I suggest, for moral meaning, a demand that sequences of real events be assessed as to their significance as elements of a moral drama"; see White, *The Content of the Form: Narrative Discourse and Historical Representation* (Baltimore: Johns Hopkins University Press, 1990), 21.

2. William Strachey, *The Historie of Travaile into Virginia Brittania*, ed. R. H. Major (London: Hakluyt Society, 1849), 42.

3. It was in the mid-seventeenth century that the meaning of "virtual" changed from its early sense of possessing virtues or powers to its later sense of maintaining an essence apart from external form. The definition of "morally virtuous" gave way to the complex indeterminacy of something "that is so in essence or effect, although not formally or actually; admitting of being called by the name so far as the effect or result is concerned" (*Oxford English Dictionary*, 2nd ed., s.v. "virtual," def. 2, 4a).

4. Mary Louise Pratt, *Imperial Eyes: Travel Writing and Transculturaion* (New York: Routledge, 1992), 201.

5. Samuel Eliot Morison, ed., *Of Plymouth Plantation, 1620–1647 by William Bradford, Sometime Governor Thereof* (New York: Alfred A. Knopf, 2002), 61.

6. Leo Marx, *The Machine in the Garden: Technology and the Pastoral Ideal in America,* 2nd ed. (New York: Oxford University Press, 2000), 41–42.

7. David Laurence, "William Bradford's American Sublime," *PMLA* 102, no. 1 (1987): 55–65.

8. Myra Jehlen, "The Literature of Colonization," in *The Cambridge History of American Literature,* vol. 1, ed. Sacvan Bercovitch (Cambridge: Cambridge University Press, 1994), 84–86.

9. Ibid., 61.

10. Ibid.

11. Isa. 13:8, King James Version.

12. See Lorenzo Veracini, *Settler Colonialism: A Theoretical Overview* (New York: Palgrave Macmillan, 2010), especially 15: "[Settler colonialism is] essentially about the establishment and consolidation of an exogenous political community following a foundative displacement."

13. J. H. Elliott, "Introduction: Colonial Identity in the Atlantic World," in *Colonial Identity in the Atlantic World, 1500–1800,* ed. Nicholas Canny and Anthony Pagden (Princeton, N.J.: Princeton University Press, 1987), 5.

14. Ibid., 8

15. Ibid., 13, 269.

16. Ibid., 4.

17. For "project," see Robert Blair St. George, "Introduction," in *Possible Pasts: Becoming Colonial in Early America,* ed. Robert Blair St. George (Ithaca, N.Y.: Cornell University Press, 2000), 5–6; for "creative adaptation," see T. H. Breen, "Creative Adaptations: Peoples and Cultures," in *Colonial British America: Essays in the New History of the Early Modern Era,* ed. Jack P. Greene and J. R. Pole (Baltimore: Johns Hopkins University Press, 1984), 195–232.

18. Elliott, "Introduction," 9.

19. Michael Zuckerman, "Identity in British America: Unease in Eden," in *Colonial Identity in the Atlantic World, 1500–1800,* ed. Nicholas Canny and Anthony Pagden (Princeton, N.J.: Princeton University Press, 1987), 158.

20. Paul Ricoeur, "Memory and Forgetting," in *Questioning Ethics: Contemporary Debates in Philosophy,* ed. Richard Kearney and Mark Dooley (New York: Routledge, 1999), 9.

21. Ibid., 8.

22. Ibid., 9.

ACKNOWLEDGMENTS

At the end of one's project, one realizes that the conventions of the "acknowledgments" genre are all founded in truth. Many debts are incurred. Institutions provide intellectual homes. Mentors are the first to see what's there, colleagues give invaluable counsel, and there are no words adequate to thank a partner. Certainly, all mistakes are one's own. And so without trying to reinvent the language of gratitude, let me try my best to give credit where credit is due.

The institutions that were home to me during this project were the American Studies Program at Yale University, the Henry E. Huntington Library, and the English Department at the University of California, Berkeley. In each of these formative intellectual environments, I found mentors and colleagues who engaged, challenged, and inspired me. It has not been a lonely journey, and I am grateful for the company. At Yale, I had the extreme good fortune to work extensively with John Demos, who took a literary reader into the historians' workshop and offered the kind of mentorship that represents the very best we do for each other in academia. As a historian, a writer, a teacher, and a friend, he has been nothing less than a guiding light. He encouraged me to dig deep and to hold on to my questions even when they seemed unanswerable. His unflagging faith in me has been a free gift that I cannot hope to repay. Elizabeth Maddock Dillon was crucial to the development of this project from its earliest to its final forms. I have often depended on her stunning intellectual clarity to show me the shape of my emerging thoughts, and on her profound understanding of our field to help me locate my work within it. I continue to learn from her at every turn. Jon Butler, Nancy Cott, John Mack Faragher, Matthew Frye Jacobson, Franny Nudelman, Laura Sanchez-Eppler, David Waldstreicher, Laura Wexler, and Bryan Jay Wolf opened my eyes to the richness and variety of American studies and provided models of pedagogy and scholarship that guide me still.

At the Huntington Library, Judith Jackson Fossett, Elliott Gorn, Karen

Halttunen, Gregory S. Jackson, Karen Lystra, Peter Mancall, Michelle Nickerson, Sharon Oster, and Mona Schulman offered friendship and encouragement over the years. Daily, in the silence of the reading room and the intensive talk of the café, I was happier for their company. My work at the Huntington was supported by the W. M. Keck Fellowship for Younger Scholars and by the Woodrow W. Wilson Foundation's Charlotte W. Newcombe Fellowship. The ongoing seminars "American Origins" and "Past Tense: Ways of Writing History" were regular touchstones, and the workshop "Writing Early American History," cosponsored by the USC–Huntington Early Modern Studies Institute and the *William and Mary Quarterly*, provided important feedback on an early version of Chapter 1. I thank the longtime director of research Robert C. Ritchie for fostering such a dynamic intellectual community at the Huntington, and I am grateful to the many scholars who came through its doors for years of lively conversation.

At Berkeley, my colleagues have inspired and helped me in countless ways. Mitchell Breitwieser and Maura Nolan have given me invaluable, sustained support and guidance on every level, for which I am enormously grateful. Dorri Beam, Catherine Gallagher, Jeffery Knapp, Scott Saul, Hertha Sweet-Wong, and Bryan Wagner all attended to large portions of the manuscript; and Stephen Best, Marcial Gonzalez, Kevis Goodman, Lyn Hejinian, Donna V. Jones, Katherine O'Brien O'Keeffe, Samuel Otter, Kent Puckett, and Janet Sorensen provided advice and assistance at critical junctures. I benefited greatly from the regular and detailed feedback, as well as the sustaining friendships, of my faculty reading group: Nadia Ellis, Eric Falci, David Landreth, Stephen Lee, David Marno, Namwali Serpell, and Emily Thornbury. American studies colleagues Michael Cohen, Beth Piatote, and Leigh Raiford have also made Berkeley a warm home to me. What may here read like a roster represents innumerable instances of kindnesses and camaraderie, and I have been extremely fortunate to live and grow among these colleagues. The financial support and leave time necessary to complete the book came from Berkeley's Megan and Peter T. Chernin Mentoring Program, the Committee on Research, the Hellman Family Fund, a Humanities Research Fellowship, and the Townsend Center for the Humanities.

I am also indebted to the larger community of Early Americanists. I especially want to thank Ralph Bauer, Kristina Bross, Susan Castillo, Jonathan Elmer, Duncan Faherty, Molly Farrell, Sandra Gustafson, Thomas Krise, Dennis Moore, Ivy Schweitzer, Cristobal Silva, and Julia Stern, who each gave me opportunities to connect to the broader community along the way.

Audiences at Berkeley, Harvard University, Indiana University at Bloomington, and Columbia University provided generous responses to the work as it emerged, as did participants at conferences of the Society of Early Americanists and the American Studies Association. Comments from anonymous readers for the journal *Early American Literature* greatly improved my work on Roanoke, part of which was published as "What Happened in Roanoke: Ralph Lane's Narrative Incursion," *Early American Literature* 48, no. 2 (2013). Parts of the "Introduction" and "Afterword" of this book also appeared in that journal under the following titles: "Keyword: Catastrophe," *Early American Literature* 46, no. 3 (2011) and "'As Dying Yet Behold We Live': Catastrophe and Interiority in *Of Plymouth Plantation*," *Early American Literature* 37, no. 1 (2002). I am grateful for permission to republish that work here.

Although this book was many years in the making, the final stages required still more hands. Jill Lepore, Max Cavitch, and an anonymous reader for the University of Pennsylvania Press read the manuscript and asked the kinds of expansive, generative questions that allowed me to cross new thresholds in revising the text. At every point in the process, I have turned to Rachel Trocchio, whose dedication, intelligence, and friendship are simply inexhaustible. Matt Seidel's attention to each word of the manuscript saved me from many false steps. My editor Bob Lockhart generously saw my work in the best possible light and guided my sense of direction as I approached the finish line. This project would never have transformed from a constant companion into a finished book without their help.

If there are words sufficient to thank my parents, Donald and Melanie Donegan, I am not writer enough to find them. They have stood behind me and beside me in ways too many to reckon. I could not find better friends than I have in my own siblings, and that is a rare blessing indeed. Cheryl, Beth, Donald, and Amie have been interested, kind, loyal, and proud, but what I mean to them has little to do with these pages; for that I am most grateful. Long ago Howard and Judy Goldsmith embraced me as a daughter, and they have supported me through a great many changes since then. Other people have held a place open for me in the pleasures of life and were always ready to welcome me back after my disappearances into the stacks or the study. Catherine Courtney, Amy Goddard Smith and John Zinman, Bekki and Steve Hambright, Karen and Steve Hillenberg, Frank and Tina Metelmann, and Cheryl and David Smith helped me return to myself again and again.

This project has grown up with my children and is better for it in every way. Zeke and Mercy have been my daily happiness and my heart's delight. While there were long stretches of time when my papers lay unmoved on my desk, the children grew and changed and surprised and enchanted me always. With them, everything is brought to light. My dear son Leo was born and died during this time, and I honor here all the ways his short life changed mine forever. Finally, I dedicate this book with love to David Gold-smith. More than anyone else, David understands what it took to arrive at this point, and more than anyone else, he made it possible. He has often wondered at my dark topics, but he can rest assured that I never could have spent so much time in seasons of misery unless I knew I could return home to seasons of joy.